# REAL-TIME SYSTEMS, ARCHITECTURE, SCHEDULING, AND APPLICATION

# REAL-TIME SYSTEMS, ARCHITECTURE, SCHEDULING, AND APPLICATION

*Editor*

**Dana Zelenko**

scitus
academics

**Real-Time Systems, Architecture, Scheduling, and Application**
Edited by **Dana Zelenko**

ISBN: 978-1-68117-656-7
Library of Congress Control Number: 2016946523


SCITUS Academics LLC,
616, Corporate Way, Suite 2, 4766,
Valley Cottage, NY 10989

www.scitusacademics.com



**Notice**



Printed in United States of America on Acid Free Paper

# PREFACE

Real-time applications are used in daily operations, such as engine and break mechanisms in cars, traffic light and air-traffic control and heart beat and blood pressure monitoring. A real-time system is one that must process information and produce a response within a specified time, else risk severe consequences, including failure. That is, in a system with a real-time constraint it is no good to have the correct action or the correct answer after a certain deadline: it is either by the deadline or it is useless. Real-Time systems are becoming pervasive. In a Real-Time System the correctness of the system behavior depends not only on the logical results of the computations, but also on the physical instant at which these results are produced. Real-Time systems are classified from a number of viewpoints i.e. on factors outside the computer system and factors inside the computer system. Special emphasis is placed on hard and soft real-time systems. A missed deadline in hard real-time systems is catastrophic and in soft real-time systems it can lead to a significant loss. Hence predictability of the system behavior is the most important concern in these systems. Predictability is often achieved by either static or dynamic scheduling of real-time tasks to meet their deadlines. Static scheduling makes scheduling decisions at compile time and is off-line.

Dynamic scheduling is online and uses schedulabilty test to determine whether a set of tasks can meet their deadlines.

*Real-Time Systems, Architecture, Scheduling, and Application* present varied aspects of real-time systems with architecture, specification and verification, scheduling and real world applications. It is convenient for advanced graduate students and researchers in comprehensive disciplines impacted by embedded computing and software. Subsequently the book emphasizes the most modern advances in real-time systems and communications networks; it serves as a vehicle for technology transition within the real-time systems community of systems architects, designers, technologists, and system analysts.

# TABLE OF CONTENTS

7

# PARALLEL IMPLEMENTATION OF BACKGROUND SUBTRACTION ALGORITHMS FOR REAL-TIME VIDEO PROCESSING ON A SUPERCOMPUTER PLATFORM

**Grzegorz Szwoch, Damian Ellwart, Andrzej Czyżewski**

Multimedia Systems Department, Gdansk University of Technology,
Narutowicza 11/12, 80-233 Gdan´sk, Poland

## ABSTRACT

Results of evaluation of the background subtraction algorithms implemented on a supercomputer platform in a parallel manner are presented in the article. The aim of the work is to chose an algorithm, a number of threads and a task scheduling method, that together provide satisfactory accuracy and efficiency of a real-time processing of high-resolution camera images, maintaining the cost of resources usage at a reasonable level. Two selected algorithms: the Gaussian mixture models and the Codebook, are presented and their computational complexity is discussed. Various approaches to the parallel implementation, including assigning the image pixels to threads, the task scheduling methods and the thread management systems, are presented. The experiments were performed on a supercomputer cluster, using a single machine with 12 physical cores. The accuracy and performance of the implemented algorithms were evaluated for varying image resolutions and numbers of concurrent processing threads. On a basis of the evaluation results, an optimal configuration for the parallel implementation of the system for real-time video content analysis on a supercomputer platform was proposed.

# KEYWORDS

Background subtraction, Parallel computing, Object detection, Gaussian mixture models Codebook

# 1. INTRODUCTION

Background subtraction is a procedure commonly used for separation of the image pixels belonging to moving objects from those representing a static background. This is one of the most frequently used algorithms in video content analysis frameworks for a detection and tracking of moving objects and an automatic event detection [5]. At the same time, it is one of the most computationally intensive image analysis procedures. Video monitoring systems for the automatic event detection require a real-time background subtraction, which is difficult to achieve with high-resolution cameras often employed in the modern video surveillance systems. A solution to this problem is either to reduce the image resolution or/and frame rate, which decreases the accuracy of the background subtraction, or to utilize parallel processing methods, dividing the task of image analysis into several concurrently running processing threads.

Recently, the authors faced a problem of implementing a background subtraction algorithm within a parallel data processing framework running on a supercomputer—a multi-node system of multi-core machines. The framework named KASKADA was designed for efficient processing of high amounts of data from multiple sources [18]. In the context of video monitoring, KASKADA will be used for concurrent analysis of the images obtained from a large number of cameras, for identifying specified objects or safety threads. The chain of the processing algorithms is run on multiple nodes of the supercomputer that communicate with each other using a message passing interface. The background subtraction algorithm is one of the initial processing stages: it receives the decoded camera images, performs the background subtraction and sends the results to further video analysis algorithms (object detection and tracking, automatic event detection, analysis of the crowd behavior, etc.), running on other nodes of the supercomputer. Multiple instances of the background subtraction algorithm have to run concurrently on separate nodes, analyzing a large number of video streams in the real time.

The implementation of a background subtraction algorithm within the KASKADA framework required answering several important questions: (1) which background subtraction algorithm is the most suitable for parallel implementation in this framework, (2) which thread management strategy is optimal, (3) how many computing units are required for real-time processing and (4) which algorithm is optimal in terms of balance between its performance and the accuracy. The aim of this article is to address these questions using a set of tests performed using the real computing system. We assumed that in a production system, a single instance of the background subtraction algorithm will be run on a single node of the supercomputer and such a solution was implemented and tested.

A variety of methods for background estimation can be found in the literature [13, 15, 16, 26]. Among all of them, the approach based on Gaussian mixture models (GMM) seems to be the most popular one. The algorithm representing the background model of a single pixel as a set of weighted Gaussian distributions was first proposed by Friedman and Russell [9], and later extended by Stauffer and Grimson [29] who proposed an efficient method of model updating. Numerous further improvements of the original GMM method were proposed. KaewTraKulPong and Bowden [12] used an expectation maximization approach for improving the learning rate of the background model. Setiawan et al. [25] applied the GMM method to an improved hue-luminance-saturation color space in order to achieve better sensitivity to color changes. An important work by Zivkovic and Van der Heijden [33] resulted in an improved adaptation of the GMM model to changes in the analyzed scene by automatic selection of the number of Gaussian components. On this, basis further work was carried out by Sicre and Nicolas [27] to further improve the model adaptation capabilities. Additionally, a modification of the GMM model adaptation process leading to reduction of the object detection errors in case of illumination variations is proposed by the authors of this work. An important problem in the background subtraction is the shadow removal, as moving shadows are assigned to the foreground in the original GMM method, so an additional procedure for removing the shadows is required. An algorithm proposed by Horprasert et al. [10] based on analysis of the color and brightness variations is often used for this task.

Another, less popular approach to the background subtraction is the Codebook algorithm proposed by Kim et al. [16]. This method represents a pixel in the background model using a set of codewords describing the color, brightness and statistical properties of the pixels.

According to its author, this method outperforms the GMM algorithm in terms of handling moving backgrounds and illumination variations, as well as in computational complexity. Kim et al. [17] improved this method for more robust background maintenance. Li et al. [19] introduced Gaussian distributions to the Codebook algorithm for quantization of the temporal series in order to reduce the rate of false-negative results. Sigari and Fathy [28] presented a two-layer implementation of the Codebook model for handling background changes. Ilyas et al. [11] improved maintenance of the codebook background model.

Several other background subtraction algorithms may be found in the literature. A survey of such methods may be found, e.g.. in works of Parks and Fels [20] or Benezeth et al. [1]. This article focuses on two chosen algorithms: the GMM, which is the most widely used, and the Codebook, because the published test results are promising.

A published work on the parallel implementation of background subtraction algorithms is mainly limited to the GPU computing area, as presented, e.g., by Fauske et al. [8] or Pham et al. [23]. The implementation of the algorithm on a parallel system with a low number (up to 12) of processing units requires a proper thread management and a task scheduling approach. The Boost Threads library is a commonly used solution for the platform-independent thread management controlled by the programmer [14]. An alternative is the automatic task scheduling, managed by an external library. The most popular solutions of this type are libraries based on the Open Multi-Processing (OpenMP) application programming interface for the shared memory multiprocessing computing [3] and the Thread Building Blocks (TBB) library [24].

The article is organized as follows. First, both the GMM and the Codebook algorithms are described. The computational complexity of both methods, as well as strategies for their parallel implementation are discussed. Next, the results of experiments in which the performance and accuracy of both algorithms were tested in different conditions are presented. The conclusions and the discussion on the practical implications of the obtained results conclude the article.

## 2. BACKGROUND SUBTRACTION ALGORITHMS

The purpose of background subtraction algorithms is to divide all the image pixels into two groups: the foreground pixels, representing moving objects, and the background pixels, belonging to the static background. This separation is necessary in order to select the pixels representing the actual moving objects for the purpose of object detection, tracking, etc. [5]. The background modeling is usually performed by constructing a background model, which may be based, e.g., on the statistical analysis of the pixel values. The actual subtraction is achieved by comparing the current pixel values with the model and making a binary foreground/background decision. The shadows of the moving objects need to be eliminated from the foreground pixels, either by the subtraction algorithm itself or by using a separate post-processing method. The result of the background subtraction usually needs to be post-processed, e.g., with the morphological operations, in order to clean the resulting binary mask (remove the noise and fill small holes). The details of the two background subtraction algorithms chosen for the evaluation are presented below.

### 2.1 Gaussian mixture model

The Gaussian mixture model proposed first by Friedman and Russell [9] is a probabilistic method used for the background modeling. This approach is based on the assumption that upon the observations made to an image pixel, the associated background representation can be chosen as the most frequent appearing value. As this ėsteem can fluctuate, even under the strictly controlled conditions, e.g., due to the image noise, the background model of each pixel is described by a Gaussian given by:

$$\eta(X, \mu, \Sigma) = \frac{1}{(2\pi)^{0.5D}|\Sigma|^{0.5}} e^{-0.5\left[(X-\mu)^T \Sigma^{-1} (X-\mu)\right]}, \tag{1}$$

where $\mu$ denotes the mean of the distribution, Σ represents the covariance matrix and $X$ stands for the pixel value. For simplification, it is assumed that the color channels are independent, then Σ=σ2·IΣ=σ2·I, where $\sigma$ is the standard deviation of the distribution. Since the real life background varies during the day and night, the Gaussian adaptation is introduced in order to handle these changes. The formula for the parameters update is given by:

$$\mu_t = (1 - \rho) \cdot \mu_{t-1} + \rho X_t \tag{2}$$

$$\sigma_t^2 = (1 - \rho) \cdot \sigma_{t-1}^2 + \rho (X_t - \mu_t)^T (X_t - \mu_t), \tag{3}$$

where $\mu_t$ and $\sigma_t$ are the mean and the standard deviation of the distribution, $\rho$ is the update factor and $X_t$ denotes the processed pixel value. This way, the background model is adjusted to reflect changes in the analyzed video content. In order to increase the model adaptation capabilities, each image point is characterized by a mixture of (typically 3–5) Gaussians. A number of Gaussians can either be constant (defined when the algorithm is run) or it can vary depending on the scene characteristics [25]. Regardless of the implementation, this approach allows for handling situations such as when an object is left or taken from the scene. Although multiple distributions are utilized, only one of them represents the current model. Hence, weight factors are assigned to each of the Gaussians to indicate their strengths. A weight adaptation procedure is defined as:

$$\omega_{k,t} = (1 - \alpha) \cdot \omega_{k,t-1} + \alpha M_{k,t}, \tag{4}$$

where $\omega_{k,t}$ is the weight of the $k$th distribution, $\alpha$ is the learning factor and $M_{k,t}$ is a binary value equal to 1 if the current pixel matched a distribution and 0 otherwise. In order to verify whether the currently analyzed pixel should be assigned to the background or foreground, its value is tested against the distributions ordered by a descending $\omega_k/\sigma_k$ factor. Typically, if the value fits the leading distribution in the range of 2.5 standard deviations (defined as the $\Delta$ parameter) from the Gaussian mean, the point is marked as belonging to the background. Otherwise, the pixel value is used to form a new distribution, which replaces the one with the lowest $\omega_k/\sigma_k$ factor.

The detection accuracy obtained utilizing this method is satisfactory in many cases. However, in the real life scenarios, changing lighting conditions can often cause the detection errors. It can be observed especially for outdoor scenes with high illumination variations. Therefore, further algorithm improvements were developed to solve this problem.

Detection errors for scenes with high illumination variations are related to the distribution adaptation process, which cannot update the model sufficiently fast to compensate the changes. This could be solved by applying a variable learning factor [30]. On the other hand, such a modification can also cause the detection errors. Higher $\rho$ values affect the distribution mean and deviation adaptation rate. Hence, in case of long-term lighting variations, the leading Gaussian can be discarded from its position (considering the $\omega/\sigma$ factor) due to the increasing deviation. This problem can be partially solved by utilizing independent adaptation factors for Gaussian mean and deviation [4]. Another modification of the GMM introduces spatial dependencies for the pixel assignment process, making it more robust [32]. On the other hand, KaewTraKulPong and Bowden [12] proposed different adaptation formulas for various processing stages to improve the initial model learning process.

The GMM modification proposed in this article applies to scenes with lighting variations. It is based on the observation that the illumination changes are smooth considering the inter-frame differences. For such conditions, the background modeling algorithm should have high adaptive capabilities. This is achieved by applying an additional post-processing stage where particular model regions are updated. To determine these regions, the pixel variability is estimated as a mean differential of the consecutive video frames in which no objects are detected:

$$\text{diff}_n = (1-\gamma)\text{diff}_{n-1} + \frac{1}{C}\gamma \sum_c \left| I_c(x,y)_n - I_c(x,y)_{n-1} \right|, \tag{5}$$

where $I(x,y)$ denotes the image point at $(x,y)$ coordinates, $\gamma$ is the pixel variance learning factor in the range (0, 1) and $C$ is the number of image color channels. This way, a matrix of values is created, size of which is equal to the analyzed image resolution. Next, each value of this matrix is thresholded ($D_{th}$) in order to determine regions characterized by a low variability. For the pixels related to the background, which fulfill this condition, an additional update process is performed. This is acquired by shifting (with a set weight) the leading distribution mean toward the actual value from the input frame. This adaptation does not change the variation of the Gaussian, hence the $\omega/\sigma$ factor for the modified distribution is constant. Due to improved adjustment capabilities of the leading distribution, it is referred to as a short-term model further on. In order to reduce local errors which can be caused by objects with the color similar to the background model, an additional Gaussian is utilized. It is considered as a long-term background representation. Adaptation of this distribution is carried out utilizing the relations described by Eqs. (2) and (3). Another advantage of this approach is that it allows for reduction of the detection sensitivity in case of scene illumination variations. It is achieved by utilizing the short- and long-term models at the same time. Since the long-term representation is independent from the regular model adaptation procedure, it can cover the same value ranges as the *k*Gaussians. Hence, in case of low image variability, the short- and long-term distributions can be similar. However, if lighting changes are present in the scene, the short- and long-term Gaussians spread, resulting in the sensitivity reduction.

## 2.2 The Codebook algorithm

The Codebook method was proposed by Kim et al. [16] for the real-time foreground–background segmentation. The author claims that this method is efficient in speed compared to the other background subtraction methods and it is more robust in scenes with illumination variations. However, so far this algorithm has not been used in video analysis systems as widely as the GMM method. The background model in the Codebook algorithm is based on representing each image pixel by a number of codewords [16]. A single codeword represents a range of color and brightness variations of the pixel and is described using a vector of nine parameters:

$$c_i = \left\langle \bar{R}_i, \bar{G}_i, \bar{B}_i, \check{I}_i, \hat{I}_i, f_i, \lambda_i, p_i, q_i \right\rangle \tag{6}$$

where $(\bar{R}_i, \bar{G}_i, \bar{B}_i)$ are the pixel values in the RGB color space, $(\check{I}_i, \hat{I}_i)$ define the lower and upper range of the brightness variations, $f_i$ counts a number of times the codeword was matched, $\lambda_i$ is the maximum negative run-length (MNRL), defined as a longest interval in which the codeword has not recurred, $p_i$ and $q_i$ store the first and the last access time of the codeword, respectively.

In the original Codebook algorithm, the background model has to be built using a number of initial image frames before the actual background subtraction may be performed. During this initial training phase, the pixel value in each image frame is compared with all the codewords representing this pixel in the background model. If a matching codeword is found, it is updated, otherwise a new codeword is created and added to the background model. A codeword $\mathbf{c}_i$ matches a pixel $(R, G, B)$ if two conditions are fulfilled. The first condition describes the color difference between the pixel and the codeword and is given by

$$\sqrt{(R^2+G^2+B^2)-\frac{(R\bar{R}+G\bar{G}+B\bar{B})^2}{\bar{R}^2+\bar{G}^2+\bar{B}^2}} \leq \varepsilon, \tag{7}$$

where $\varepsilon$ is a constant threshold that defines the maximum allowed color variation. The second condition is related to the brightness variations and it is introduced in order to take the illumination changes and shadows into account. The condition is given by:

$$\alpha\hat{I} \leq \sqrt{R^2+G^2+B^2} \leq \min\left\{\beta\hat{I}, \frac{\check{I}}{\alpha}\right\}, \tag{8}$$

where $\alpha$ and $\beta$ are constants (the shadow and the highlight threshold, respectively) that limit the range of the pixel brightness variations.

If a matching codeword is found according to Eqs. (7) and (8), its $(R, G, B)$ values are updated with the current pixel values, using a running average. The brightness range of the codeword is extended if the pixel brightness was outside this range. The statistic parameters of the codeword (the update times and MNRL) are updated accordingly. If none of the codewords representing the pixel were matched, a new codeword is created and initialized with the current pixel values and the current frame number, then the codeword is added to the background model [16]. Therefore, during the training phase, new codewords are added each time the color or the brightness of the pixel change considerably.

After the training period is finished, the background model is pruned by eliminating the codewords with MNRL exceeding the threshold, which is typically equal to half of the training time. Then, the detection phase is performed simply by finding the matching codeword using the two conditions described before. If a match is found, the pixel is assigned to the background and the matching codeword is updated. If no match is found, the pixel is assigned to the moving object, but no codeword is added to the model. This approach has a drawback: the background model does not adapt to the scene and illumination changes. Therefore, a more complex approach to the background subtraction, utilizing the method proposed by Kim is used for the background maintenance [17].

Two layers are added to the background model, already containing the permanent background layer obtained during the training: a long-term background (the codewords added to the model after the training is finished) and a cache (the codewords created during the detection phase, but not added to the background). Therefore, the modified detection procedure is organized as follows.

- The search for a matching codeword is performed in all model layers.
- If a match was found in the permanent or the long-term model layer, the pixel is assigned to the background.
- If a matching codeword was not found or the only match was found in the cache, the pixel is assigned to the moving object (foreground).
- The matching codeword, if found, is updated.
- If no matching codeword was found, a new codeword is created and put in the cache.
- The codewords in the cache that were not updated during the time $T_{\text{h}}$ are removed.
- The codewords that remain in the cache longer than the time $T_{\text{add}}$ are moved to the long-term model layer, from this time on, they represent the background.
- The codewords in the long-term layer that were not updated for a defined time $T_{\text{del}}$ (usually much longer than $T_{\text{h}}$) are removed from the model.

With this procedure, adaptation of the background to the scene and illumination changes is achieved, at a cost of increased computational complexity. For the proper adaptation of the model to varying conditions, the threshold parameters need to be adjusted according to the character of variations.

In the original Codebook method, the background subtraction during the training phase is not possible. This is a drawback in comparison to the GMM method. Therefore, we modified the training phase by selecting the matched codewords with MNRL lower than the half of the elapsed training time as those representing the background, and the remaining ones as representing the moving objects. With this modification, a coarse background subtraction may be performed during the training phase. Additionally, in order to reduce the memory usage, the codewords are not added to the model if the elapsed training time is larger than the maximum allowed MNRL, since these codewords would be removed after the training anyway.

## 2.3 Morphological processing

The background subtraction result obtained using any of the described methods is a binary mask with the background and foreground pixels encoded using different values (usually 0 for the background and 255 or 1 for the foreground). The raw binary mask obtained from the background subtraction usually requires a post-processing before it may be used by the following video analysis algorithms. Due to imperfections of the background subtraction algorithms, the mask is distorted by the noise—single pixels or small groups of pixels being the false-positive results of the algorithm—and holes—a similar effect for the false-negative results. A common method of removing this noise and holes is using a morphological processing [6]. Two typical morphological operations used for this task are the dilation which increases the number of foreground pixels and closes small holes, and the erosion—a dual operation that reduces the number of foreground pixels and removes the noise. Since these operations distort the background subtraction result, they need to be performed together in a sequence. Typically, first the morphological opening (the erosion followed by the dilation) is performed for removing the noise, then the morphological closing (the dilation followed by the erosion) for closing small holes. All the morphological operations are usually performed using the same structuring element. In the presented work, a 3 × 3 pixels structuring element was used. The cleaned mask is passed as an input to the next processing stage, which usually performs the mask segmentation and extracts the connected components representing the moving objects. At this stage, groups of the false-positive pixels are removed by imposing a limit on the minimum connected component area.

# 3. ANALYSIS OF THE COMPUTATIONAL COMPLEXITY

There are two factors determining the time needed to process a single image frame with the background subtraction algorithm. The first one is the image resolution—the number of pixels to process. Assuming that no image pixels are removed from processing (masked out), all the pixels have to be processed independently, so the increase in image resolution results in a prolonged processing time (the relation should be linear in case of a sequential processing). The second, more important factor is the image content variability, which affects the processing time of a single pixel. If the scene in the sequence of images is 'empty' and stable, the processing time for each pixel should be identical (provided that a stable background model is already constructed). In practical situations, the motion occurs only in parts of the image and the changeability of the image content is usually not uniform—there are stable regions and the parts with different rate of content changes. Some of these changes may be recurring, other may be the short-term ones. This has a serious impact on the processing time of a single pixel.

## 3.1 The GMM algorithm

Complexity of the GMM method depends on many factors. It is assumed that color images are processed and the model for each of the image pixels is already created. The processing time $T$ is defined as:

$$T = T_M + kT_U, \tag{9}$$

where $T_M$ represents the time needed to find a matching Gaussian, $k$ is the number of distributions, and $T_U$ is the time required for the model update process. During the matching stage (corresponding to the $T_M$ time), each image pixel is compared with $k$ Gaussians. To assess whether the current pixel fits a particular distribution, its value is compared with the mean and the standard deviation of this distribution. This process is repeated for $k$ existing distributions, until a match is found. In order to improve the performance, the Gaussians are typically sorted in the order of decreasing $\omega/\sigma$ factor. Hence, the most probable match can be acquired in the first iteration. In case the analyzed pixel does not match any of the Gaussians, a new distribution is created replacing one of the existing, which is characterized by the lowest $\omega/\sigma$ factor.

The second GMM processing stage (corresponding to $T_U$ time) is related to the model update procedure. First, for the matching Gaussian, its parameters are adjusted according to Eqs. (2) and (3). Additionally, the resulting Gaussian variance is tested against a set minimum value. Next, regardless of whether a match was previously found or a new distribution was created, the distributions weights are updated according to Eq. (4).

The described procedure is carried out for each image pixel. However, the time required to analyze different image regions can vary significantly due to various scene characteristics. The more frequent movement can be observed in the image, the more difficult it is to model the background. Hence, more operations are required to be carried out, extending the processing time. This generally leads to increased $T_M$ time, since $T_U$ depends mostly on the number of Gaussian distributions. The modifications introduced to the original GMM method require extra calculations to be performed. However, in experiments with the adjusted adaptation method, fewer distributions are utilized (three instead of five). This compensates the time needed to carry out the additional update stage. Hence, both these methods are considered as one during the efficiency evaluation. Additional operations are needed to detect the shadowed regions falsely recognized as objects in the object detection stage.

## 3.2 The Codebook algorithm

In the Codebook algorithm, the total processing time of a single image pixel is a sum of the times needed to find a matching codeword (if any) and updating the matching codeword (if it was found) or creating and adding a new codeword to the model (in case a match was not found). Because the creation of a new codeword is simple, this factor was excluded from the analysis. The times needed for the memory allocation and restructuring of the codebook (removing the stale codewords, moving the codewords between the layers, etc.) were also omitted.

Searching for a matching codeword requires testing the brightness and color conditions for each codeword in the model, until a codeword with the matching color and brightness is found in any layer of the model (either the permanent or the long-term one, but not in the cache). Since the color condition described by Eq. (7) requires performing a considerably larger number of operations than the brightness condition expressed by Eq. (8), searching for a matched codeword is started with the brightness condition and, if it is fulfilled, the color condition is tested next. Because both the conditions have to be fulfilled in order to match the codeword, the non-matching codewords are discarded from the further analysis after the simpler condition was not met, which reduces the overall computation time.

There are two important factors that affect the analysis time of a single image pixel. First, the number of codewords representing the pixel is not constant in time, it depends on the image changeability and the rates of the codebook updating, from a single codeword in the stable regions to five or even more codewords in the highly variable regions (especially when the codebook cleaning is performed rarely). This is an important difference compared to the original GMM method in which the number of distributions per pixel is constant. Second, the analysis time of a single codeword depends on the number of codewords for which testing of both conditions was necessary. Therefore, the processing time in different regions of the image may differ significantly. If the time needed for testing the brightness and the color condition are denoted as $T_B$ and $T_C$, respectively, and the update time is $T_U$, the total processing time for a single image pixel can be expressed as:

$$T = N_B T_B + N_C(T_B + T_C) + N_U(T_B + T_C + T_U), \quad (10)$$

where $N_B$ is the number of codewords rejected after testing the brightness condition, $N_C$ is the number of codewords rejected after testing both conditions, $N_U$ is one if a matching codeword was found (so that it needs updating) and zero otherwise. In order to reduce the processing time, a matched codeword is moved to the front of the codebook, so that it is tested as the first one in the next image frame (because this codeword is a most likely match for the next image).

As a practical example of the relations discussed above, a camera view consisting of two regions will be presented. One of these regions is stable, e.g., a wall of a building in a constant lighting conditions, while the other is constantly changing, e.g., a busy sidewalk with people in different color clothing, moving continuously. In the first region, a matching codeword will be usually found and updated in the first step, so $T_1 = (T_B + T_C + T_U)$. In the second region, the processing time will be usually larger than $T_1$, but it cannot be predicted. The second codeword may be matched (in case of a recurrent movement) or none of the codewords may match. In the worst case, all the codewords may be rejected after testing both conditions, so that $T_{max} = N \cdot (T_B + T_C)$, where $N$ is the number of codewords representing the pixel. This may happen if a number of objects of a similar brightness but different color move through the observed region, so that a large number of codewords is created.

The observation that the processing time depends on variability of the image content has serious implications on load balancing in the parallelized algorithm. This problem will be discussed further in the article.

# 4. PARALLELIZATION STRATEGIES

The background subtraction algorithms described earlier—the GMM and the Codebook—perform independent analysis of each pixel, i.e., the result of analysis of a given pixel does not depend on the analysis result of any other pixel. Therefore, both algorithms are suitable for implementation in Single Instruction Multiple Data systems, as well as for a multi-threaded, parallel processing. In a massively parallel approach, each pixel could be analyzed in a separate thread. While this approach may be suitable for GPU computing, it is impractical in systems with a limited number of processing units. Therefore, the image is typically divided into several parts and each part is assigned to a processing thread. The main problem is a proper choice of the thread management and task scheduling methods. Four possible choices are presented in Table 1.

Two approaches to the thread management are possible: a manual and an automatic one. In the manual method, the programmer creates and manages the threads, e.g., using the Boost Threads library [14], and controls the task scheduling (assigning the image sections to the processing threads). This approach has an advantage of a complete control over the parallel processing. The automatic method utilizes a framework for parallel processing, e.g., using the OpenMP API [3], which performs the thread management and task scheduling using the black-box approach. This method is easier to implement, but the programmer loses the complete control over the process.

**Table 1** Possible implementation of thread management and task scheduling systems for parallel background subtraction in video

| | **Thread management** | |
|---|---|---|
| | **Manual** | **Automatic** |
| Task scheduling | | |
| Static | Threads managed by the programmer, e.g., with*boost::threads* | Pre-allocation of image parts, OpenMP: *#pragma parallel for schedule (static)* |
| Dynamic | As above + task scheduling system written by the programmer | Image rows assigned to threads on demand by OpenMP: *#pragma parallel for schedule (dynamic)* |

The task scheduling may be done using different approaches. Sections of the image may be assigned to the threads a priori, before the processing is started, e.g., the image may be cut into four horizontal stripes and each part is processed by a separate thread. An alternative approach is to assign smaller chunks of data to threads, e.g., a single row of pixels may be initially given to each thread. When a thread finishes its work, it receives another row of pixel to process. This procedure is repeated until the whole image is processed. This approach should, in theory, provide a better work balancing between threads, at a cost of overhead related to more complex thread management. In the OpenMP API, these two approaches are named the static and the dynamic task scheduling, respectively [3]. The dynamic approach is easy to implement in the automatic thread management, in OpenMP it only requires adding a single pragma command to the code. Using the dynamic method with the manual thread management is possible, but requires additional work needed for creating an own thread management system. Figure 1 presents simplified block diagrams of both task scheduling methods.

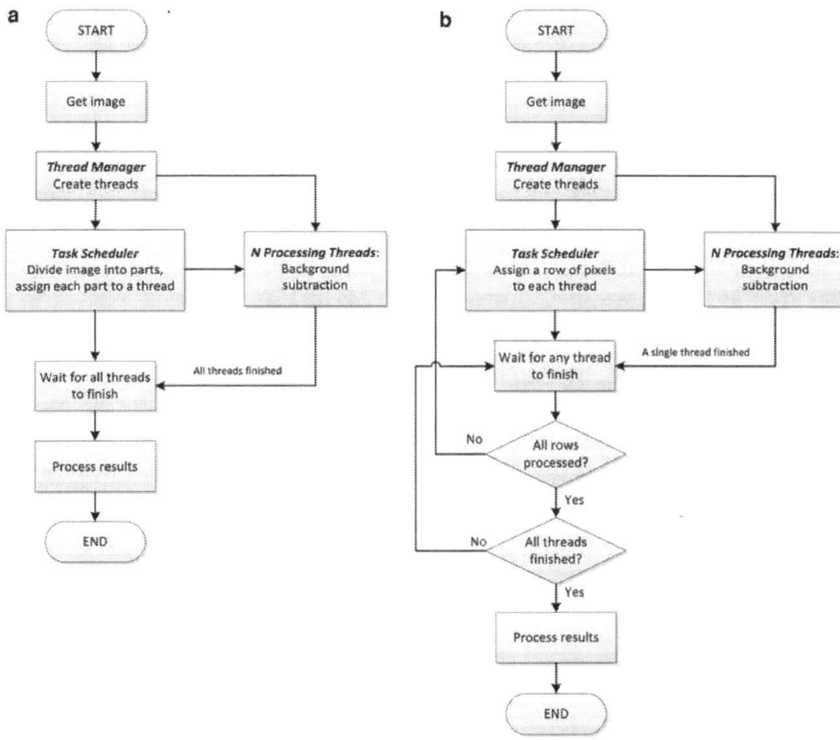


**Figure. 1** Simplified block diagrams of the parallel background subtraction in image frames using **a** the static and **b** the dynamic task scheduling methods

As it was discussed previously, in both background subtraction algorithms, especially in the Codebook method, the processing time of a single pixel varies according to the rate of image changeability. This is important when a parallelization strategy is selected. The most intuitive approach is to use manually managed threads with the static task scheduling, e.g., to create four threads and assign a horizontal image strip for each thread. However, let us discuss what happens if one of these strips contains changing content (e.g., a busy street) and the others are static (the sky, buildings, a lawn, etc.). If the static approach is used, the thread which receives the 'street' part will have to work longer (more codewords or Gaussians to check) and the other threads will finish their work earlier and they will be idle, resulting in a poor work balance. Therefore, the dynamic approach seems to be more suitable for the background subtraction. The preliminary experiments showed that even in case of more uniform movement in the image, the dynamic approach was more efficient than the static one [7]. This is further verified in the experiments described in this article.

OpenMP was employed for the task scheduling in the background subtraction, because it allows for selection of either the dynamic or the static scheduling method. Since the processing algorithm analyzes the image by rows (the outer loop) and then each row by pixel (the inner loop), it was decided to parallelize the outer loop iterations (*pragma parallel for*), so that a single row of pixels is assigned to a thread at a given time. It was previously verified that assigning larger data chunks to threads (more than one pixel row) does not improve performance of the algorithm [7]. Moreover, the OpenMP library also provides a guided task scheduling method, which in theory should balance the advantages and disadvantages of the static and dynamic approaches [3]. However, the guided method in the current implementation of the GOMP library used for tests does not perform better than the static one [7].

The morphological processing is parallelized using the same approach. The static task scheduling method is sufficient in this case, because the processing times for different pixels are comparable. Because the output value depends on the input values of pixels in the neighborhood, each dilation/erosion operation has to be run separately, in sequence.

# 5. EXPERIMENTS

## 5.1 Performance testing

The performance of the background subtraction algorithms was tested on a live 'supercomputer' system using the KASKADA framework. A single computing node contained two six-core CPUs in Xeon EM64T architecture, running at 2.27 GHz, with 16 GB RAM, controlled by the Debian Linux operating system. The whole system consists of 192 nodes connected with Infiniband network and its computing power is rated at 20.9 TFLOPS [31]. The algorithms were written in C++ language and compiled with the GNU compiler in version 4.3.2 with the parameters tuned to the supercomputer architecture. The GOMP library (an implementation of the OpenMP API) was used for the parallel task scheduling.

In the tests, a camera recording of HD resolution (1,920 × 1,200 pixels, 25 fps) and several downscaled versions of the same recordings were processed. Since it was not possible to find a suitable HD recording in the available benchmark sets, a typical recording from the city traffic-monitoring camera, with an uniform movement of vehicles in the camera frame was chosen. The initial 100 frames of the recording were used for the background model training and the actual background subtraction was timed in the remaining 1,400 frames. For each image resolution, seven values of concurrently running processing threads, from 1 to 12, were tested. The hyperthreading capabilities of the CPUs were not used, only the physical cores were employed. Two task scheduling methods: the static and the dynamic one, were evaluated using the OpenMP system. Each test run (for a given resolution, task scheduling method and number of threads) was repeated 12 times and the measured running times were expressed in a number of frames processed per second (fps). Only the background subtraction procedure was timed, other operations related to video decoding, memory buffer management, etc., were not included in measurements, because they are common for each tested algorithm in all configurations. In each test run, the lowest and the highest recorded fps values were discarded and the remaining 10 test results were averaged.

The results of the performance testing for the original GMM and the Codebook algorithms are presented in Fig. 2. The modified GMM algorithm performed similarly to the original one so it was omitted for the result clarity. Surprisingly, the observed performance of the GMM algorithm was significantly better compared with the Codebook algorithm. In many cases, the GMM algorithm was 3–4 times faster. A higher complexity of a single pixel processing, varying number of the codewords per pixel and the need for constant memory allocations and deallocations are the most probable reasons for the observed worse performance of the Codebook algorithm. The GMM method, with a fixed number of Gaussians per pixel, was faster despite the need for performing an additional shadow removal. For lower image resolutions (up to 800 × 450), a single thread is sufficient to achieve the processing speed exceeding twice the source fps value if the GMM algorithm is used. For larger resolutions, 4–6 threads are needed for similar processing fps. However, in case of the HD recording, the GMM algorithm was not able to achieve satisfactory fps value. The Codebook algorithm needed 8–12 threads in order to achieve the same performance level as the GMM with 2 or 4 threads.

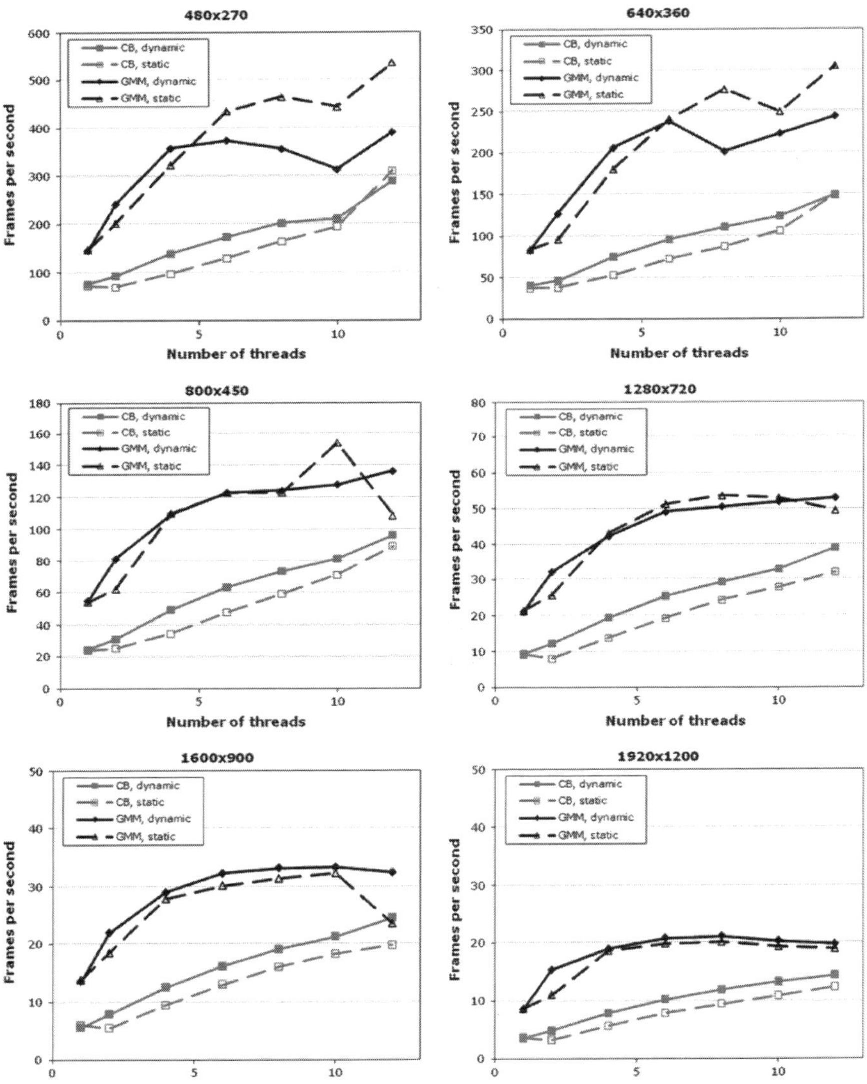


**Figure. 2** Results of performance testing of the parallel GMM and Codebook algorithms, using the static and the dynamic task scheduling in OpenMP, expressed as frames processed per second versus the number of processing threads. The *Y* scale is different for each subplot in order to provide better visualization of the results

In terms of the parallel processing, increasing the number of threads for the Codebook algorithm resulted in reduction of the processing time and the relation was, in most of the cases, almost linear, although the fps values obtained for higher resolutions are not satisfactory. With the GMM algorithm, increasing the number of threads gives a performance boost up to eight threads and using more than six threads is not significantly beneficial. This is especially evident for the lower image resolutions, where too many threads decrease the algorithm performance. However, this effect is observed for very large fps values (more than 150), so it has no practical implications. The most important observation is that for the HD recording, using more than four threads do not improve the processing time in a significant way. One possible explanation for the abovementioned effects is that the payload related to running and managing a larger number of threads is not balanced by the decrease in the actual processing time of a single thread. It should be noted that when the input image is divided into more than four parts, decrease in the chunk size for a single thread is not as significant as when two or four threads are used instead of one, especially for lower image resolutions. Also, when the number of the processing threads exceeds the number of the physical cores of a single CPU (which is equal to six), some hardware issues, especially related to the memory access, may influence the results. However, these details are difficult to test and the authors of this article did not have access to the low level of the system architecture, they were only able to implement the tested algorithms in a way that the internal organization of data structures or the order of pixel processing do not influence the performance of the algorithm.

Comparing the dynamic and the static task scheduling methods, it may be observed that the dynamic approach improves the performance of the Codebook algorithm, being 1.3–1.6 times faster than the static one when two to six threads are used. The difference decreases with the rising number of threads. For the low resolutions and a high number of threads, the overhead of the dynamic method is too high. For the GMM method, both approaches yield comparable results in the range of up to 200 fps values, the dynamic method is marginally better for the lower number of threads. Therefore, the static approach is sufficient in case of the GMM method, while for the Codebook algorithm the dynamic method improves its performance.

## 5.2 Accuracy of background subtraction

In order to evaluate the detection accuracy of both implemented methods, the experiments using a set of benchmark videos were carried out. A precise and objective evaluation of the object detection results is a difficult task. Most authors verify the algorithms on the basis of a single selected video frame. However, techniques based on the virtual scenes can also be found in the literature [2]. In this work, the following approach was utilized. Two recordings from the PETS2001 [21] and two recordings from the PETS2006 [22] datasets were chosen. Two of the selected video samples from the PETS2006 dataset represent a typical indoor scene (S1-T1-C3, S3-T7-A3) with medium intensity of the object movement and a stable lighting. Both recordings from the PETS2001 dataset depict an outdoor scene with a parking lot (ds1_ts_c2, ds3_ts_c1). The second of these videos represents difficult conditions for object detection: illumination variations caused by the clouds moving on the sky on a sunny day. Such a dataset allows for evaluating the algorithms in different conditions. The parameters of the test videos are presented in Table 2.

For the purpose of assessment of the object detection accuracy, the ground truth data was prepared. In order to obtain it, a set of images in 60 frames intervals was extracted from each of the analyzed recordings. These images were then manually processed and, as a result, the masks denoting the foreground objects were created. This way, 223 images representing the ground truth data were acquired.

For the assessment of the object detection results, the following three measures based on errors of type I and II were calculated:

$$\text{Precision} = \frac{\text{TP}}{\text{TP} + \text{FP}} \tag{11}$$

$$\text{Recall} = \frac{\text{TP}}{\text{TP} + \text{FN}} \tag{12}$$

$$\text{Accuracy} = \frac{\text{TP} + \text{TN}}{\text{TP} + \text{FP} + \text{FN} + \text{TN}}, \tag{13}$$

where TP pixels correctly assigned to the foreground (true-positive result), TN pixels correctly assigned to the background (true-negative), FP pixels incorrectly assigned to the foreground (false-positive), FN pixels incorrectly assigned to the background (false-negative).

**Table 2** Characterization of the dataset utilized for the algorithm quality assessment

| **Dataset** | **Video name** | **Resolution** | **Fps** | **Scene characteristics** |
|---|---|---|---|---|
| PETS 2001 | ds1_ts_c 2 | 768 × 576 | 25 | Outdoor, parking lot, low illumination variations |
| PETS 2001 | ds3_ts_c 1 | 768 × 576 | 25 | Outdoor, parking lot, high illumination variations |
| PETS 2006 | S1-T1-C3 | 720 × 576 | 25 | Indoor, train station, constant illumination |
| PETS 2006 | S3-T7-A3 | 720 × 576 | 25 | Indoor, train station, constant illumination |

The precision factor denotes the rate of the correct detection results in relation to the whole foreground area. The recall parameter indicates the degree of the relevant detections. The accuracy is a more comprehensive measure, which shows the overall similarity of the result to the ground truth data. All of these parameters should be maximized for the optimal algorithm. These factors were calculated for each of the prepared ground truth data.

In order to acquire the object detection results from the implemented algorithms, all four test recordings were analyzed by three algorithms (the original GMM, the modified GMM and the Codebook). Identical algorithm parameters, listed in Table 3, were used for each of the processed videos. During the preliminary experiments, various parameter values were tested. The chosen settings allow for achieving a compromise between the results acquired for all four analyzed recordings.

**Table 3** Object detection algorithms settings utilized during the carried out experiments

| **Method** | **Codebook** | **GMM** | **Modified GMM** |
|---|---|---|---|
| | $\alpha = 0.7$ | $\rho$ = 0.0005 | $\rho = 0.0005$ |
| | $\beta = 1.2$ | $\alpha$ = 0.0005 | $\alpha = 0.0005$ |
| | $\varepsilon_1 = 20$ | $k = 5$ | $k = 3$ |
| | $\varepsilon_2 = 20$ | $T = 0.5$ | $T = 0.5$ |
| | $T_h = 20$ | $\Delta = 2.5$ | $\Delta = 2.5$ |
| | $T_{add} = 100$ | | $\gamma = 0.075$ |
| Parameters | $T_{del} = 100$ | | $D_{th} = 5$ |

The aggregated results for each of the recordings are illustrated in Fig. 3. Analyzing the precision plot, it can be observed that for all the four videos, the modified version of the GMM method gives the best results in terms of the mean precision and the result stability. Additionally, the high precision stability related to low deviation of the measure for the utilized benchmark data is achieved. A high precision value means that more pixels were correctly assigned to the foreground and at the same time, fewer pixels were incorrectly excluded from the background. For the adjusted GMM method, this outcome is related to better adaptation capabilities. Hence, the static image regions observed under the changing illumination were still recognized as the background elements. The most significant differences between the regular and the modified GMM method (in the favor of the second) are noticeable for the recording with high lighting variations.

The recall plot depicts the rate of how many of the relevant results were correctly denoted. In other words, it is related to the sensitivity of the algorithm. Hence, the higher the recall is, the more objects are reliably detected. The results show that the regular GMM method is the most sensitive of all the evaluated object detection algorithms. This outcome agrees with the predictions regarding the modified GMM approach since the adjustments were designed to lower the algorithm sensitivity. The Codebook method turns out to perform worst, similarly as for the precision factor. However, in the case of the outdoor recording with illumination changes, it outperforms the regular GMM algorithm significantly.

The accuracy factor is an overall score which describes the rate of correct classifications to both categories, which in this case are the background and the foreground. In terms of the accuracy factor, all the assessed algorithms produce comparable results. Only for the recording where the dynamic illumination changes are present, relevant differences can be seen. The mean accuracy value for the Codebook and for the modified GMM method are similar. However, the Codebook algorithm produces less stable results.

The optimal object detection algorithm should be characterized by maximized values of the precision, recall and accuracy factors. Hence, a summary of the results with the scores from each processed video aggregated is presented in Fig. 4. Analyzing the overall score, it can be stated that the best results for the prepared dataset in terms of the object detection quality can be achieved with the modified GMM method, followed by the regular GMM algorithm and the Codebook as the least accurate one.

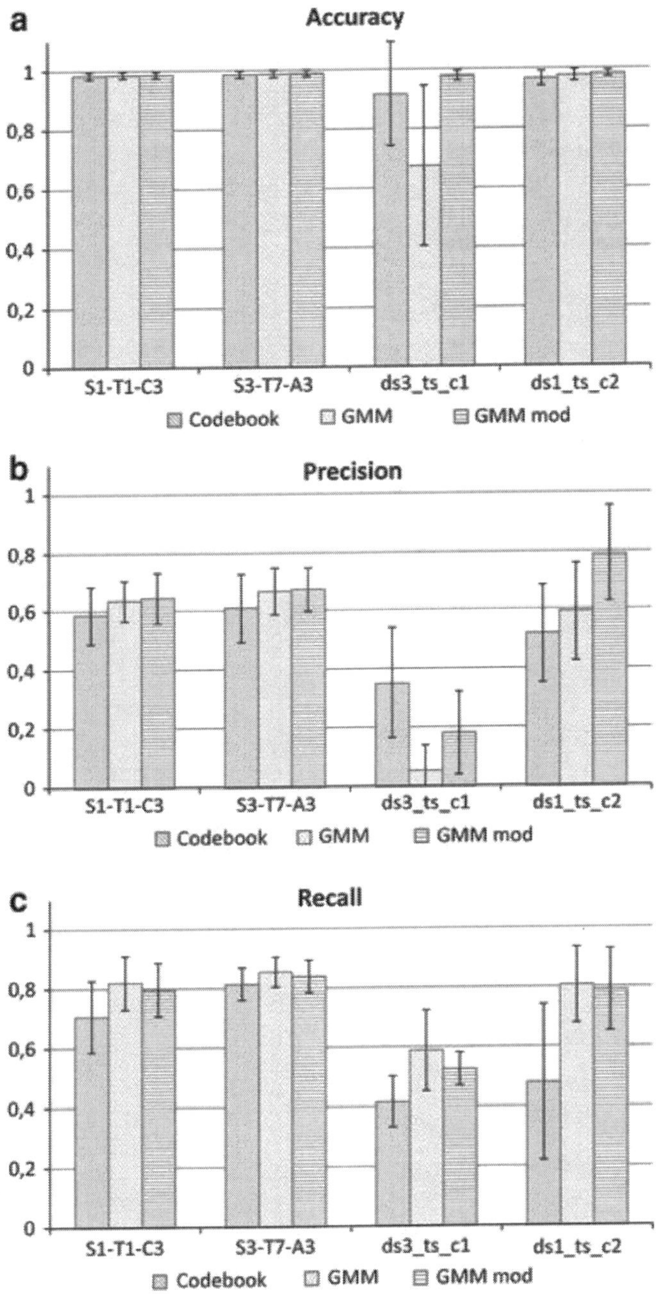


**Figure. 3** Results of object detection quality testing of the Codebook, GMM and modified GMM algorithms. Precision, recall and accuracy are expressed for each of the four recordings as a mean value with a standard deviation *bar*

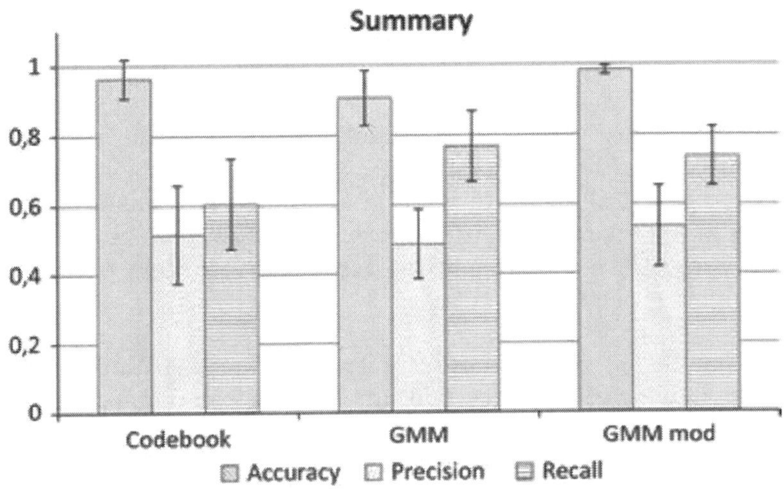


**Figure. 4** The summary of object detection quality testing of Codebook, GMM and modified GMM algorithms. The averaged results for all the analyzed recordings are presented

# 6. CONCLUSIONS

The task of the authors was to implement the background subtraction algorithm in a parallel manner, within the framework for a complex multimedia stream processing running on a supercomputer. In order to realize this task, a sufficiently accurate algorithm, a method of parallel implementation and a strategy of assigning the image pixels to the threads had to be chosen. The authors have not found such a research in the published works, therefore the results, which may be useful for other researchers implementing the background subtraction procedure on a parallel system, were presented in this article. The authors also proposed an improvement to the original GMM algorithm making it more robust in difficult lighting conditions and also a modification of the training phase in the Codebook algorithm.

Two background subtraction algorithms were tested—the GMM (in two versions: the original one and the proposed modification) and the Codebook—and the accuracy and performance of their parallel implementation on a supercomputer platform for the real-time video processing were evaluated. The GMM algorithm proved to be significantly more efficient than the Codebook. For the high-resolution images, the rate of processed frames per seconds could not achieve the source fps rate, despite increasing the number of processing threads running concurrently on the separate physical processing units. For the lower image resolutions, two to six threads provide a sufficient performance, and increasing the number of threads above this level does not reduce the processing time. The Codebook algorithm is too slow for a practical application in the real-time video analysis system. This method has some potential, but the algorithm requires reworking in order to reduce the complexity, especially regarding the memory management procedures.

In terms of the object detection accuracy, all tested algorithms provide a satisfactory level of the correct results. When all three measures—the overall accuracy, precision and recall—are taken into account, the GMM algorithm provides the best results for both the indoor and outdoor videos, and it outperforms the original GMM method in case of difficult lighting conditions.

On a basis of the performed efficiency and accuracy tests, the GMM algorithm with the proposed modification was selected for the parallel implementation on a supercomputer. Because the conducted research employs mainly cameras of PAL (768 × 576) and higher resolutions, six physical CPU cores for six processing threads should be sufficient for obtaining the processing fps rate at a level suitable for the real-time processing, without the need for decreasing resolution or dropping frames. An automatic thread management with OpenMP API is used, because it provides good performance and reduces the amount of work related to adapting the algorithm for parallel implementation. It was also decided to use the dynamic task scheduling, as the overhead related to the resource management is not significant and the dynamic approach may be useful in case of camera scenes with movement limited to some horizontal image sections.

In the future, the authors plan to test the performance of the background subtraction algorithms together with other video processing algorithms, such as object tracking, classification and event detection, running on other supercomputer nodes and communicating with a message passing interface system. The future work will also focus on processing high-resolution images using multiple supercomputer nodes in order to avoid the observed effect of saturated performance of the algorithm. Additionally, the authors plan to test the performance of the background subtraction algorithms implemented on GPU devices in order to compare the results with these presented in this article and to asses the capabilities of the modern GPU devices for the real-time processing of high-resolution video streams from cameras.

## ACKNOWLEDGMENTS

Research funded within the project No. POIG.02.03.03-00-008/08, entitled "MAYDAY EURO 2012—the supercomputer platform of context-depended analysis of multimedia data streams for identifying specified objects or safety threads". The project is subsidized by the European regional development fund and by the Polish State budget.

## REFERENCES

1. Benezeth, Y., Jodoin, P.-M., Emile, B., Laurent, H., Rosenberg, C.: Comparative study of background subtraction algorithms. J. Electron. Imaging 19(3) (2010).

2. Brutzer, S., Hoeferlin, B., Heidemann, G.: Evaluation of Background subtraction techniques for video surveillance. In: Proceedings of 24th IEEE Conference on Computer Vision and Pattern Recognition, 1937–1944 (2011)

3. Chapman, B., Jost, G., van der Paas, R.: Using OpenMP. Portable shared memory parallel programming. MIT Press, Cambridge (2007)

4. Chen, G., Yu, Z., Wen, Q., Yu, Y.: Improved Gaussian mixture model for moving object learning. Artif Intell Comput Intell LNCS **7002/2011**, 179–186 (2011).

5. Czyżewski, A., Szwoch, G., Dalka, P., et al.: Multi-stage video analysis framework. In: Lin, W. (ed.) Video Surveillance, pp. 147–172. Intech (2011)

6. Dougherty, E., Lotufo, R.: Hands-on morphological processing. SPIE Press, Bellingham (2003)

7. Dziech, A., Czyżewski, A. (eds.): Performance evaluation of the parallel codebook algorithm for background subtraction in video stream.

Multimedia Communications, Services and Security, Communications in Computer and Information Science, Springer **149**, 149–157 (2011)

8. Fauske, E., Eliassen, L.M., Bakken, R.H.: A comparison of learning based background subtraction techniques implemented in CUDA. In: Proceedings of Norwegian Artificial Intelligent Symposium (NAIS), pp. 181–192, Trondheim (2009)

9. Friedman, N., Russell, S.: Image segmentation in video sequences: a probabilistic approach. In: Proceedings of 13th Conference on Uncertainty in Artificial Intelligence (1997)

10. Horprasert, T., Harwood, D., Davis, L.S.: A statistical approach for real-time robust background subtraction and shadow detection. In: Proceedings of IEEE Frame Rate Workshop, Kerkyra, pp. 1–19 (1999)

11. Ilyas, A., Scuturici, M., Miguet, S.: Real time foreground-background segmentation using a modified Codebook Model. In: Proceedings of Sixth IEEE International Conference on Advanced Video and Signal Based Surveillance AVSS, pp. 454–459, Genova (2009)

12. KaewTraKulPong, P., Bowden, R.: An improved adaptive background mixture model for real-time tracking with shadow detection. In: Proceedings of 2nd European Workshop on Advanced Video Based Surveillance Systems (2001)

13. Karasulu, B.: Review and evaluation of well-known methods for moving object detection and tracking in videos. J. Aeronaut. Space Technol. **4**, 11–22 (2010)

14. Kempf, B.: The Boost Threads library. C/C++ Users J. **20**(5), 6–13 (2002)

15. Kim, K., Davis, L.S.: Object detection and tracking for intelligent video surveillance. Multimed Anal Process Commun **346**, 265–288 (2011)

16. Kim, K., Chalidabhongse, T.H., Harwood, D., Davis, L.: Real-time foreground-background segmentation using codebook model. Real-time Imaging **11**, 167–256 (2005)

17. Kim, K., Harwood, D., Davis, L.: Background updating for visual surveillance. In: Bebis, G., Boyle, R., Koracin, D., Parvin, B. (eds.) Advances in Visual Computing, LNCS, vol. 3804, pp. 337–346. Springer, Heidelberg (2005)

18. Krawczyk, H., Proficz, J.: KASKADA—Multimedia processing platform architecture. In: Proceedings of International Conference on Signal Processing and Multimedia Applications (SIGMAP), Athens, pp. 26–31 (2010)

19. Li, Y., Chen, F., Xu, W., Du, Y.: Gaussian-Based Codebook Model for video background subtraction. Advances in Natural Computation, LNCS, vol. 4222, pp. 762–776, Springer (2006)

20. Parks, D.H., Fels, S.S.: Evaluation of background subtraction algorithms with post-processing. In: Proceedings of IEEE Fifth International Conference on Advanced Video and Signal Based Surveillance AVSS, pp. 192–199, Sanfa Fe (2008)

21. PETS 2001 dataset.: 2nd IEEE international workshop on performance evaluation of tracking and surveillance (PETS 2001), Kauai, Hawaii (2001). http://www.cvg.cs.rdg.ac.uk/PETS2001/pets2001-dataset.html. Accessed 4 Dec 2012

22. PETS 2006 dataset.: 9th IEEE international workshop on performance evaluation of tracking and surveillance (PETS 2006), New York (2006). http://www.cvg.rdg.ac.uk/PETS2006/data.html. Accessed 4 Dec 2012

23. Pham, V., Vo, P., Hung, V.T., Bac, L.H.: GPU Implementation of extended Gaussian Mixture Model for Background Subtraction. IEEE RIVF International Conference on Computing and Communication Technologies, Research, Innovation, and Vision for the Future (RIVF), pp. 1–4, Hanoi (2010)

24. Reinders, J.: Intel threading building blocks. Outfitting C++ for multi-core processor parallelism. O'Reilly Media, Sebastopol (2007). ISBN 10: 0-596-51480-8. http://shop.oreilly.com/product/9780596514808.do

25. Setiawan, N.A., Seok-Ju, H., Jang-Woon, K., Chil-Woo, L.: Gaussian mixture model in improved HLS color space for human Silhouette extraction. Advances in artificial reality and tele-existence, Lecture notes in computer science, vol. 4282, Springer, pp. 732–741 (2006)

26. Shimada, A., Taniguchi, R.: Hybrid background model using Spatial-Temporal LBP. Advanced Video and Signal Based Surveillance (2009)

27. Sicre, R., Nicolas, H.: Improved Gaussian mixture model for the task of object tracking. Lecture Notes in Computer Science, vol. 6855/2011, pp. 389–396 (2011).

28. Sigari, M.H., Fathy, M.: Real-time background modeling/subtraction using Two-Layer Codebook Model. In: Proceedings of International Multi-Conference of Engineers and Computer Scientists IMECS, pp. 1–5. Hong Kong (2008)

29. Stauffer, C., Grimson, W.E.: Adaptive background mixture models for real-time tracking. In: Proceedings of IEEE Conference on Computer Vision and Pattern Recognition, pp. 246–252. USA (1999)

30. Suo, P., Wang, Y.: An improved adaptive background modelling algorithm based on Gaussian mixture model, ICSP (2008)

31. TASK: Galera plus. http://www.task.gda.pl/kdm/kdm/gplus (in Polish)

32. Wang, J., Dong, L.: Moving objects detection method based on a fast convergence Gaussian mixture model. In: 3rd International Conference on Computer Research and Development, pp. 269–273. China (2011)

33. Zivkovic, Z., Van der Heijden, F.: Efficient adaptive density estimation per image pixel for the task of background subtraction. Pattern Recogn. Lett. **27**(7), 773–780 (2006)

2

# ARCHITECTURE DESIGN OF THE HIGH-THROUGHPUT COMPENSATOR AND INTERPOLATOR FOR THE H.265/HEVC ENCODER

**Grzegorz Pastuszak, Maciej Trochimiuk**

Institute of Radioelectronics, Warsaw University of Technology, Nowowiejska 15/19, 00-665 Warsaw, Poland

## ABSTRACT

This paper presents the architecture of the high-throughput compensator and the interpolator used in the motion estimation of the H.265/HEVC encoder. The architecture can process 8×8 blocks in each clock cycle. The design allows the random order of checked coding blocks and motion vectors. This feature makes the architecture suitable for different search algorithms. The interpolator embeds 64 multiplierless reconfigurable filter cores to support computations for different fractional-pel positions. Synthesis results show that the design can operate at 200 and 400 MHz when implemented in FPGA Arria II and TSMC 90 nm, respectively. The computational scalability enables the proposed architecture to trade the throughput for the compression efficiency. If 2160p@30fps video is encoded, the design clocked at 400 MHz can check about 100 motion vectors for 8×8 blocks.

## KEYWORDS

Video coding, Interpolation, Motion estimation, H.265/HEVC, FPGA, Very large-scale integration (VLSI)


## 1. INTRODUCTION

The latest research and standardization efforts in video coding have lead to the specification of the H.265/HEVC standard [1, 2]. In terms of the rate-distortion efficiency, it provides the improvement of about 35–50 % over its predecessor H.264/AVC [3] at the price of increased computational complexity. Although the general structure of encoder and decoder remains the same, there are many changes in the algorithm of each module. In the case of the subpixel motion estimation and compensation, the size of prediction blocks can be selected from 8×4/4×8 to 64×64. Also, there are new interpolation schemes to compute fractional-pel positions. Compared to H.264/AVC, the new interpolation provides the improvement of inter coding by 0.144 dB, on average [4]. H.264/AVC and H.265/HEVC standards employ fractional-sample interpolation of reference pictures with the quarter-pixel accuracy. The H.264/AVC standard uses six-tap luma filtering of half-pel positions followed by linear interpolation for quarter-pel positions. Chroma samples are computed by weighed interpolation of four closest integer-pel samples. In H.265/HEVC, seven-tap and eight-tap filters are used for the luma interpolation of half-pel and quarter-pel positions, respectively. Chroma samples are computed using four-tap filters. Filter coefficients are provided in Table 1.

Design and implementation of digital filters is a thoroughly explored issue, especially for small-tap filters. Moreover, digital signal processors are well suited for high-speed filtering since their architectures are adjusted to vector and matrix computations using many parallel multiply-and-accumulate units. Nevertheless, computational resources of processors are often not sufficient to support compression-efficient encoding, especially for high resolutions. Therefore, dedicated hardware accelerators are necessary.

Except one design [5], architectures for the motion estimation consist of two parts assigned to the integer-pel and fractional-pel search [6–15]. This approach requires separate reference-pixel buffers for each part. The integer-pel part usually applies the hierarchical strategies to extend the search range, which involves quality losses. Most architectures use non-adaptive search patterns and their resource consumption is large [6–10]. The architecture supporting Multipoint Diamond Search proposed in [11] requires less resource. However, it supports only 16×16 blocks, limiting the compression efficiency.

**Table 1** Filter coefficients in the H.265/HEVC interpolator

| Filter type | Reference sample index | | | | | | | |
|---|---|---|---|---|---|---|---|---|
| | −3 | −2 | −1 | 0 | 1 | 2 | 3 | 4 |
| Luma 1/4 | −1 | 4 | −10 | 58 | 17 | −5 | 1 | |
| Luma 1/2 | −1 | 4 | −11 | 40 | 40 | −11 | 4 | −1 |
| Luma 3/4 | | 1 | −5 | 17 | 58 | −10 | 4 | −1 |
| Chroma 1/8 | | | −2 | 58 | 10 | −2 | | |
| Chroma 1/4 | | | −4 | 54 | 16 | −2 | | |
| Chroma 3/8 | | | −6 | 46 | 28 | −4 | | |
| Chroma 1/2 | | | −4 | 36 | 36 | −4 | | |
| Chroma 5/8 | | | −4 | 28 | 46 | −6 | | |
| Chroma 3/4 | | | −2 | 16 | 54 | −4 | | |
| Chroma 7/8 | | | −2 | 10 | 58 | −2 | | |

Some high-throughput interpolators have been proposed in the literature for H.264/AVC [5–9]. Their scheduling assumes two successive steps, one for the half-pel interpolation and another for the quarter-pel interpolation. This approach is natural in terms of the specification of quarter-pel computations which refer to the results of half-pel computations. This dataflow cannot be applied directly in H.265/HEVC since quarter-pel samples are computed using separate filters. In particular, more filters are needed in the second step. Furthermore, the hardware cost increases due to a larger number of filter taps and much higher throughputs required (more partitioning modes). Some interpolator architectures have been described in publications [12–15]. They achieve throughputs suitable for video resolutions from 1080 to 4320p. Their scheduling assumes that interpolation is performed only around one point selected at the integer-pel stage for a given prediction unit. This limits the search flexibility and scalability. Moreover, three designs [12–14] are based on the assumption that the size of prediction units is selected. If the processing of more sizes has to be performed, the throughput is decreased accordingly. One design [15] supports three prediction block sizes (16×16, 32×32, and 64×64). On the other hand, it consumes a large amount of hardware resources. In general, obtaining a compression-efficient and high-throughput implementation requires more hardware resources and increases power consumption. Therefore, there is a need for solutions optimizing these parameters.

This work presents the high-throughput architecture of the compensator and the interpolator dedicated to the H.265/HEVC encoder. Similarly to the previous work dedicated to H.264/AVC [5], the modules can check one motion vector for an 8×8 block in each clock cycle. This feature makes the architecture suitable for different fast search algorithms as the order of motion vectors does not affect the architecture. Moreover, the computational scalability enables the tradeoff between the throughput for the compression efficiency. The present work has three novel contributions. Firstly, the fine-level search range is extended, whereas the memory cost is reduced. Secondly, the interpolation for a given prediction block can be performed in parallel with the integer-pel search. Thirdly, the proposed reconfigurable filter core for H.265/HEVC can process both luma and chroma.

The proposed dataflow reduces the size of on-chip memories 16 times while preserving the random order of checked coding blocks and fractional-accuracy motion vectors. The interpolator embeds 64 multiplierless reconfigurable filter cores to support computations for different fractional-pel positions.

The rest of the paper is organized as follows: Sect. 2 reviews previous developments on the hardware design of the adaptive motion estimation. Section 3 describes the new architecture of the motion estimation system for H.265/HEVC. Scheduling of the interpolation is presented in Sect. 4. Section 5 concentrates on the design of the reconfigurable filter core used in the interpolator. Section 6 provides implementations results. Finally, the paper is concluded in Sect. 7.

## 2. DESIGN FOR ADAPTIVE MOTION ESTIMATION

The adaptive computationally scalable motion estimation algorithm allows the H.264/AVC encoders to achieve efficiencies close to optimal in real-time conditions [16]. The algorithm can employ different search strategies to adapt to local motion activity, and the number of checked search points is set by the encoder controller for each macroblock. The algorithm can achieve results close to optimum even if the number of search points assigned to macroblocks is strongly limited and varies with time. The block diagram of the architecture supporting the adaptive computationally scalable motion estimation at the fine level [5] is depicted in Fig. 1. For clarity, the coarse-level engine is omitted. Note that the coarse level in the hierarchical motion estimation enables a wider search range at the lower accuracy of motion vectors. The architecture includes the interpolator and the motion vector generator. The remaining elements build the compensator. The design allows the adaptive search for both integer-pel and fractional-pel positions as the interpolated pixels are loaded to 64 on-chip memories along with integer-pel ones. Particularly, the interpolator processes the reference area prior to the search algorithm performed by the motion vector generator and the compensator. Each memory keeps every eighth sample both in the horizontal and vertical dimension, and each fraction-pel sample is stored in the same memory as its closest top-left integer neighbor. In general, samples for a given MV can belong to four adjacent 8×8 blocks (see Fig. 2a, b). Since MVs vary in the whole search range, data control is enhanced. Firstly, integer parts of read address coordinates are incremented for memories keeping samples located at the bottom and right sides of the 8×8 search-area grid lines. Secondly, two shifters rotate samples between block positions in the horizontal and vertical dimension to restore their space consistency (see Fig. 2c, d).

Original pixels and intra predictions are buffered in the same memories as the interpolated reference area. As a consequence, the joint size of the memories is significant even when the search range is small. For example, each of the 64 memory modules needs 16k bits when using one reference frame and the search range of [−8, 7] in both dimensions. In the case of the H.265/HEVC encoder, the memory capacity would be much greater since the processing on 16×16-pixel macroblocks is replaced by coding tree units with sizes up to 64×64 pixels. Taking into account the wider search range of [−32, 31] in both dimensions, the memory capacity could be increased 16 times. If the architecture is restricted to the luma component, the increase can be reduced to four. However, such a design still would be inefficient in terms of silicon area and power consumption. The interpolator developed for the considered H.265/HEVC architecture is about three to four times more complex [4] than that used in H.264/AVC. This increase stems from the greater number and order of interpolation filters applied.

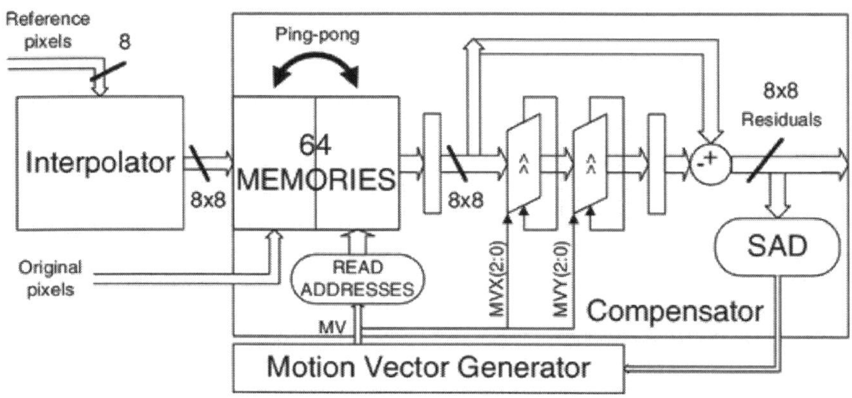


**Figure. 1** Architecture of the adaptive motion estimation system

## 3. NEW ARCHITECTURE

The dataflow is modified to reduce the memory capacity in the H.265/HEVC adaptive ME system described in the previous section. Instead of storing interpolated pixels in the memories, the architecture can compute fractional-pel samples after reading integer-pel ones from the memories. For a given search range, this approach decreases the memory space assigned to luma samples 16 times. The interpolated area of each chroma component occupies the same memory space as luma one regardless of the chroma subsampling format. If the interpolation is performed after reading (as in the modified architecture), the reduction of the memory space for chroma is greater than for luma. Particularly, the 4:2:0 video format enables the 64-fold reduction. The lower memory cost allows wider search ranges, subsequently removing the need for the hierarchical search.

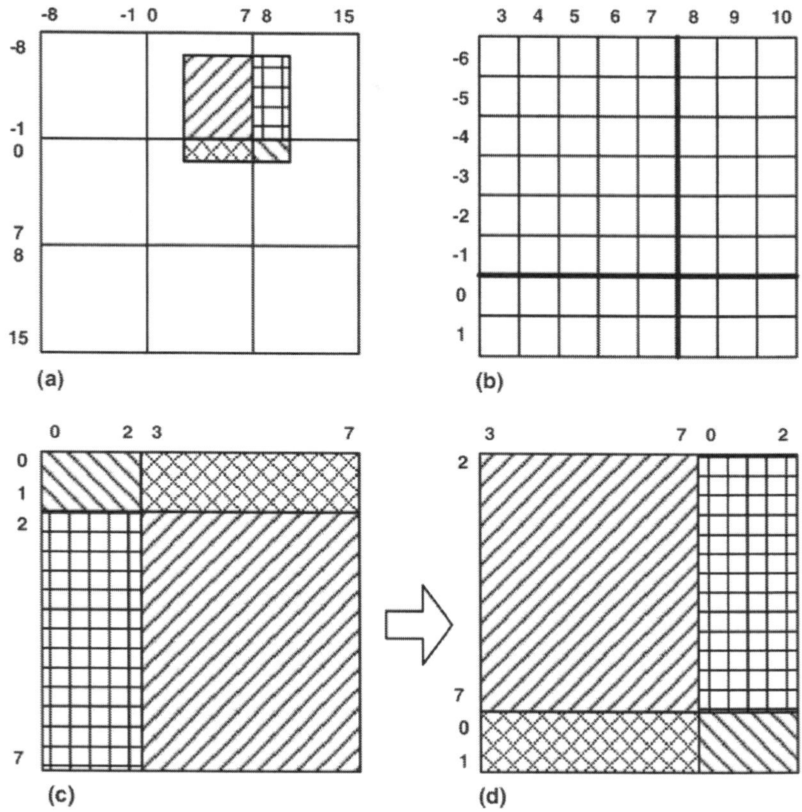


**Figure. 2** Sample arrangement of the 8×8 block for MV = (3, −6): **a** location within search area; **b** block samples with their search-area indices; **c** block samples read from memories with 2D memory indices; **d** block samples after the rotation with 2D memory indices

The proposed architecture embeds 64 memory modules to store the 256×160 reference pixels (luma and chroma). Instead of the ping-pong scheme, data access is based on 'moving windows', as shown in Fig. 3. The memory space is divided into four subspaces each of which has the size of 64×160 pixels. One of the subspaces is assigned to the write port, whereas the remaining ones to the read port. The assignment is fixed until the processing for a given coding tree unit is in progress. When the motion estimation for the next coding tree unit is started, the windows are moved right by 64 pixels (the width of one subspace). The subspace assigned to the write port is filled with reference pixels which become the part of the search area for the next three coding tree units. In the meantime, the read port is used to access the search area. The size of the 192×160-pixel area assigned to the read port enables the search range of (−64, 63) × (−48, 47).

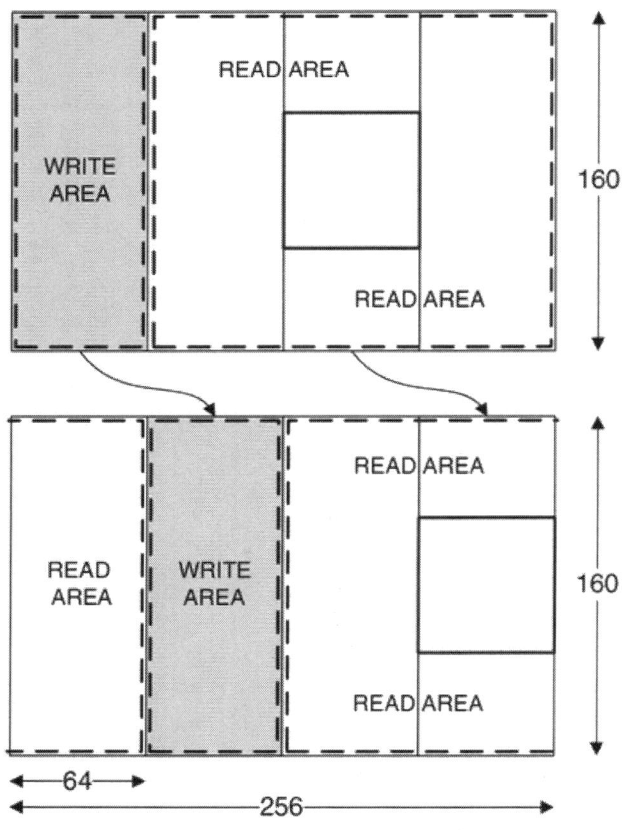


**Figure. 3** The assignment of the write and read ports to memory subspaces in the 'moving widows' scheme

In the adaptive computationally scalable motion estimation system applied for the H.264/AVC [5], original and reference 8×8 blocks are read alternately from the same memories. This dataflow is inconvenient for high-resolution videos since the throughput is limited by memory access. In the proposed architecture, separate memories for original and reference pixels allow a doubled access rate. If MVs are checked for the same 8×8 blocks continuously, the memory with original samples should remain unchanged. This gives the opportunity to reduce power consumption.

The interpolation using reference samples read from memories has a significant impact on the architecture of the adaptive ME system, which is depicted in Fig. 4. The main path of the compensator bypasses the interpolator and can support the integer-pel motion estimation with the throughput of one 8×8 block per clock cycle. For fractional-pel luma, two or four 8×8 blocks are forwarded to the interpolator in successive clock cycles. The interpolated blocks appear at the interpolator output after a number of clock cycles. The delay is dependent on the interpolation type, as described in the following section.

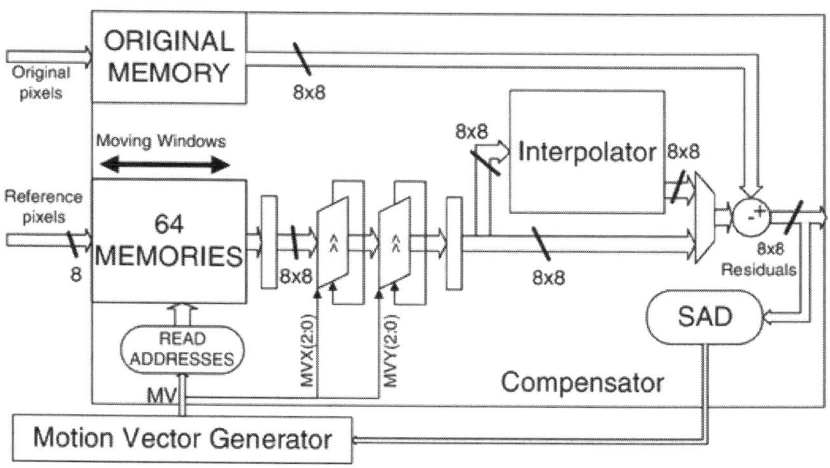


**Figure. 4** Architecture of the adaptive motion estimation system with the interpolation on samples read from memories

The general architecture of the interpolator is depicted in Fig. 5. To process blocks of 8×8 samples, the interpolator embeds 64 reconfigurable filters. The reconfiguration allows the computation of four fractional-pel positions (e.g., 0, 1/4, 1/2, and 3/4) for both luma and chroma samples. The filters take samples from 15×8 input registers. Register control is accomplished by a set of multiplexers. Firstly, data kept in input registers remain unchanged if the interpolation is performed for either horizontally or vertically neighboring fractional samples in consecutive clock cycles. Secondly, chroma samples are written to the input register through shifting by two horizontal/vertical positions. Thirdly, if a motion vector has both components with non-zero fractions, the feedback loop is selected as the input to registers after the horizontal processing. Fourthly, 8×8 blocks at the input and output interfaces can be transposed to select between the horizontal and vertical interpolation.

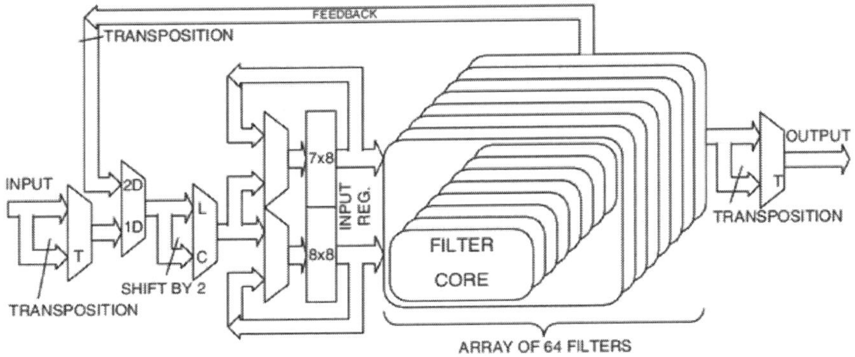


**Figure. 5** Interpolator architecture. Each connection carries an 8×8 sample block

# 4. SCHEDULING

Interpolation filters specified in H.265/HEVC refer up to eight samples located in row/column at neighboring pixel positions. Apart from the corresponding integer-pel position, three preceding and four following samples are accessed. Thus, the 1D horizontal and vertical interpolations can be accomplished with access to the 15×8 and 8×15 areas, respectively. To access the area in the same clock cycle, the interpolator architecture embeds 15×8 input 16-bit registers. Provided that 8×8 blocks appear at the interpolator input, two cycles are taken to load the registers. The blocks are taken from the main datapath in the compensator, and their location can be identified by specific motion vectors, as shown in Fig. 6. For the convenience, the following description will refer to motion vector differences (MVDs) from the integer-pel position around which the fractional-pel search is executed. If the compensator provides two adjacent 8×8 blocks obtained for MVDs equal to (−3, 0) and (5, 0), the interpolator can compute MVDs equal to

(0, 1/4), (0, 1/2), and (0, 3/4). The two accessed blocks allow the horizontal extension required by filters. Decrementing the horizontal MV components of input blocks [i.e., (−4, 0) and (4, 0)] allows the computation for negative fractional-pel positions. The 1D vertical interpolation involves two modifications compared to the horizontal one. Firstly, components of MVDs are exchanged, i.e., vertically adjacent blocks are accessed. Secondly, both 8×8 input blocks and the interpolation result are transposed.

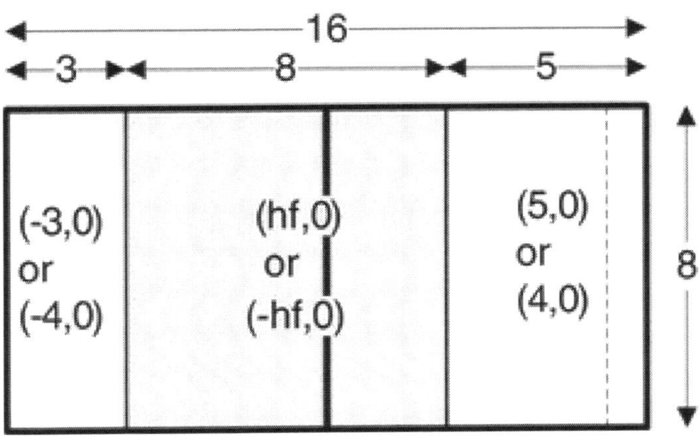


**Figure. 6** Locations of input and output blocks for the 1D horizontal interpolation. '*hf*' denotes any of fractions 1/2, 1/4, and 3/4. The *dashed line* indicates the 15×8 area

The 2D interpolation of an 8×8 luma block requires access to the 15×15 area due to the extension by three and four positions in both dimensions. Therefore, the compensator must provide four adjacent reference 8×8 blocks, as illustrated in Fig. 7. MVDs shown in the figure allow the interpolation for fractional-pel positions located on the bottom-right side of the integer-pel search centre (positive fractions). The computation for other sides is possible by decrementing one or both MVD components. The horizontal interpolation is executed separately for upper and lower blocks for a selected horizontal fraction (hf). Two vertically adjacent 8×8 blocks are computed and used in the following vertical phase. As the wiring between input registers and the filter array is fixed to support the horizontal processing, the transposition is applied before (the feedback) and after (final result) the vertical interpolation.

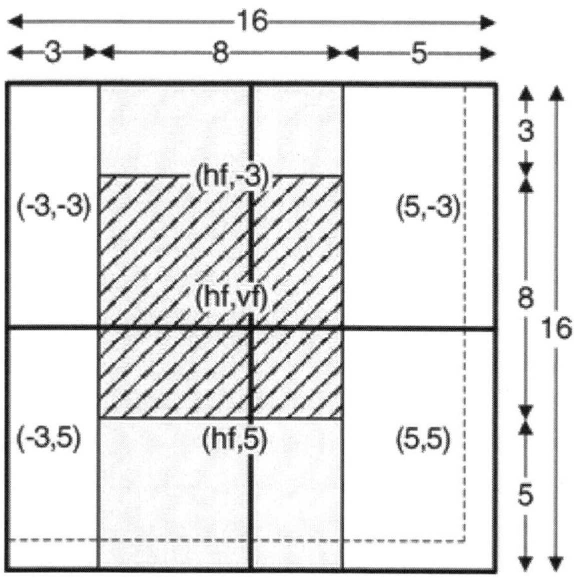


**Figure. 7** Locations of input and output blocks for the 2D interpolation. '*hf*' and '*vf*' denote any of fractions 1/2, 1/4, and 3/4. *Dashed lines* indicate the 15×15 area

The example of the fractional-pel search pattern is shown in Fig. 8. In the first phase, only 1D processing is used. The remaining phases involve the 2D interpolation. The timing diagram of 1D and 2D interpolations is depicted in Figs. 9 and 10, respectively. In the first case, the architecture computes 12 fractional-pel positions forming the cross pattern (squares in Fig. 8). Results appear at the interpolator output three clock cycles after the second 8×8 block at the input. The delay stems from three pipeline/register stages embedded in the datapath. Based on two 8×8 input blocks, three fractional-pel positions are computed in successive clock cycles. When blocks for the three positions are released, next two input blocks appear at the input. In this case, residuals are computed for blocks released from the interpolator output rather than from the integer-pel datapath of the compensator. Therefore, providing input blocks to the interpolator involves two additional clock cycles only at the beginning of the 1D interpolation.

Although input blocks are determined for the interpolator, they can also be utilized to check corresponding integer-pel positions.

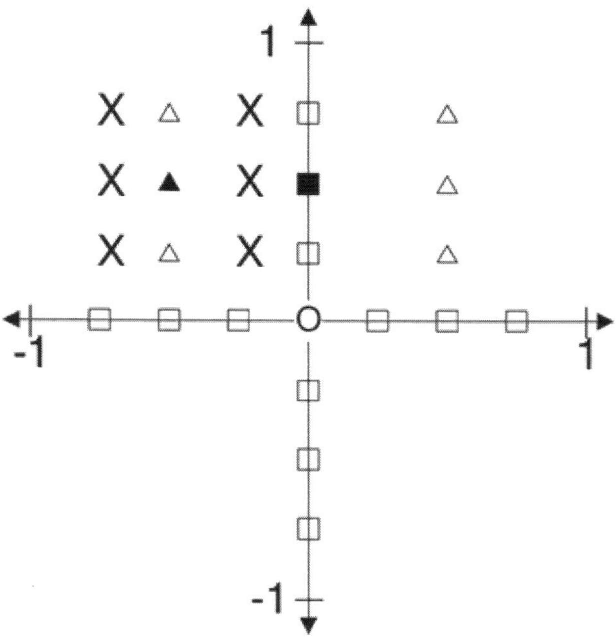


**Figure. 8** Example of the fractional-pel search pattern. *Squares, triangles,* and *crosses* indicate the first, the second, and the third phase, respectively. *Black elements* indicate the best points found in corresponding phases

Figure 10 depicts the 2D interpolation for luma and chroma. The architecture performs the horizontal and vertical processing in two consecutive phases. In the first phase for luma, four adjacent 8×8 blocks included in the 16×16 area are loaded into the 15×8 input register in four clock cycles. When each of the two block pairs is written, the horizontal interpolation is started. 1D results appear at the filter output with the two-cycle delay. They are fed back to input registers. The vertical interpolation starts when both results are written into input registers. 8×8 predictions appear at the interpolator output with a two-cycle delay. Three vertically neighboring fractional-pel positions can be computed in successive clock cycles.

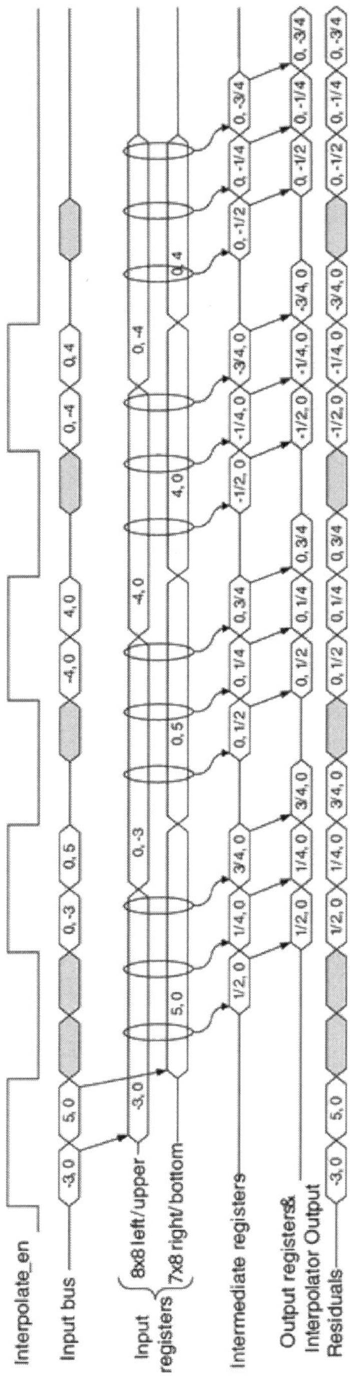


**Figure. 9** Timing diagram of successive 1D interpolations

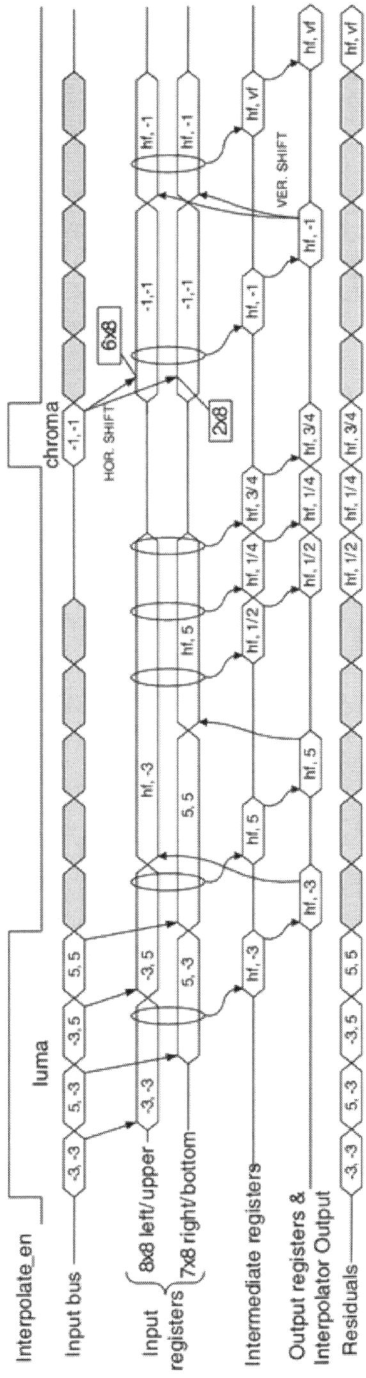


**Figure. 10** Timing diagram of the 2D interpolation

The interpolation for chroma (4:2:0) differs from that for luma. Only one 8×8 is received at the beginning. It is sufficient to compute the 4×4 fractional-pel output. The input block is obtained for the MVD equal to (−1, −1) and must be written to registers with a shift by two horizontal positions. This operation adjusts the input domain to active filter taps, as access to two left register columns is required only for luma. The analogous operation is accomplished while feeding the registers before the vertical processing. Only four columns of the filter array are used due to the smaller size of the output block. Moreover, the bottom row of filters is also not utilized. Therefore, the architecture employs only 4×7 filters supporting the chroma interpolation.

The 1D and 2D interpolation introduces the delay between receiving of input blocks and releasing of fractional-pel results. In the meantime, data appearing in the main path of the compensator bypass the interpolator. Such data are in grey in Figs. 9 and 10. Since the integer-pel path in the compensator does not communicate with the interpolator, corresponding clock cycles can be utilized to check some integer-accuracy motion vectors for other prediction blocks. Such interleaved processing requires the two-thread motion vector generator.

# 5. RECONFIGURABLE FILTER STRUCTURE

Interpolation filters specified in H.265/HEVC have seven or eight taps as shown in Table 1. The hardware architecture can map each tap into a separate multiplier with results summed by three-level adder tree (see Fig. 11). If the design must work at high frequencies, the filter structure should be pipelined. Successive pipeline stages should be balanced in terms of critical path delays. The most obvious approach is to place registers after the multiplications and between particular tree stages. As signal delays in carry chains of cascaded arithmetic circuits overlap to a large extent, the number of stages can be limited and balanced with the stage having the longest path (e.g., multiplication).

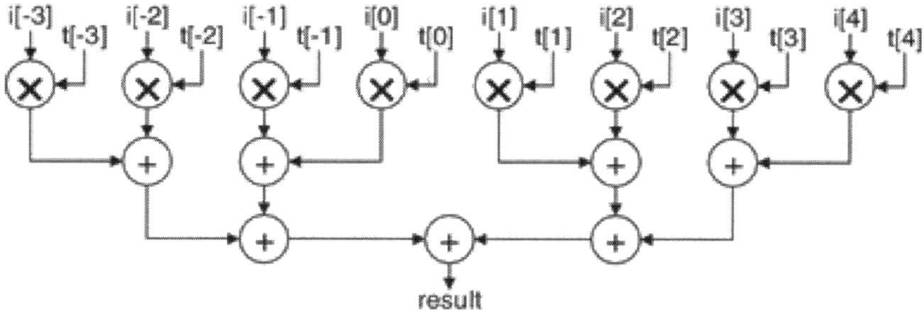


**Figure. 11** Straightforward architecture of the 8-tap interpolation filter

FPGA devices usually have DSP units dedicated to filter implementations. Such units embed multipliers, adder trees, and internal pipeline registers allowing the operation at high frequencies. Such resources enable the straightforward implementation of the fractional sample interpolation. Apart from high speed, implementations based on DSP units utilize few general-purpose resources such as logic elements. However, the number of DSP units in FPGA devices is limited, and they can be utilized in other modules of the H.265/HEVC encoder, i.e., the forward/inverse transform and the (de)quantization. Therefore, the implementation based on regular logic elements can better fit FPGA resources.

In ASIC implementations, the incorporation of regular multipliers is inefficient when coefficients are constant or limited to a narrow set of values. A better approach is to design adder/subtractor trees with dataflow reconfigured by multiplexers. This approach can also be used in FPGA devices when there is insufficient availability of DSP units. The multiplexers can change the actual filter coefficients by shifting and switching between the intermediate branches of the tree. For example, it is possible to add samples corresponding to the same coefficient values at the first stage (the property of symmetrical filters). In general, there are many possible filter implementations based on the adder/subtractor tree. However, preferred solutions should minimize the amount of utilized resources. The design of particular filters exploits some well-known optimization techniques. Firstly, filter coefficients which are equal to a power of two do not require multiplication circuits as hardwired-shifting can yield the result. Secondly, multiplications are equivalent to additions/subtractions of the same sample up-shifted by different position numbers. Thirdly, an input sample or intermediate results can be directed to different adder/subtractor nodes to balance the tree. Fourthly, the reconfiguration of the filter coefficients can be realized by multiplexing. Fifthly, when two filters have the same coefficient values with the inverted order, it is possible to share resources by changing the assignment of the input samples with multiplexers.

Figure 12 depicts the proposed structure of the reconfigurable filter based on the adder/subtractor tree. The full-featured filter embeds 22 adders/subtractors at two pipeline stages. If only luma is supported, the number of adders/subtractors is decreased to 17. The dataflow is reconfigured by five types of multiplexers:

- NI multiplexers select between non-inverted and inverted order of input samples. This selection allows the same dataflow for filter pairs with the mirrored order of coefficients. In particular, the I input is active when processing element implements the 3/4 luma filter or the 5/8, 6/8, or 7/8 chroma filters. Otherwise, the N input is selected.

- OE multiplexers are utilized only for chroma to select between odd (O) and even (E) numerators of fractional-pel positions. The O input is selected when the circuit is configured as the 1/8, 3/8, 5/8, or 7/8 filters. Otherwise, the E input is selected.

- HQ multiplexers select between half- and quarter-pel configurations. The H input is selected when the circuit is configured as the half-pel luma filter or the 3/8, 4/8, or 5/8 chroma filters. Otherwise, the Q input is selected.

- LC multiplexers select between luma (L) and chroma (C) interpolation modes.

- The SAT multiplexer accomplishes the saturation of the final result to avoid overflow and underflow.

Interpolation filters in H.265/HEVC involve the increase of the output bit accuracy to avoid underflow and overflow. In extreme cases, the output requires additional seven bits compared to the input accuracy. Additionally, the sign bit must be taken into account. Therefore, 16 bits are needed to represent samples after the 1D interpolation before the rounding operation. In the second phase of the 2D interpolation on 16-bit signed data, the output accuracy is increased by seven bits to 23 bits. Consecutive stages of the adder/subtractor tree gradually increase the range to 23 bits at the 2D output. To keep the same output range for the 1D and 2D processing, eight-bit integer-pel samples are written to input registers before the interpolation with shifting up by six bit positions.

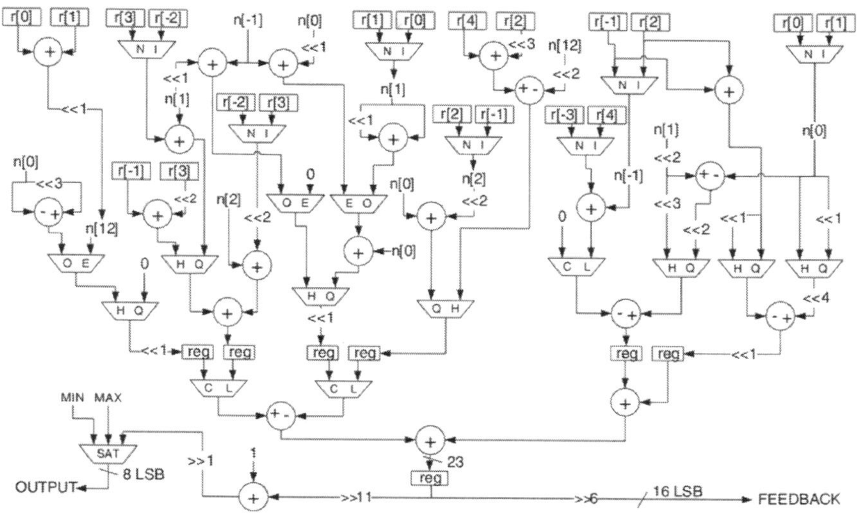

**Figure. 12** Architecture of the reconfigurable filter. Indices of input registers ($r[x]$) are relative and depend on the position in the filter array

# 6. IMPLEMENTATION RESULTS

The architecture of the compensator and the interpolator is specified in VHDL and verified with the HM 13 reference model [2]. The synthesis is performed for FPGA and ASIC technologies using the Altera Quartus II software (ver. 12.0) and Synopsys Design Compiler (ver. 2012.06-SP5), respectively. Particularly, FPGA synthesis is performed for Aria II GX FPGA devices (speed grade 4), whereas TSMC 90 nm is selected as the ASIC technology. Implementation results are summarized in Table 2. As can be seen, the main contribution to the resource consumption is from the interpolator, which embeds 64 reconfigurable filter cores. The full-featured filter needs 488 ALUTs and 4524 gates for FPGA and ASIC technologies, respectively. If only luma is supported, the resources are decreased significantly to 325 ALUTs and 3452 gates. The joint resource consumption for the compensator and the interpolator is close to that for the whole motion estimation system since the motion vector generator is expected to utilize less logic [5]. For the ASIC technology, the design can operate at the frequency of 400 MHz. This performance enables the encoder to allocate about 400 and 100 clock cycles per each

8×8 block for 1080p@30fps and 2160p@30fps, respectively. One motion vector (integer-pel or fractional-pel) can be checked almost in each clock cycle. The compression efficiency of this approach will depend on the search algorithm accomplished by the motion vector generator. The estimated power consumption of the ASIC implementation is equal to 11.4 and 244.2 mW for the interpolator and the compensator, respectively. The high power consumption of the compensator is caused by memories keeping reference pixels.

**Table 2** Synthesis results

| Technology | Units | Module | |
|---|---|---|---|
| | | Compensator | Interpolator |
| Arria II GX | Logic (ALUT) | 4 247 | 28 757 |
| | Clock (MHz) | 200 | 200 |
| TSMC 90 nm | Logic (gate) | 42 519 | 277 074 |
| | Clock (MHz) | 400 | 400 |
| | Memory (kB) | 64 + 12 | – |

The compensator incorporates 64 two-port memory modules to store reference pixels. Each module has the size of 1kB. This capacity allows the search range of (−64, 63) × (−48, 48) for both luma and chroma. Wider ranges are possible at the cost of the increased memory size. The original pixels are stored in a separate memory of a capacity of 12 kB.

Byun et al. [10] presented the H.265/HEVC integer-pel full search architecture supporting all prediction unit sizes at the range of (−32, 31) × (−32, 31). The design consumes 3.56 Mgates and 23 kB memories. The hardware cost of the motion estimation system described in this paper is much smaller even if the motion vector generator would be several times more complex than that developed for H.264/AVC [5]. Moreover, the search range is wider. Low-power integer-pel design was proposed by Sanchez et al. [11]. Its resource consumption is relatively low (50k gates and 82k bit memories). However, it supports only 16×16 blocks and a narrow search range, which does not exploit the compression potential of H.265/HEVC.

The proposed architecture for H.265/HEVC interpolator is compared with other designs in Tables 3 and 4. The tables include implementation results for our previous architecture [4] generating fractional-pel samples before storing them into 64 on-chip memories. Although the proposed architecture needs more resources in the interpolator, it significantly reduces the size of the memories in the compensator, as described in Sect.3. The maximal working frequency of the proposed architecture is the highest within the ASIC comparison. Three implementations [12–14] offer lower parallelism. As a consequence, declared throughputs are achieved when the size of the prediction unit is selected prior to the interpolation. One design supports 4320p@30fps video with the interpolation for three prediction unit sizes (64×64, 32×32, and 16×16). On the other hand, it consumes a large amount of resources, and its design efficiency is the lowest. Moreover, adapted simplifications involve quality losses. Only one of the architectures [13] has a significantly better design efficiency (parallelism/resources). However, it requires additional memories and the control logic. Most referred designs support only the luma interpolation [12, 14, 15]. One ASIC design [15] implements filters specified in Working Draft 3. The FPGA implementation proposed by Afonso et al. [12] achieves a high frequency due to deep pipelining and the better device. The proposed architecture can also be modified to operate at higher frequencies by the insertion of registers. This modification would not increase the logic resources since at least one flip-flop is embedded in each ALUT.

**Table 3** Comparison with other FPGA architectures

| Design | Afonso [12] | Pastuszak [4] | This work |
|---|---|---|---|
| Technology | Stratix III | Arria II GX | Arria II GX |
| Clock (MHz) | 403 | 200 | 200 |
| Resources (ALUT) | 4077 + 16547 | 18 831 | 28 757 |
| Parallelism (sample/clock) | 27 | 64 | 64 |
| 1,000 × parallelism/resources | 1.31 | 3.40 | 2.26 |
| Features | Luma | Luma and chroma | Luma and chroma |

**Table 4** Comparison with other ASIC architectures

| Design | Diniz [13] | Guo [14] | He [15] | Pastuszak [4] | This work |
|---|---|---|---|---|---|
| Technology (nm) | TSMC 150 | SMIC 90 | 65 | TSMC 90 | TSMC 90 |
| Clock (MHz) | 312 | 250 | 188 | 400 | 400 |
| Resources (gate) | 30 209 | 32 496 | 1 183 000 | 224 094 | 277 074 |
| Parallelism (sample/clock) | 12 | 8 | 16×12 | 64 | 64 |
| 1,000 × parallelism/resources | 0.3972 | 0.2462 | 0.1623 | 0.2856 | 0.2310 |
| Throughput | 2160p@30fps | 2160p@60fps | 4320p@30fps | 1080p@30fps | 2160p@30fps |
| Features | Luma and chroma | Luma | Luma | Luma and chroma | Luma and chroma |

The proposed architecture can support many search algorithms owing to the flexibility in the order of checked motion vectors. Therefore, the compression efficiency depends on the selected algorithm and the number of clock cycles assigned to particular coding tree units. To estimate the efficiency achievable with the architecture, the reference model HM13 is used for the low-delay configuration defined in Common Test Conditions. Five 1080p sequences [19] are evaluated with 50 frames and TZ Search. The software is modified to model a limited number of checked integer-pel motion vectors. The limitation is set to 50 or 100 for each 8×8 prediction block. The first corresponds to the half of clock cycles allocated in the case of the 2160p video coding. The remaining cycles can be utilized for the subpixel estimation, chroma, and additional estimation for larger prediction units. For larger prediction blocks, only common motion vectors checked for four smaller prediction blocks are taken into account. The reference scenario has no limitations on the number of checked motion vectors. Evaluation results are summarized in Table 5 in terms of Bjontegaard Delta Rate [20]. Although losses in the compression efficiency are not large, there is a space to develop more robust search algorithm. In particular, the correlation between smaller prediction blocks should be utilized to obtain more predictions for larger blocks.

**Table 5** Evaluation results for BD-rate for different numbers of checked integer-pel MVs

| Sequence | BD-rate | |
|---|---|---|
| | 50 MVs | 100 MVs |
| Blue sky | 1.36 | 0.46 |
| Ducks take off | 0.32 | 0.04 |
| Station2 | 1.65 | 0.26 |
| Rush hour | 4.02 | 0.38 |
| Tractor | 2.43 | 0.74 |
| Average | 1.96 | 0.38 |

The real-time H.265/HEVC encoding of 1080p videos can also be obtained using the parallel processing on CPU and GPU platforms [17, 18]. On the other hand, the compression efficiency of such implementations is significantly lower compared to the HM reference software (0.7–0.92 dB).

# 7. CONCLUSION

The architecture of the compensator and the interpolator is developed for the H.265/HEVC adaptive motion estimation. The design performs interpolation on reference pixels read from on-chip memories. This allows much wider search ranges and reduced memory sizes. The design achieves the high utilization of hardware resources, thanks to interleaving of integer- and fractional-pel computations. The design can check about 100 motion vectors for each 8×8 block when encoding 2160p@30fps video at the 400 MHz. Future research will concentrate on the development of an efficient search strategy able to support different prediction block sizes.

# REFERENCES

1. ITU-T Recommendation H.265 and ISO/IEC 23008-2 MPEG-H Part 2, High efficiency video coding (HEVC), (2013)

2. HEVC software repository: HM-10.0 reference model. Available: https://hevc.hhi.fraunhofer.de/svn/svn_HEVCSoftware/branches/HM-10.0-dev/

3. ITU-T Rec. H.264 and ISO/IEC 14496-10 MPEG-4 Part 10, Advanced video coding (AVC), (2005)

4. Pastuszak, G., Trochimiuk, M.: Architecture design and efficiency evaluation for the high-throughput interpolation in the hevc encoder. Euromicro Conf. Digit. Syst. Des. (DSD) **2013**, 423–428 (2013)

5. Pastuszak, G., Jakubowski, M.: Adaptive computationally-scalable motion estimation for the hardware H.264/AVC encoder. IEEE Trans. Circuits Syst. Video Technol. **23**(5), 802–812 (2013)

6. Chen, T.-C., Chien, S.-Y., Huang, Y.-W., Tsai, C.-H., Chen, C.-Y., Chen, T.-W., Chen, L.-G.: Analysis and architecture design of an HDTV720p 30

frames/s H.264/AVC encoder. IEEE Trans. Circuits Syst. Video Technol. **16**(6), 673–688 (2006)

7. Liu, Z., Song, Y., Shao, M., Li, S., Li, L., Ishiwata, S., Nakagawa, M., Goto, S., Ikenaga, T.: HDTV1080p H.264/AVC encoder chip design and performance analysis. IEEE J. Solid-State Circuits **44**(2), 594–608 (2009)

8. Yang, C., Goto, S., Ikenaga, T.: High performance VLSI architecture of fractional motion estimation in H.264 for HDTV, In: IEEE International Symposium on Circuits and Systems (ISCAS 2006), pp. 21–24 (2006)

9. Oktem, S., Hamzaoglu, I.: An efficient hardware Architecture for quarter-pixel accurate H.264 motion estimation, In: 10th Euromicro Conference on Digital System Design, pp. 1142–1143 (2007)

10. Byun, J., Jung, Y., Kim, J.: Design of integer motion estimator of HEVC for asymmetric motion-partitioning mode and 4 K-UHD. Electron. Lett. **49**(18), 1142–1143 (2013)

11. Sanchez, G., Porto, M., Agostini, L.: A hardware friendly motion estimation algorithm for the emergent HEVC standard and its low power hardware design, In: IEEE International Conference on Image Processing, pp. 1991–1994 (2013)

12. Afonso, V., Maich, H., Agostini, L., Franco, D.: Low cost and high throughput FME interpolation for the HEVC emerging video coding standard, In: IEEE Fourth Latin American Symposium on Circuits and Systems (LASCAS) (2013)

13. Diniz, C. M., Shafique, M., Bampi, S., Henkel, J.: High-throughput interpolation hardware architecture with coarse-grained reconfigurable datapaths for HEVC, In: IEEE International Conference on Image Processing, pp. 2091–2095 (2013)

14. Guo, Z., Zhou, D., Goto, S.: An optimized MC interpolation architecture for HEVC, In: IEEE International Conference on Acoustics, Speech and Signal Processing, pp. 1117–1120 (2012)

15. He, G., Zhou, D., Chen, Z., Zhang, T., Goto, S.: A 995Mpixels/s 0.2nJ/pixel fractional motion estimation architecture in HEVC for Ultra-HD, In: IEEE Asian Solid-State Circuits Conference, pp. 301–304 (2013)

16. Jakubowski, M., Pastuszak, G.: An adaptive computation-aware algorithm for multi-frame variable block-size motion estimation in H.264/AVC, In: International Conference on Signal Processing and Multimedia Applications (SIGMAP '09), pp. 122–125 (2009)

17. Wang, X., Song, L., Chen, M., Yang, J.: Paralleling variable block size motion estimation of HEVC on CPU plus GPU platform, In: IEEE International Conference on Multimedia and Expo Workshops (ICMEW) (2013)

18. Wang, X., Song, L., Chen, M., Yang, J.: Paralleling variable block size motion estimation of HEVC on multi-core CPU plus GPU platform, In: IEEE International Conference on Image Processing (ICIP), pp. 1836–1839 (2013)

19. Xiph.org: Test media, available on-line at http://media.xiph.org/video/derf/ (2011)

20. Bjontegaard, G.: Calculation of Average PSNR differences Between RD-Curves, In: ITU-T VCEG-M33, VCEG 13th Meeting (2001)

3

# ALGORITHM AND ARCHITECTURE DESIGN OF THE MOTION ESTIMATION FOR THE H.265/HEVC 4K-UHD ENCODER

**Grzegorz Pastuszak, Maciej Trochimiuk**

Institute of Radioelectronics, Warsaw University of Technology, Nowowiejska 15/19, 00-665 Warsaw, Poland

## ABSTRACT

This paper presents the algorithm and the architecture of the high-throughput motion estimation system for the H.265/HEVC encoder. The design allows the processing of 2160p@30fps videos at the clock frequency of 400 MHz. The architecture embeds two parallel processing paths for the integer-pel and the fractional-pel motion estimation. The paths share the same memories. Access conflicts are avoided by the use of dual-port modules and register buffers for reused samples. In each clock cycle, the integer-pel and the fractional-pel path can evaluate one and four motion vectors for an 8 × 8 luma block, respectively. A separate interpolator for chroma additionally increases the throughput. The integer-pel path supports test zone search for 8 × 8 prediction blocks. The motion estimation for larger blocks is performed by the utilization of results of the 8 × 8 search. The search for rectangular PUs is performed only at the fractional-pel level and reuses partial costs computed for square PUs. As a consequence, a significant amount of computation is saved. Synthesis results show that the design can operate at 200 and 400 MHz when implemented in FPGA Arria II and TSMC 90 nm, respectively. The implemented algorithm is verified in the HM16 software. If 2160p@30fps videos are encoded with the low-delay configuration, BD-PSNR and BD-rate are equal to −0.026 dB and 1.64 %, respectively.

## KEYWORDS

Video coding Motion estimation Interpolation H.265/HEVC FPGA Very large-scale integration (VLSI)

## 1. INTRODUCTION

Research and standardization efforts in video coding led to the specification of the H.265/HEVC standard [1,2] in 2013. At the same quality of the reconstructed video, the standard provides an improvement in compression efficiency of about 35–50 % compared to its predecessor H.264/AVC [3]. However, the better compression efficiency is achieved at the price of increased computational complexity. Although the general structure of the encoder and the decoder remains the same, there are many changes in the algorithm. Instead of 16 × 16-pixel macroblocks, the new standard applies coding tree units (CTUs), which can be up to 64 × 64 pixels in size. Each CTU can be recursively split into square coding units (CUs) with the minimal size of 8 × 8 pixels. Each 2N × 2N CU can be partitioned into predictions units (PUs). N can be equal to 4, 8, 16, or 32. There are eight allowable partition shapes: two square shapes (2N × 2N and N × N), two symmetric rectangular shapes (N × 2N and 2N × N), and four asymmetric rectangular shapes (2N × 3N/2, 2N × N/2, 3N/2 × 2N, and N/2 × 2N). Each inter PU has a separate motion vector (MV). Similar to H.264/AVC, the H.265/HEVC allows quarter pixel accuracy MVs. There are new interpolation schemes to compute fractional-pel positions. In particular, 7-tap and 8-tap filters are used for the luma interpolation of half-pel and quarter-pel positions, respectively. Chroma samples are computed using 4-tap filters. Although design and implementation of digital filters is a thoroughly explored issue, high-throughput video encoders require some effort to obtain efficient hardware solutions.

With the exception of our previous designs [4, 5], architectures for the motion estimation (ME) consist of two parts assigned to the integer-pel and fractional-pel search [6–15]. This approach requires separate reference pixel buffers for each part. The integer-pel part usually applies the hierarchical strategies to extend the search range, which involves quality losses. Most architectures use non-adaptive search patterns and their resource consumption is large [6–10]. The architecture supporting Multipoint Diamond Search proposed in [11] requires less resource; however, it only supports 16 × 16 blocks, limiting the compression efficiency.

Some high-throughput interpolators have been proposed in literature for H.264/AVC [5–9]. Their scheduling assumes two successive steps, one for the half-pel interpolation and another for the quarter-pel interpolation. This approach is natural in terms of the specification of quarter-pel computations which refer to results of half-pel computations. This dataflow cannot be applied directly in H.265/HEVC since quarter-pel samples are computed using separate filters. In particular, more filters are needed in the second step. Furthermore, the hardware cost increases due to a larger number of filter taps and much higher throughputs required (more partitioning modes). Some interpolator architectures designed for H.265/HEVC have been described in literature [12–15]. They achieve throughputs suitable for video resolutions from 1080p to 4320p. All the designs neglect the interpolation for merge modes. Three designs [12–14] are based on the assumption that the size of prediction units is selected at the integer-pel ME. If the processing of more sizes has to be performed, the throughput is decreased accordingly. One design [15] supports three prediction block sizes (16 × 16, 32 × 32, and 64 × 64); however, it consumes a large amount of hardware resources. Generally, a compression-efficient and high-throughput implementation requires more hardware resources and increases power consumption. Therefore, there is a need for solutions in which these parameters are optimized.

This study presents the high-throughput ME architecture dedicated to the H.265/HEVC encoder. Similar to the previous works [4, 5], the architecture can check one integer-pel motion vector for an 8 × 8 block in each clock cycle. As an arbitral order of motion vectors is allowed, the architecture supports the test zone search (TZS) algorithm used in the HM software. A significant amount of computation is saved for 16 × 16 and 32 × 32 prediction blocks by the exploitation of results of the 8 × 8-block search. In the case of rectangular PUs, only MVs checked for the fractional-pel ME of 2N × 2N PUs are evaluated, which additionally reduces the complexity at small quality losses.

The present study has four novel contributions at the architecture level. Firstly, the use of dual-port memories and register buffers for reused data allows shared and conflict-free access from two processing paths corresponding to the integer-pel and the fractional-pel search. Secondly, the extension of the interpolation to 9 × 9 blocks allows the evaluation of four 8 × 8 fractional-pel blocks at a small increase in the resource cost. Thirdly, the architecture enables the two-dimensional continuous interpolation of 9 × 9 blocks with reconfigurable and dedicated filter cores. Fourthly, the separate chroma interpolator additionally increases the throughput and design flexibility.

The rest of the paper are organized as follows: Sect. 2 reviews previous developments on the hardware design of the adaptive motion estimation. Section 3 describes the new architecture of the H.265/HEVC motion estimation system. The applied scheduling is described in Sect. 4. Section 5 presents the motion estimation algorithm executed by the proposed architecture. Section 6 provides implementation results. Finally, the paper is concluded in Sect. 7.

## 2. DESIGN FOR ADAPTIVE MOTION ESTIMATION

The adaptive computationally scalable motion estimation algorithm allows video encoders to achieve close to optimal efficiencies in real-time conditions [16]. The algorithm can employ different search strategies to adapt to local motion activity, and the number of checked search points is set by the encoder controller for each macroblock. The algorithm can achieve results close to optimum even if the number of search points assigned to macroblocks is strongly limited and varies with time.

The block diagram of the architecture supporting the adaptive computationally scalable motion estimation for the H.265/HEVC encoder [4] is depicted in Fig. 1. The architecture embeds the interpolator and the motion vector generator. The remaining elements build the compensator. The design allows the adaptive search for both integer-pel and fractional-pel positions. The fractional-pel search is performed around some MVs selected at the integer-pel stage. However, the integer-pel estimation is interrupted whenever data are submitted or released from the interpolator because of the sharing of the same memories and the residual computation. As a consequence, less clock cycles can be utilized at both stages of the motion estimation. Higher throughputs are achieved when interpolated pixels are stored in the memories. On the other hand, the interpolation before writing into the memories involves a large memory cost [5]. This disadvantage is of particular importance in the case of the H.265/HEVC encoder, in which the processing of 16 × 16-pixel macroblocks is replaced by CTUs with sizes up to 64 × 64 pixels.

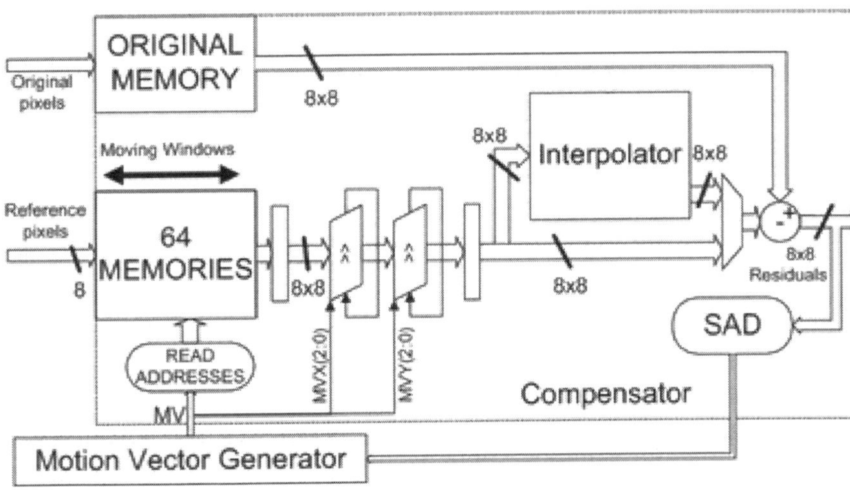


**Figure. 1** Architecture of the adaptive motion estimation system for the H.265/HEVC encoder [4]

In order to process blocks of 8 × 8 samples, the interpolator embeds 64 reconfigurable filters [4]. The reconfiguration allows the computation of four fractional-pel positions (e.g., 0, 1/4, 1/2, and 3/4) for both luma and chroma samples. The number of filters corresponds to the size of blocks processed in the main path. Although the interpolation parallelism is high, the throughput is limited by the reading of 8 × 8 blocks at the input. In particular, two and four 8 × 8 blocks must be read to obtain the 1D and 2D interpolation of three fractional-pel positions for one block, respectively. More clock cycles are utilized when the interpolation is performed in two dimensions. If 100 cycles are available for each 8 × 8-pixel block (2160p@30fps), the interpolation around two integer-pel MVs can be performed for luma. Particularly, one 1D luma interpolation with the cross pattern takes 16 cycles, whereas 2D interpolation for nine positions takes 27 cycles. Two corresponding chroma blocks are interpolated in 10 cycles for one position. Totally, 96 out of 100 cycles are utilized for the luma and chroma interpolation. 54 cycles are available for the integer-pel search interleaved with memory reads for the fractional-pel estimation. Although the throughput is significantly improved compared to other designs [12–14], it is still insufficient to evaluate the greater number of PU sizes. Additional interpolations are indispensable to support merge modes.

The compensator embeds 64 memory modules to store 256 × 160 reference pixels (luma and chroma) [4]. Data access is based on 'moving windows,' as shown in Fig. 2. The memory space is divided into four subspaces each of which are 64 × 160 pixels in size. One of the subspaces is assigned to the write port, whereas the remaining ones to the read port. The assignment is fixed until the processing for a given CTU is in progress. When the motion estimation for the next CTU is started, the windows are moved right by 64 pixels (the width of one subspace). The subspace assigned to the write port is filled with reference pixels which become part of the search area for the next three coding tree units. In the meantime, the read port is used to access the search area. The size of the 192 × 160-pixel area assigned to the read port enables the search range of (−64, 63) × (−48, 47). Each of 64 memories keeps every eighth integer-pel sample both in the horizontal and vertical dimension. Generally, samples for a given MV can belong to four adjacent 8 × 8 blocks (see Fig. 3a, b). Since MVs vary in the whole search range, the data control is enhanced. Firstly, integer parts of read address coordinates are incremented for memories keeping samples located at the bottom and right sides of the 8 × 8 search area grid lines. Secondly, two shifters rotate samples between block positions in the horizontal and vertical dimension to restore their spatial consistency (see Fig. 3c, d).

# 3. NEW ARCHITECTURE

In the architecture described in the previous section [4], the integer-pel and the fractional-pel search share the same processing path with the interleaved processing. As a consequence, the number of clock cycles assigned to the integer-pel estimation is decreased almost by half, which has a negative impact on the compression efficiency. The main bottleneck is introduced by the memory read port able to provide one 8 × 8 block in each clock cycle. In order to resolve the problem, the new architecture incorporates dual-port memory modules instead of two-port ones. The main advantage of dual ports is that they can operate in either the read or the write mode. In the architecture, the first port is assigned to the integer-pel path, whereas the second is used as the input to the interpolator. The interpolator incorporates the register buffer at the inputs stage to reuse samples from the second path. Since the interpolator does not read data in each clock cycle, some cycles can still be utilized to write the reference pixels for the following CTUs. The same approach is applied to the memory storing original samples.

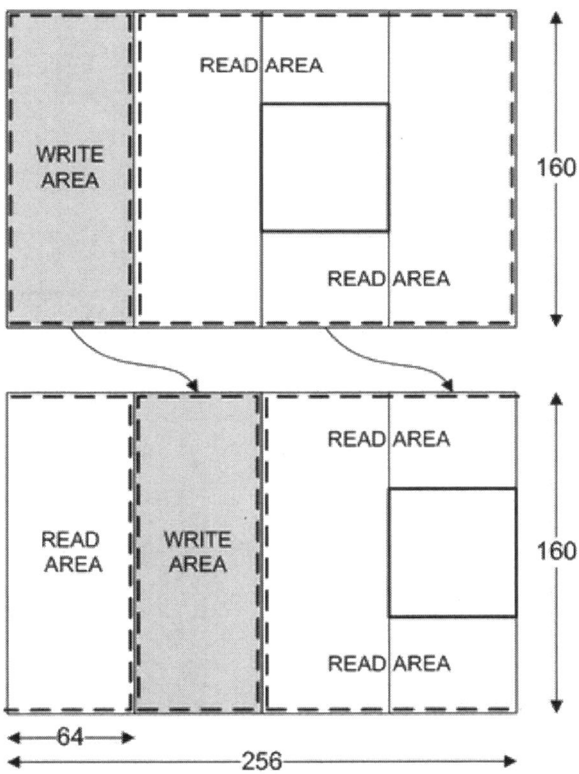


**Figure. 2** The assignment of the write and read ports to memory subspaces in the 'moving widows' scheme [4]

The new architecture of the motion estimation system is depicted in Fig. 4. The architecture embeds two processing paths (integer-pel and fractional-pel) which read data from original sample and reference sample memories through separate ports. The integer-pel path operates as the loop where the search process can be adapted according to the result obtained for previous MVs. Particularly, the MV generator supports the TZ search algorithm for 8 × 8 blocks. The module embeds two finite state machines which determine MVs for the integer-pel and the fractional-pel path. The fractional-pel path includes an interpolator for luma samples. Although the path cannot be fed in each clock cycle due to the memory writing, the continuous processing is allowed by the buffering and the reusing of reference data in the interpolator.

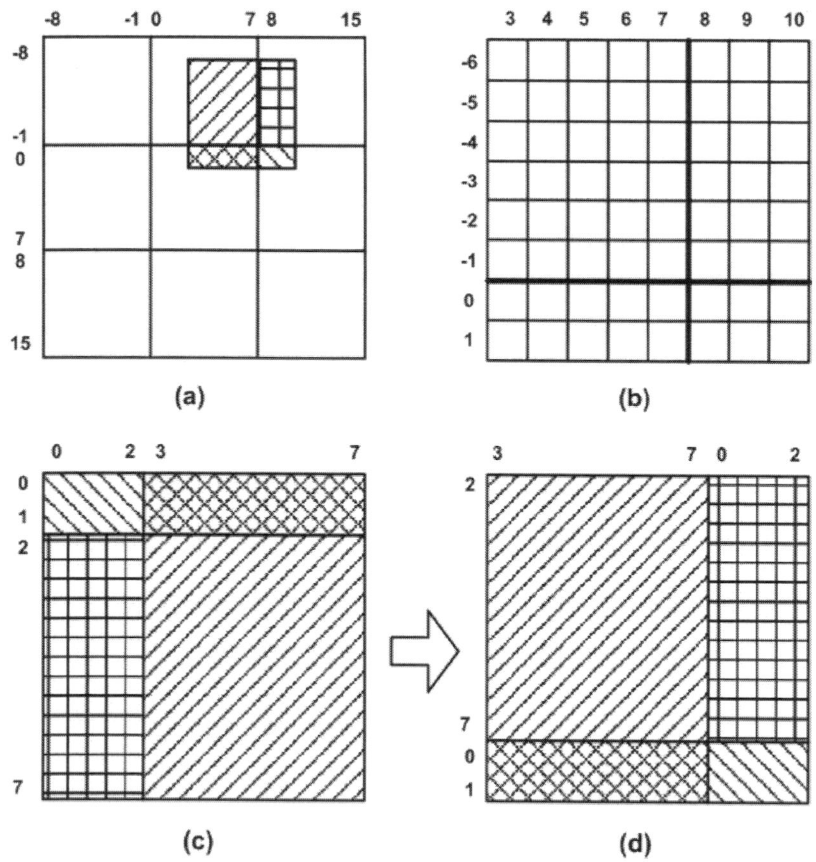


**Figure. 3** Sample arrangement of the 8 × 8 block for MV = (3,−6): **a** location within search area; **b** block samples with their search area indices; **c** block samples read form memories with 2D memory indices; **d** block samples after the rotation with 2D memory indices

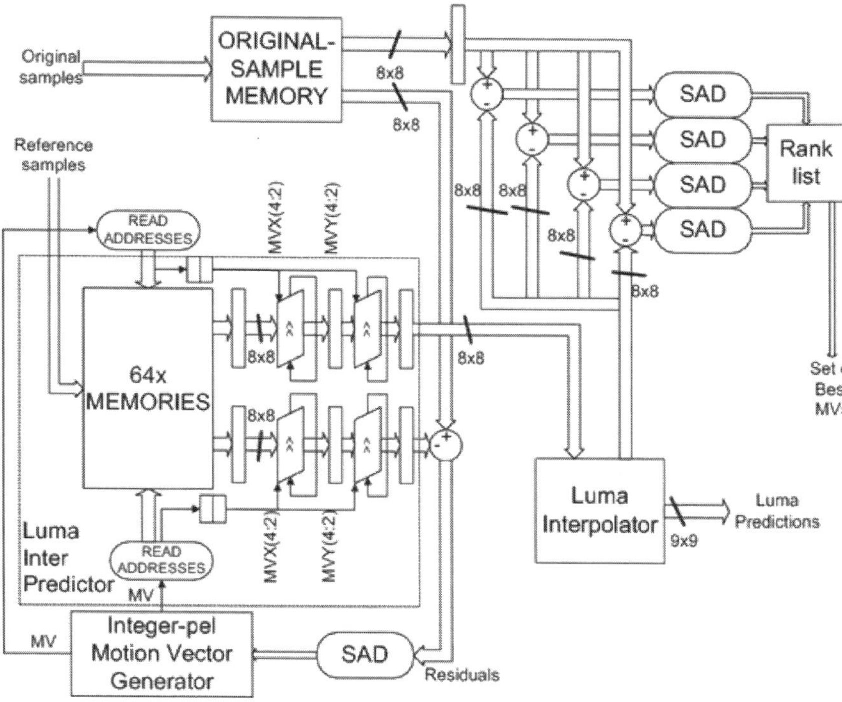


**Figure. 4** Architecture of the motion estimation system with two processing paths corresponding to the interpolation and the integer-pel search

The luma interpolator can release 9 × 9 blocks in successive clock cycles. Each one includes four overlapping 8 × 8 blocks, as shown in Fig. 5. The common area for all the blocks has 7 × 7 samples. The four 8 × 8 blocks correspond to fractional accuracy MVs whose horizontal and/or vertical components differ by 1. As a consequence, it is possible to simultaneously check four fractional-pel MVs around an integer-pel MV. The computation of 9 × 9 blocks increases the parallelism of the fractional-pel path four times at a relatively small increase of the hardware cost. With the assumption that the interpolator embeds separate horizontal and vertical filters, their number increases from 64 to 72 and 81, respectively. Four 8 × 8 candidate blocks distinguished within the 9 × 9 block are subtracted from original samples. Four results are used to compute sum of absolute differences (SAD). SADs increased by corresponding MV bit costs are compared one another. Based on the comparisons, the rank list is built. The rank is used to preselect the group of four candidate MVs worth analyzing with the rate-distortion criterion. Actually, the rank list is used for square PUs. For each rectangular partition, only one best candidate MV is selected.

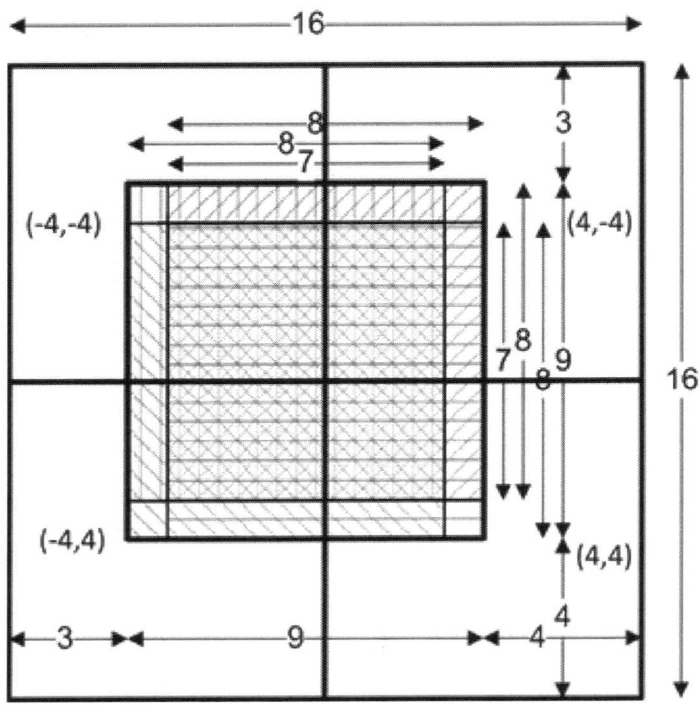


**Figure. 5** Locations of input and output blocks for the 2D interpolation. 9 × 9 block released from the luma interpolator includes four overlapping 8 × 8 blocks

9 × 9 blocks released from the interpolator must be written to a buffer to wait for the end of the preselection process. Some predictions corresponding to preselected MV candidates should be kept until they are forwarded to the reconstruction loop and the rate-distortion optimization. The buffer is outside the ME system and will be used to integrate with other encoder modules [17].

The new architecture of the luma interpolator is depicted in Fig. 6. The architecture incorporates separate stages for horizontal and vertical interpolation. Four successive 8 × 8 input blocks are written into the input ring buffer composed of four 16 × 4 register groups. The ring can reuse the four written blocks. When the blocks are reused, reference memories can be written with new data. One group of registers provides samples to 36 horizontal filters. The filters interpolate one 9 × 4 block in each clock cycle. Each horizontal filter can be reconfigured to support quarter-pel and half-pel interpolations. Additionally, the filters can be configured as the bypass path when the horizontal MV component is integer. Actually, filter cores do not support the interpolation for 3/4 positions. This interpolation is obtained by the horizontal transposition of samples at the input and the output. This method is also applied in the chroma interpolator.

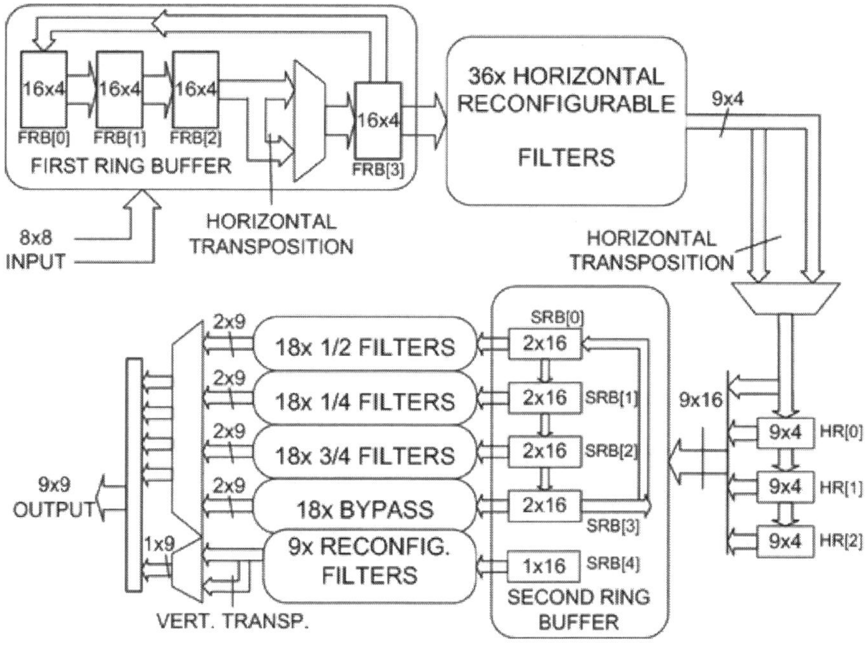


**Figure. 6** Architecture of the luma interpolator. *FRB* first ring buffer, *SRB* second ring buffer, *HR* horizontal register

The horizontal interpolator computes the 9 × 16 sample array in four clock cycles and then forwards it to the vertical stage. The vertical interpolator can be implemented as the 9 × 9 array of reconfigurable filters which determine a 9 × 9 block for one fractional-pel MV in each clock cycle. However, the hardware cost of 81 reconfigurable filters is significant. To save resources, the vertical stage incorporates 54 dedicated and nine reconfigurable filters. Each of three fractional-pel interpolations (1/4, 1/2, and 3/4) is performed with 18 dedicated filters. Separate bypass paths transfer 18 samples not interpolated vertically. Each bypass path includes the rounding adder and the range limiter. Nine reconfigurable filters perform all interpolations for the most right column in three cycles. The fourth cycle is utilized to transfer nine samples through the bypass path. The remaining eight columns are horizontally rotated between registers feeding dedicated filters and the bypass path. In particular, the register content is moved by two columns in each clock cycle. Each register column is assigned to one of the three groups of dedicated filters or to the bypass path. As a consequence, the 9 × 9 blocks released from the vertical stage consists of samples interpolated for four fractional-pel MVs. Thus, SADs must be accumulated in parallel for 16 fractional-pel MVs in four clock cycles. One multiplexer at the interpolator output is used to restore locations of four 2 × 9 sample groups. Another multiplexer vertically transposes positions in the most right column if the result for the 3/4 interpolation is released.

Inter-chroma predictions are obtained with MVs inferred from luma for a given CU size. Therefore, the required throughput of the chroma interpolation is much smaller than that of luma. The chroma interpolator embeds 12 reconfigurable filter cores assigned to two processing stages, as shown in Fig. 7. Eight cores interpolate chroma samples horizontally, whereas the vertical stage incorporates the remaining four cores. The chroma interpolator can provide four samples in each clock cycle. The inter-chroma predictor embedding the interpolator is designed as a separate processing path with dedicated 16 memories. The chroma predictor applies similar dataflow as in the case of the luma path. However, the prediction is determined only for one MV.

Figures 8, 9, 10, 11 show architectures of particular filter cores incorporated to the design. All the filters are implemented with two pipeline stages not shown in the figures for the clarity. Particularly, one stage includes one or two layers of adders/subtractors. The architecture of one reconfigurable filter used at the horizontal stage of the luma interpolator is depicted in Fig. 8. The filter supports half-pel (H) and quarter-pel (Q) interpolation. The reconfiguration between the two types of the interpolation is performed with seven multiplexers. Additional three multiplexers allow the transfer of one sample when the horizontal interpolation is not used. In this case, inputs indicated as I (integer) in Fig. 8 are selected. The half of 10 two-input multiplexers have one input fixed to zero. As a consequence, the multiplexers are reduced to AND gates. Similar reductions are achieved for five multiplexers in the chroma filter.

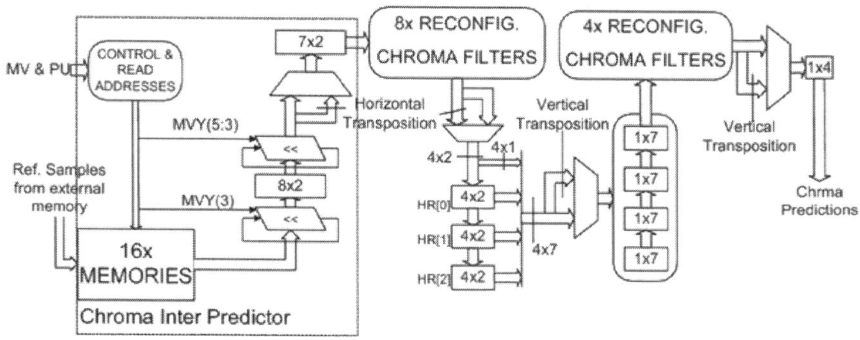


**Figure. 7** Architecture of the chroma inter predictor

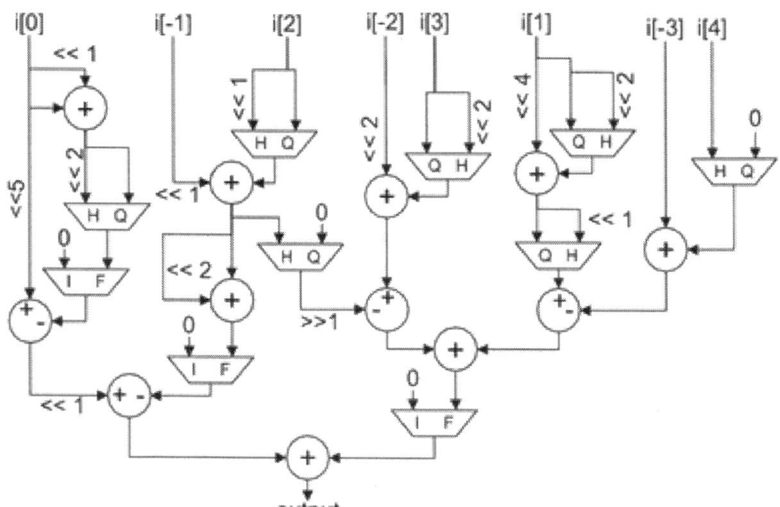


**Figure. 8** Architecture of the reconfigurable luma filter

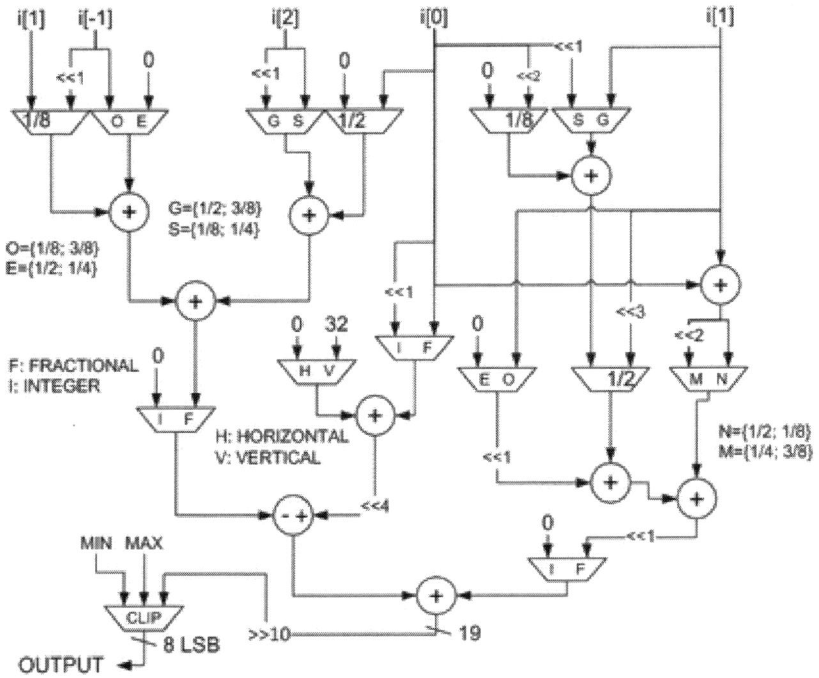


**Figure. 9** Architecture of the reconfigurable chroma filter

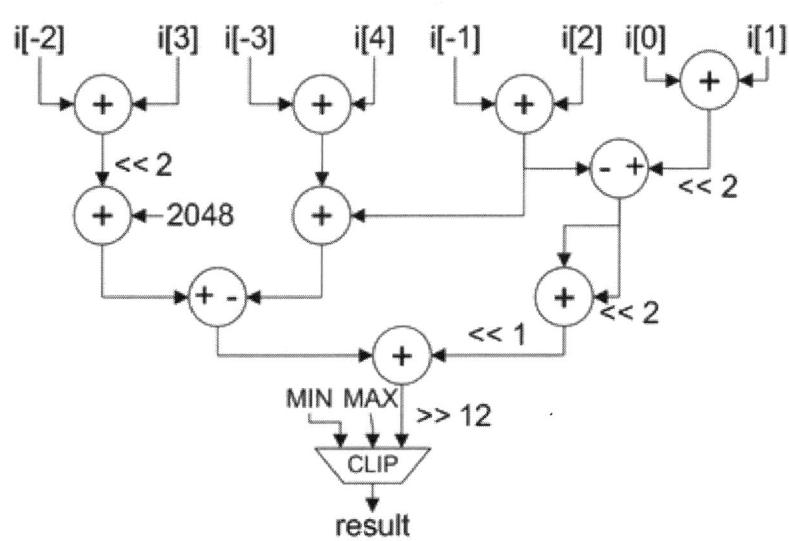


**Figure. 10** Architecture of the dedicated half-pel luma filter

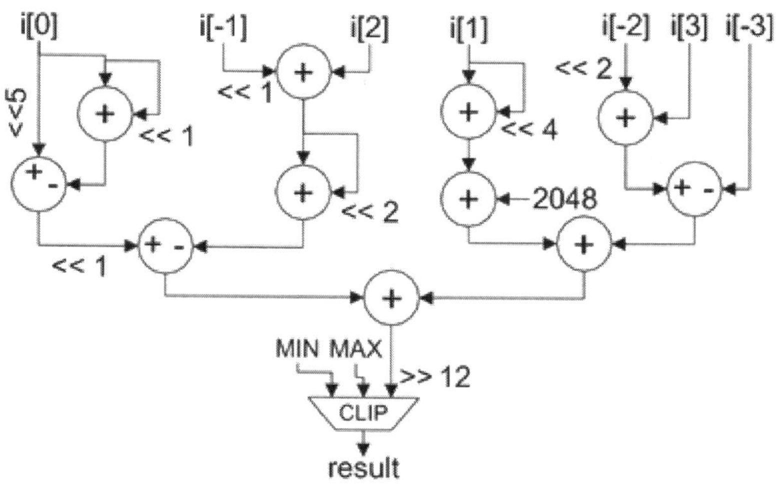


**Figure. 11** Architecture of the dedicated quarter-pel luma filter

The design of reconfigurable filters is well suited to FPGA devices since multiplexers are embedded in the same logic cell as the following adder/subtractor. The luma and chroma filter cores embed 12 and 10 adders/subtractors, respectively. The previous architecture required 22 adders/subtractors for the filter supporting both luma and chroma and 17 for luma. Therefore, the significant reduction of resources is achieved when the filter is limited to the luma processing.

Figures 10 and 11 depict architectures of dedicated filters used at the vertical stage for the half-pel and quarter-pel interpolation, respectively. The half-pel filter embeds 10 adders/subtractors whereas the quarter-pel filter consumes one more. Dedicated filters embed the rounding adder in the tree. The output multiplexer accomplishes the clipping (CLIP) of the final result to avoid overflow and underflow.

## 4. SCHEDULING

The ME system is pipelined based on 32 × 32 units, as shown in Fig. 12. Four parts of 64 × 64 PUs are processed only for the merge mode in relevant time intervals. To support 2160p@30fps video at 400 MHz, the number of clock cycles assigned to one unit is 1600. It means that 100 cycles are assigned to one 8 × 8 input block at each stage. The integer-pel ME allocates most cycles to the 8 × 8 search. The best MVs found for 8 × 8 blocks are used for the 16 × 16 search, in particular, four MVs are evaluated for one 16 × 16 block. Similarly, the best four MVs found at the 16 × 16 search are evaluated for one 32 × 32 block. Since eight MVs are assigned to larger PUs, the 8 × 8 search can utilize 92 MVs. For lower resolutions, more MVs are checked.

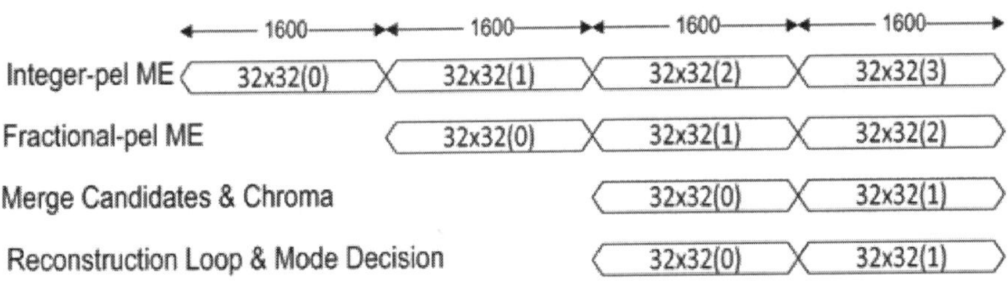


**Figure. 12** Scheduling of the motion estimation

The fractional-pel ME needs 16 clock cycles to evaluate 64 MVs around one integer-pel MV. Thus, the search can be performed around six MVs for a given 8 × 8 block. However, some cycles are required to interpolate MVs identified for the merge mode, in particular, four cycles are utilized to obtain the 8 × 8 interpolation for one MV. If the merge MV falls in the range of the regular fractional ME, no additional cycles are required. It is assumed that 48 cycles are allocated to regular fractional ME around three integer-pel MVs (8 × 8, 16 × 16, and 32 × 32 PUs). The remaining 52 cycles are utilized to process 13 merge mode candidates determined for different CU divisions. The regular factional-pel ME for a given PU is skipped if its range matches that for a larger PU. Saved cycles are utilized to evaluate more merge mode MVs. Since the availability of most of merge MVs depends on the mode decision for preceding CUs/PUs, merge mode candidates are evaluated at the same stage as the reconstruction loop and the CU/PU mode decision.

Interpolation filters specified in H.265/HEVC refer up to eight luma samples located in row/column at neighboring pixel positions. Therefore, the 2D interpolation of one sample requires access to the 8 × 8 reference block. If four blocks are accessed, the output can be extended to the 9 × 9 block. Provided that 8 × 8 blocks appear at the interpolator input, four cycles are taken to load the input registers. The location of the blocks can be identified by specific MVs, as shown in Fig. 5. For convenience, the following description will refer to motion vector differences (MVDs) relative to the integer-pel position around which the fractional-pel search is executed. If two horizontally adjacent 8 × 8 blocks are obtained for MVDs equal to (−4, 0) and (4, 0), the interpolator can compute MVDs equal to (1/4, 0), (1/2, 0), (3/4, 0), (−1/4, 0), (−1/2, 0), and (−3/4, 0). The same rule applies to the vertical processing. Four reference blocks required for the 2D interpolation have the following MVD: (−4, −4), (4, −4), (−4, 4), and (4, 4).

The luma interpolator can provide one 9 × 9 block in each clock cycle. As discussed in Sect. 3, the 9 × 9 block includes four overlapping 8 × 8 blocks. Thus, blocks for all 64 fractional-pel MVD around an integer-pel MV can be released in 16 successive cycles. The interpolation process is divided into four phases. In each phase, the interpolator computes the block for MVDs having the same horizontal fraction. Figure 13 shows the pattern used to generate fractional-pel samples around the integer-pel MV located in the middle. The pattern is regular and independent on the cost obtained for particular MVDs. Moreover, the pattern extends the fractional-pel search to MVDs whose horizontal or vertical component is equal to −1. Since the search is full, the compression efficiency is improved by 0.03 dB, on average. In the case of the merge mode, the design must interpolate samples with one of four phases used for the full search. Although the 8 × 8 block should be interpolated only for one MVD, one phase provides 16 MVDs. This is utilized to evaluate more MVDs and merge candidates (if they fall in the range).

The timing diagram of 2D luma interpolation is depicted in Fig. 14. To perform the interpolation around one integer-pel MV, four reference blocks are read form the input. The figure shows MVD corresponding to the blocks. In the timing diagram, there are some clock cycles when reference blocks are not read from memories. Such periods are utilized to write new data.

To perform the luma interpolation, four 8 × 8 reference blocks are taken from the input and written to the first ring buffer. The buffer consists of four register groups (FRB[0]–FRB [3]), each of which keeps four 16 sample rows. In each clock cycle, the rows are vertically rotated between register groups. Row indices are indicated in Fig. 14. Each reference block is simultaneously written to two register groups. Since each row is composed of samples taken from two reference blocks, two groups are half-filled with new samples in one cycle. Due to the rotation, the first/third block is written to FRB[0] and FRB [1], whereas the second/fourth block is written to FRB [1] and FRB [2]. If the 3/4 interpolation is performed, samples written to FRB [3] registers are horizontally transposed. The FRB [3] registers feed horizontal filters. The filtering result is obtained with the delay of two clock cycles. Horizontally interpolated samples corresponding to four rows are written to horizontal registers (HR) in each clock cycle. Every fourth clock cycle, 12 rows kept in HR and four rows available at filter outputs are forwarded to the second ring buffer (SRB). The buffer feeds 63 vertical filters and 18 bypass paths. The SRB is composed of nine columns. Eight of them are horizontally rotated by two positions in each clock cycle. Each two of six columns are assigned to a group of 18 dedicated filters supporting one particular type of the interpolation (either 1/2, 1/4, or 3/4). Two columns are assigned to 18 bypass paths. Similar to the horizontal stage, the filtering result is obtained with the delay of two clock cycles. The rotation in the second ring buffer allows the processing of eight columns with each filter type. On the other hand, multiplexers are required at outputs to restore appropriate locations of columns in the 9 × 9 block. One of nine columns is not rotated, and it feeds nine reconfigurable filters. The filters are reconfigured in each clock cycle to support one particular type of the interpolation. For the 3/4 interpolation, samples kept in SRB [4] are vertically transposed.

# 5. SEARCH STRATEGY

The proposed ME architecture can check an 8 × 8 prediction for one integer-pel MV and four fractional-pel MVs in each clock cycle. In practice, the number of evaluated MVs is limited and depends on the clock frequency and the video resolution. If the motion estimation operates at the frequency of 400 MHz and processes 2160p@30fps videos, the number of integer-pel MVs per each 8 × 8 block in the original image is about 100. This number should be allocated to all evaluated PUs corresponding to the block. Taking into account wider search ranges required for the 2160p@30fps resolution, numbers of MVs allocated to particular PUs can be too small to achieve a high compression efficiency. In the case of the fractional-pel ME, the available number of clock cycles can also limit the efficiency. Other limitations stem from the encoder dataflow, which introduces the delay between the ME and the final mode decision (based on the rate-distortion optimization). The delay causes some MV predictions to be unknown at the ME. Thus, costs of evaluated MVs cannot be estimated reliably.

Moreover, the determination of predictions for merge modes must follow the mode decision for preceding blocks.

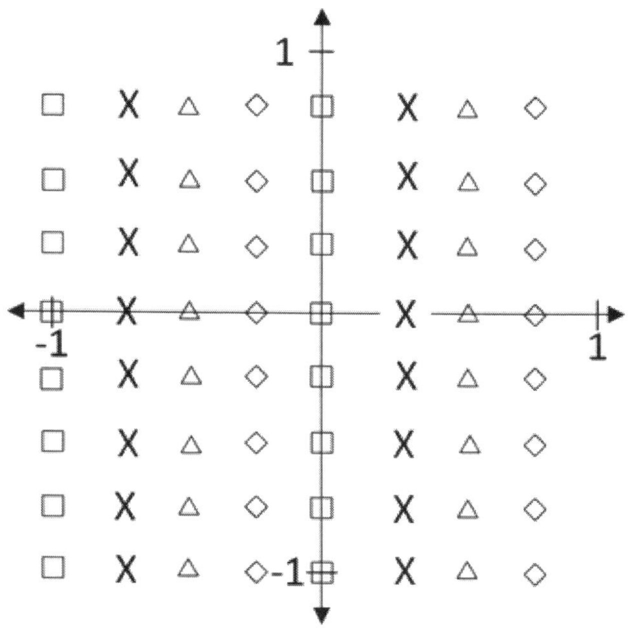


**Figure. 13** Fractional-pel search pattern. *Squares, triangles, crosses,* and *diamonds* indicate the first, the second, the third, and the fourth phase, respectively

Taking into account the limitations described above, the proposed search strategy introduces the following simplifications to the motion estimation algorithm applied in the HM software:

- The search range is set to (−64, 63) × (−64, 63).
- Test zone search is performed only for 8 × 8 PUs. It is interrupted when the number of checked MVs achieves the limit specified for a given resolution. The limit corresponds to the number of clock cycles assigned in the hardware architecture (e.g., 92 for 2160p@30fps). If some 8 × 8 PUs within the 32 × 32 unit do not utilize all allowable cycles, the remaining cycles are added to continue the interrupted search. This reallocation makes losses in the compression efficiency negligible.

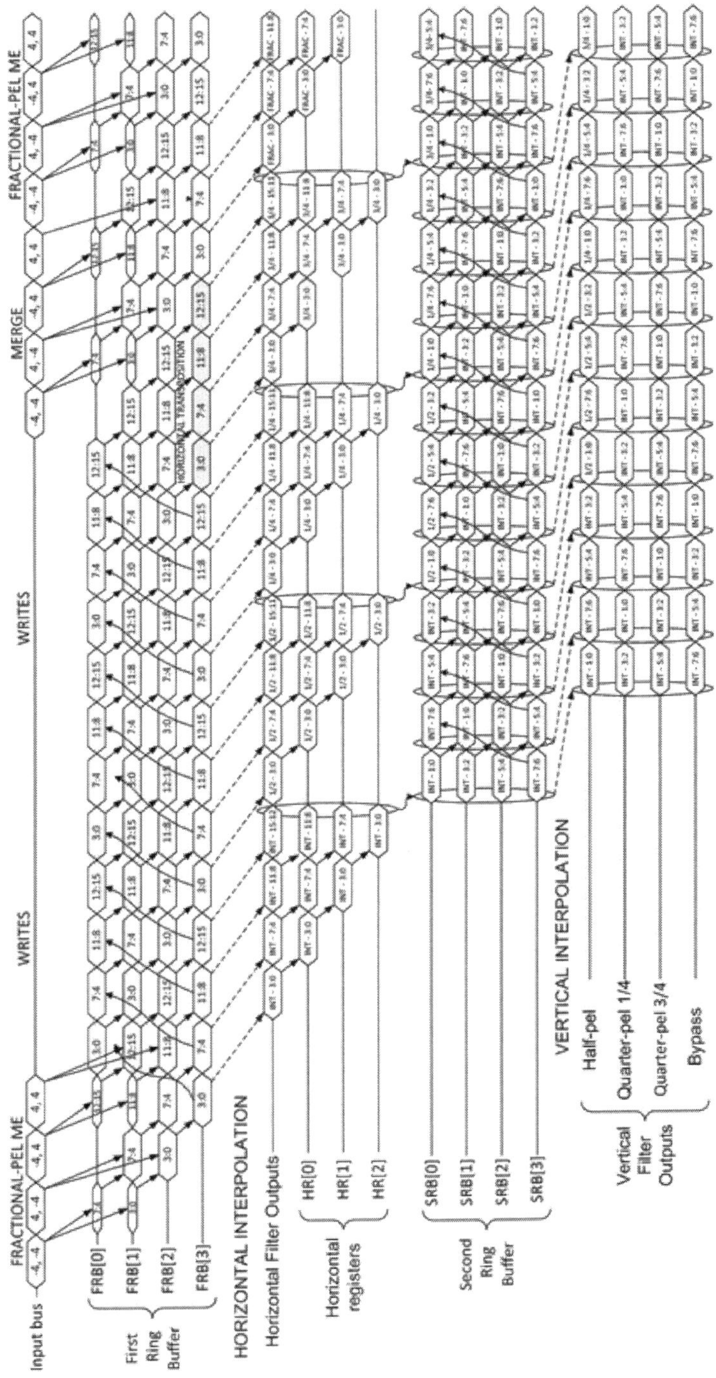


**Figure. 14** Timing diagram of the 2D luma interpolation

- The integer-pel motion estimation for 16 × 16 PUs is performed by utilizing results from the 8 × 8 search. Four MV candidates are taken from MVs found for 8 × 8 blocks included in a given PU.

- The integer-pel motion estimation for 32 × 32 PUs is performed by utilizing results from the 16 × 16 search. MV candidates are determined according to the rule applied in the 16 × 16 search.

- Rectangular PUs are evaluated within the range of the fractional-pel estimation corresponding 2N × 2N PUs. Although this simplification significantly reduces the ME complexity, it has a small impact on the average compression efficiency (0.3 %).

- MV costs are estimated based on results of the 8 × 8 search if a neighbor belongs to the same CTU. In this case, MV differences are computed with the assumption that neighbors are 8 × 8 blocks. In the remaining cases, actual MV predictors are taken from adjacent CTUs.

- Only merge mode candidates are evaluated for 64 × 64 PUs and their rectangular partitions. The exclusion of the 64 × 64 search decreases the compression efficiency by 0.8 % (−0.02 dB), on average.

- At least three merge mode candidates are evaluated for each PU if the video resolution is 2160p@30fps. More candidates can be processed if any of the three following conditions are true: First, merge MVs fall in the range of the fractional-pel search for the same or a larger PU. Second, fractional-pel search for a given PU matches that for a larger PU. Third, the resolution is lower than 2160p@30fps. The conditions stem from the scheduling and allow a better utilization of available clock cycles. In particular, more merge modes are evaluated to avoid the redundant processing and/or no-operation cycles.

- The final MV is not selected with sum of absolute transformed differences (SATD) used in the HM software. Instead, candidate MVs are selected based on SAD at the fractional-pel stage. Four candidates are selected for square PUs. The remaining (rectangular) PUs have one candidate MV. It is assumed that corresponding predictions are used in the mode selection based on the rate-distortion analysis. This approach decreases the compression efficiency by 0.3 % compared to the use of SATD.

The reuse of results of the 8 × 8 search saves a significant amount of computations. Particularly, eight integer-pel MVs are evaluated for larger PUs including a given 8 × 8 block. Moreover, MVs for the larger PUs are reused for smaller ones.

To estimate the efficiency achievable with the architecture, the reference model HM16 is used with the low-delay configuration defined in Common Test Conditions [18] and one reference frame. The software is modified according to the simplifications described above. Sequences assigned to different video classes are coded. Apart from classes A–E specified in Common Test Conditions, a separate group of 2160p (4K) sequences is also evaluated. The sequences are taken from two video repositories [19, 20]. The first [19] includes six sequences: Bosporus, Jockey, Honey Bee, Shake and Dry, Ready Steady Go, and Yacht Ride. The second group [20] includes Crowd Run, Ducks Take Off, In To Tree, and Park Joy. Sequences in the first and the second group are originally captured at 120 and 50 fps, respectively. To provide reliable results, their frame rate is decreased to 30 and 25 fps by coding every fourth and second frame, respectively. Evaluation results are summarized in Table 1 in terms of Bjontegaard Measures [21]. As can be seen, losses in the compression efficiency are relatively small. The largest loss is obtained for small-resolution sequences (classes C and D). It is caused by the impact of the smallest PUs, which are less frequently selected compared to the HM software.

**Table 1** Evaluation results for BD-PSNR and BD-Rate

| Class | Resolution | BD-PSNR [dB] | BD-rate (%) |
|---|---|---|---|
| A | 2560 × 1600 | −0.033 | 1.45 |
| B | 1920 × 1080 | −0.031 | 1.56 |
| C | 832 × 480 | −0.103 | 2.92 |
| D | 416 × 240 | −0.148 | 4.15 |
| E | 1280 × 720 | −0.069 | 2.98 |
| 4 K | 3840 × 2160 | −0.026 | 1.64 |
| Average | | −0.068 | 2.45 |

# 6. IMPLEMENTATION RESULTS

The architecture of the motion estimation system is specified in VHDL and verified with the modified HM16 reference model [2]. Apart from memory mapping, the VHDL description is independent on the technology selected. The synthesis is performed for FPGA and ASIC technologies using the Altera Quartus II software (ver. 13.1) and Synopsys Design Compiler (ver. 2013.03-SP5-4), respectively. Particularly, FPGA synthesis is performed for Aria II GX FPGA devices (speed grade 5), whereas TSMC 90 nm is selected as the ASIC technology. Implementation results are summarized in Table 2. As can be seen, the main contribution to the resource consumption is from the luma interpolator, which embeds 45 reconfigurable and 54 dedicated filters. The reconfigurable filter at the horizontal stage needs 157 ALUTs and 1517 gates for FPGA and ASIC technologies, respectively. At the vertical stage, resources consumed by each of nine reconfigurable filters are increased to 272 ALUTs and 3049 gates, respectively. The increase stems from the greater number of bits used to represent inputs and intermediate results. Dedicated filters consume less resource (116-166 ALUTs or 1747-2080 gates). The previous version of the interpolator [4] embeds 64 reconfigurable filters, each of which requires much more resources compared to filters used in the new design. For example, the fully featured filter in the previous design consumes 488 ALUTs or 4524 gates. The new architecture reduces the resource consumption mainly by the incorporation of dedicated filters for luma and separate chroma filters.

For the ASIC technology, the design can operate at the frequency of 400 MHz. This performance enables the encoder to allocate about 100 clock cycles per each 8 × 8 block if the resolution is 2160p@30fps. The estimated power consumption of the ASIC implementation is equal to 293 mW. The high power consumption is caused by memories keeping reference and original pixels. The FPGA implementation can operate at 200 MHz. As a consequence, the throughput is decreased by half.

The luma and chroma paths incorporate 64 dual-port and 16 two-port memory modules, respectively. The modules store reference pixels. Each module in the luma path is 0.75 kB in size. In the case of the chroma path, the size is 1.5 kB. The joint capacity of 72 kB allows the search range of (−64, 63) × (−64, 63) for both luma and chroma. Wider ranges are possible at the cost of the increased memory size. The original luma samples are stored in a separate dual-port memory with a capacity of 4 kB. This capacity is sufficient to keep samples for one CTU.

Since the ME system is pipelined based on 32 × 32 units, the assignment of memory subspaces is swapped between four processing stages (the writing, the integer-pel ME, the fractional-pel ME, and the merge mode evaluation).

Byun et al. [10] presented the H.265/HEVC integer-pel full search architecture supporting all prediction unit sizes with the range of (−32, 31) × (−32, 31). The design consumes 3.56 M gates and 23 kB memories. The hardware cost of the motion estimation system described in this paper is much smaller (422.7 k gates and 76 kB memories). Moreover, the search range is wider [(−64, 63) × (−64, 63)]. The low-power integer-pel design was proposed by Sanchez et al. [11]. Its resource consumption is relatively low (50 k gates and 82 kbit memories). However, it supports only 16 × 16 blocks and a narrow search range, which does not exploit the compression potential of H.265/HEVC.

The proposed architecture for H.265/HEVC interpolator is compared with other designs in Tables 3, 4. The proposed architecture has the highest throughput of 260 fractional-pel samples per clock cycle (4 blocks × 64 luma samples + 4 chroma samples). Taking into account the luma and chroma interpolation, the previous architecture [4] consumes slightly more resources. Since the proposed one significantly increases the throughput, the parallelism-to-resource ratio is several times higher. The ratio is also much higher compared to other designs. Moreover, the proposed design achieves this ratio for the 2D interpolation, whereas the ratio for most others takes into account the 1D parallelism. The maximal working frequency of the proposed architecture is the highest within the ASIC comparison. Although three implementations [12–14] require less resource, they offer much lower parallelism. As a consequence, declared throughputs are achieved when the size of the prediction unit is selected prior to the interpolation. One design [15] supports 4320p@30fps video with the interpolation for three PU sizes (64 × 64, 32 × 32, and 16 × 16). On the other hand, it consumes a large amount of resources, and its design efficiency is the lowest. Moreover, adapted simplifications involve quality losses, and implemented filters are specified in Working Draft 3. Since one of the architectures [13] requires additional memories and the control logic, its actual design efficiency (parallelism/resources) is lower. Compared to the previous version of the interpolator [4], the power consumption of the new one is higher for the ASIC technology. It stems from the continuous processing at all pipeline stages, which increases the switching activity of the circuit.

**Table 2** Resource consumption for FPGA and ASIC technologies

| Module | Arria II GX (ALUT) | TSMC 90 nm (gate) | Memory (kB) | Power (mW) |
|---|---|---|---|---|
| MV generator | 3598 (7.71 %) | 27,836 (6.59 %) | – | 3.1 |
| Luma predictor | 3412 (7.32 %) | 28,982 (6.86 %) | 48 | 164.7 |
| Luma interpolator | 24,202 (51.89 %) | 240,072 (56.80 %) | – | 30.2 |
| Cost estimator | 12,143 (26.03 %) | 97,124 (22.98 %) | 4 | 27.1 |
| Chroma predictor | 546 (1.17 %) | 3264 (0.77 %) | 24 | 65.4 |
| Chroma interpolator | 2742 (5.88 %) | 25,386 (6.00 %) | – | 2.5 |
| Total | 46,643 | 422,664 | 76 | 293.0 |

**Table 3** Comparison with other FPGA architectures

| Design | Afonso [12] | Pastuszak [4] | This study |
|---|---|---|---|
| Technology | Stratix III | Arria II GX | Arria II GX |
| Clock (MHz) | 403 | 200 | 200 |
| Resources (ALUT) | 4077 + 16547 | 28,757 | 26,944 |
| Parallelism (sample/clock) | 27 (1D) | 64 (1D) | 260 (2D) |
| 1000 × parallelism/resources | 1.31 | 2.26 | 9.64 |
| Throughput | 2160p@30fps | 1080p@60fps | 1080p@60fps |
| Dynamic power (mW) | 379 | 182 | 171 |
| Features | Luma | Luma and chroma | Luma and chroma |

**Table 4** Comparison with other ASIC architectures

| Design | Diniz [13] | Guo [14] | He [15] | Pastuszak [4] | This study |
|---|---|---|---|---|---|
| Technology (nm) | TSMC 150 | SMIC 90 | 65 | TSMC 90 | TSMC 90 |
| Clock (MHz) | 312 | 250 | 188 | 400 | 400 |
| Resources (gate) | 30,209 | 32,496 | 1,183,000 | 277,074 | 265,458 |
| Parallelism (sample/clock) | 12 (1D) | 8 (1D) | 16 × 12 (2D) | 64 (1D) | 260 (2D) |
| 1000 × parallelism/resources | 0.3972 | 0.2462 | 0.1623 | 0.2310 | 0.9794 |
| Throughput | 2160p@30fps | 2160p@60fps | 4320p@30fps | 2160p@30fps | 2160p@30fps |
| Power (Mw) | – | – | 198.6 | 11.4 | 30.2 |
| Features | Luma and chroma | Luma | Luma | Luma and chroma | Luma and chroma |

Most referenced designs support only the luma interpolation [12, 14, 15]. The FPGA implementation proposed by Afonso et al. [12] achieves a high frequency due to deep pipelining and the better device. The proposed architecture can also be modified to operate at higher frequencies by the insertion of registers. This modification would not increase the logic resources since at least one flip-flop is embedded in each ALUT. However, the power consumption would be increased. Moreover, the gain in the frequency would not compensate the increased latency of the deeply pipelined processing path composed of the luma predictor, the interpolator, and the cost estimator. The latency of the path affects timing constraints corresponding to the final mode decision and the availability of corresponding MVs. Thus, it would be difficult to determine merge mode candidates and MV costs for the highest throughput.

Although the hardware cost of the interpolator is decreased compared to the previous one [4], the proposed ME system is more complex. Particularly, the compensator in the previous architecture consumes 42.5 k gates, whereas the inter luma/chroma predictor and the cost estimator in the new one require 129.4 k gates. There are two main reasons of the increase. First, separate processing paths for the integer-pel and the fractional-pel are used. Second, four costs are simultaneously evaluated in the fractional-pel path. Since most logic resources are contributed by interpolators (265.5 k gates), the increased complexity in the remaining modules is relatively small in terms of the whole ME system. The throughput is increased by the factor of 1.85 (100/54) and 3.1 (100/32) for the integer-pel and fractional-pel processing, respectively.

# 7. CONCLUSION

The ME architecture is developed for the H.265/HEVC encoder. The design embeds two parallel processing paths for the integer-pel and the fractional-pel motion estimation. The paths share the same dual-port memories. Internal buffers and the scheduling allow the writing of reference samples through the port assigned to the fractional-pel path. The architecture supports TZS for 8 × 8 prediction blocks. The motion estimation for larger blocks is performed by utilizing results of the 8 × 8 search. The search for rectangular PUs is performed only at the fractional-pel level and reuses partial costs computed for 2N × 2N PUs. The design achieves the best ratio of the throughput to hardware resources compared to other designs. The design can check about 100 integer-pel MVs for each 8 × 8 input block when encoding 2160p@30fps video at the 400 MHz. Within future works, the proposed ME system will be integrated with the intra encoder [17] to support inter modes.

## ACKNOWLEDGMENTS

This research was supported in part by PL-Grid Infrastructure.

## REFERENCES

1. ITU-T Recommendation H.265 and ISO/IEC 23008-2 MPEG-H Part 2, High efficiency video coding (HEVC) (2013)

2. HEVC software repository—HM-16.0 reference model. https://hevc.hhi.fraunhofer.de/trac/hevc/browser/tags/HM-16.0 (2015). Accessed 29 June 2015

3. ITU-T Rec. H.264 and ISO/IEC 14496-10 MPEG-4 Part 10, Advanced video coding (AVC) (2005)

4. Pastuszak, G., Trochimiuk, M.: Architecture design of the high-throughput compensator and interpolator for the H.265/HEVC encoder. J. Real Time Image Process. Online first articles (2014)

5. Pastuszak, G., Jakubowski, M.: Adaptive computationally-scalable motion estimation for the hardware H.264/AVC encoder. IEEE Trans. Circuits Syst. Video Technol. **23**(5), 802–812 (2013)

6. Chen, T.-C., Chien, S.-Y., Huang, Y.-W., Tsai, C.-H., Chen, C.-Y., Chen, T.-W., Chen, L.-G.: Analysis and architecture design of an HDTV720p 30 frames/s H.264/AVC encoder. IEEE Trans. Circuits Syst. Video Technol. **16**(6), 673–688 (2006)

7. Liu, Z., Song, Y., Shao, M., Li, S., Li, L., Ishiwata, S., Nakagawa, M., Goto, S., Ikenaga, T.: HDTV1080p H.264/AVC encoder chip design and performance analysis. IEEE J. Solid-State Circuits **44**(2), 594–608 (2009)

8. Yang, C., Goto, S., Ikenaga, T.: High performance VLSI architecture of fractional motion estimation in H.264 for HDTV. In: IEEE International Symposium on Circuits and Systems (ISCAS 2006) pp. 21–24 (2006)

9. Oktem, S., Hamzaoglu, I.: An efficient hardware architecture for quarter-pixel accurate H.264 motion estimation. In: 10th Euromicro Conference on Digital System Design, pp. 1142–1143 (2007)

10. Byun, J., Jung, Y., Kim, J.: Design of integer motion estimator of HEVC for asymmetric motion-partitioning mode and 4K-UHD. Electron. Lett. **49**(18), 1142–1143 (2013)

11. Sanchez, G., Porto, M., Agostini, L.: A hardware friedly motion estimation algorithm for the emergent HEVC standard and its low power hardware design. In: IEEE International Conference on Image Processing, pp. 1991–1994 (2013)

12. Afonso, V., Maich, H., Agostini, L., Franco, D.: Low cost and high throughput FME interpolation for the HEVC emerging video coding standard. In: IEEE Fourth Latin American Symposium on Circuits and Systems (LASCAS) (2013)

13. Diniz, C. M., Shafique, M., Bampi, S., Henkel, J.: High-throughput interpolation hardware architecture with coarse-grained reconfigurable datapaths for HEVC. In: IEEE International Conference on Image Processing, pp. 2091–2095 (2013)

14. Guo, Z., Zhou, D., & Goto, S.: An optimized MC interpolation architecture for HEVC. In: IEEE International Conference on Acoustics, Speech and Signal Processing, pp. 1117–1120 (2012)

15. He, G., Zhou, D., Chen, Z., Zhang, T., Goto, S.: A 995Mpixels/s 0.2nJ/pixel fractional motion estimation architecture in HEVC for Ultra-HD. In: IEEE Asian Solid-State Circuits Conference, pp. 301–304 (2013)

16. Jakubowski, M., Pastuszak, G.: An adaptive computation-aware algorithm for multi-frame variable block-size motion estimation in H.264/AVC. In: International Conference on Signal Processing and Multimedia Applications (SIGMAP '09), pp. 122–125 (2009)

17. Pastuszak, G., Abramowski, A.: Algorithm and architecture design of the H.265/HEVC intra encoder. IEEE Transactions on Circuits and Systems for Video Technology, pp. 1 (2015.

18. Bossen, F.: Common test conditions and software configurations, JCT-VC-L1100. JCT-VC, Geneva (2013)

19. Ultra video group, test sequences: (online). http://ultravideo.cs.tut.fi/#testsequences (2015). Accessed 29 June 2015

20. Xiph.org: test media, http://media.xiph.org/video/derf/ (2011). Accessed 29 June 2015

21. Bjontegaard, G.: Calculation of average PSNR differences between RD-Curves. In: ITU-T VCEG-M33, VCEG 13th Meeting

4

# A STATE-OF-THE-ART SURVEY ON REAL-TIME ISSUES IN EMBEDDED SYSTEMS VIRTUALIZATION

**Zonghua Gu, Qingling Zhao**

College of Computer Science, Zhejiang University, Hangzhou, China

## ABSTRACT

Virtualization has gained great acceptance in the server and cloud computing arena. In recent years, it has also been widely applied to real-time embedded systems with stringent timing constraints. We present a comprehensive survey on real-time issues in virtualization for embedded systems, covering popular virtualization systems including KVM, Xen, L4 and others.

## KEYWORDS

Virtualization; Embedded Systems; Real-Time Scheduling

## 1. INTRODUCTION

Platform virtualization refers to the creation of Virtual Machines (VMs), also called domains, guest OSes, or partitions, running on the physical machine managed by a Virtual Machine Monitor (VMM), also called a hypervisor. Virtualization technology enables concurrent execution of multiple VMs on the same hardware (single or multicore) processor. Virtualization technology has been widely applied in the enterprise and cloud computing space. In recent years, it has been increasingly widely deployed in the embedded systems domain, including avionics systems, industrial automation, mobile phones, etc. Compared to the conventional application domain of enterprise systems, virtualization in embedded systems must place strong emphasis on issues like real-time performance, security and dependability, etc.

A VMM can run either on the hardware directly (called bare-metal, or Type-1 virtualization), or run on top of a host operating system (called hosted, or Type-2 virtualization). Another way to classify platform-level virtualization technologies is full virtualization vs paravirtualization. Full virtualization allows the guest OS to run on the VMM without any modification, while paravirtualization requires the guest OS to be modified by adding hypercalls into the VMM. Representative Type-2, full virtualization solutions include KVM, VirtualBox, Microsoft Virtual PC, VMWare Workstation; Representative Type-1, paravirtualization solutions include Xen, L4, VMWare ESX. There are some research attempts at constructing Type-1, full virtualization solutions, e.g., Kinebuchi et al. [1] implemented such a solution by porting the QEMU machine emulator to run as an application on L4Ka::Pistachio microkernel; in turn, unmodified guest OS can run on top of QEMU; Schild et al. [2] used Intel VT-d HW extensions to run unmodified guest OS on L4. There are also Type-2, para-virtualization solutions, e.g., VMWare MVP (Mobile Virtualization Platform) [3], as well as some attempts at adding para-virtualization features to Type-2 virtualization systems to improve performance, e.g., task-grain scheduling in KVM [4].

Since embedded systems often have stringent timing and performance constraints, virtualization for embedded systems must address real-time issues. We focus on realtime issues in virtualization for embedded systems, and leave out certain topics that are more relevant to the server application space due to space constrains, including: power and energy-aware scheduling, dynamic adaptive scheduling, multicore scheduling on high-end NUMA (Non-Uniform Memory Access) machines, nested virtualization, etc. In addition, we focus on recent developments in this field, instead of presenting a historical perspective.

This paper is structured as follows: we discuss hard real-time virtualization solutions for safety-critical systems in Section 2; Xen-based solutions in Section 3, including hard real-time and soft real-time extensions to Xen; KVM-based solutions in Section 4; micro-kernel based solutions represented by L4 in Section 5; other virtualization frameworks for embedded systems in Section 6; OS virtualization in Section 7; task-grain scheduling in Section 8; the Lock-Holder Preemption problem in Section 9; and finally, a brief conclusion in Section 10. (The topics of Sections 8 and 9 are cross-cutting issues that are not specific to any virtualization approach, but we believe they are of sufficient importance to dedicate separate sections to cover them.)

## 2. HARD REAL-TIME VIRTUALIZATION FOR SAFETY-CRITICAL SYSTEMS

The ARINC 653 standard [5] defines a software architecture for spatial and temporal partitioning designed for safety-critical IMA (Integrated Modular Avionics) applications. It defines services such as partition management, process management, time management, inter and intra-partition communication. In the ARINC 653 specification for system partitioning and scheduling, each partition (virtual machine) is allocated a time slice, and partitioned are scheduled in a TDMA (Time Division Multiple Access) manner. A related standard is the Multiple Independent Levels of Security (MILS) architecture, an enabling architecture for developing security-critical applications conforming to the Common Criteria security evaluation. The MILS architecture defines four conceptual layers of separation: separation kernel and hardware; middleware services; trusted applications; distributed communications. Authors from Lockheed Martin [6] presented a feasibility assessment toward applying the Microkernel Hypervisor architecture to enable virtualization for a representative set of avionics applications requiring multiple guest OS environments, including a mixture of safety-critical and non-safety-critical guest OSes. Several commercial RTOS products conform to the ARINC 653 standard, including LynuxWorks LynxOS-178, Green Hills INTEGRITY-178B, Wind River VxWorks 653, BAE Systems CsLEOS, and DDC-I DEOS, etc. Many vendors also offer commercial virtualization products for safety-critical systems, many by adapting existing RTOS products. For example, LynuxWorks implemented a virtualization layer to host their LynxOS product, called the LynxSecure hypervisor that supports MILS and ARINC 653. WindRiver [7] provides a hypervisor product for both its VxWorks MILS and VxWorks 653 platforms, including support for multicore. Other similar products include: Greenhills INTEGRITY MultiVisor [8], RealTime Systems GmbH Hypervisor [9], Tenasys eVM for Windows

[10], National Instruments Real-Time Hyper Hypervisor [11], Open Synergy COQOS [12], Enea Hypervisor [13], SysGO PikeOS [14], IBV Automation GmbH QWin etc. VanderLeest [15], from a company named DornerWorks, took a different approach by adapting the open-source Xen hypervisor to implement the ARINC 653 standard.

XtratuM [16] is a Type-1 hypervisor targeting safety critical avionics embedded systems. It runs on LEON3 SPARC V8 processor, a widely used CPU in space applications. It features temporal and spatial separation, efficient scheduling mechanism, low footprint with minimum computational overhead, efficient context switch of the partitions (domains), deterministic hypervisor system calls. Zamorano et al. [17,18] ported the Ada-based Open Ravenscar Kernel (ORK+) to run as a partition on XtratuM, forming a software platform conforming to the ARINC 653 standard. Campagna et al. [19] implemented a dual-redundancy system on XtratuM to tolerate transient faults like Single-Event-Upset, common on the high-radiation space environment. Three partitions are executed concurrently, two of them run identical copies of the application software, and the third checks consistency of their outputs. The OVERSEE (Open Vehicular Secure Platform) Project [20] aims to bring the avionics standard to automotive systems by porting FreeOSEK, an OSEK/VDX-compliant RTOS, as a paravirtualized guest OS running on top of the XtratuM hypervisor [21]. While most ARINC-653 compliant virtualization solutions are based on para-virtualization, Han et al. [22] presented an implementation of ARINC 653 based on Type-2, full virtualization architectures, including VM-Ware and VirtualBox.

Next, we briefly mention some virtualization solutions for safety-critical systems that are not specifically designed for the avionics domain, hence do not conform to the ARINC-653 standard. Authors from Indian Institute of Technology [23] developed SParK (Safety Partition Kernel), a Type-1 para-virtualization solution designed for safety-critical systems; an open-source RTOS uC/ OS-II and a customized version of saRTL (stand-alone RT Linux) are ported as guest OSes on SParK. Authors from CEA (Atomic Energy Commission), France [24] developed PharOS, a dependable RTOS designed for automotive control systems featuring temporal and spatial isolation in the presence of a mixed workload of both time-triggered and event-triggered tasks. They adapted Trampoline, an OSEK/VDX-compliant RTOS, as a paravirtualized guest OS running on top of PharOS host OS to form a Type-2 virtualization architecture. To ensure temporal predictability, Trampoline is run as a timetriggered task within PharOS. Authors from PUCRS, Brazil [25] developed Virtual-Hellfire Hypervisor, a Type-1 virtualization system based on the microkernel HellfireOS featuring spatial and temporal isolation for safety-critical applications. The target HW platform is HERMES Network-on-Chip with MIPS-like processing elements [26].

# 3. XEN-BASED SOLUTIONS

Cherkasova et al. [27] introduced and evaluated three CPU schedulers in Xen: BVT (Borrowed Virtual Time), SEDF (Simple Earliest Deadline First), and Credit. Since the BVT scheduler is now deprecated, we only discuss Credit and SEDF here.

The default scheduling algorithm in Xen is the Credit Scheduler: it implements a proportional-share scheduling strategy where a user can adjust the CPU share for each VM. It also features automatic workload balancing of virtual CPUs (vCPUs) across physical cores (pCPUs) on a multicore processor. This algorithm guarantees that no pCPU will idle when there exists a runnable vCPU in the system. Each VM is associated with a weight and a cap. When the cap is 0, VM can receive extra CPU time unused by other VMs, i.e., WC (Work-Conserving) mode; when the cap is nonzero (expressed as a percentage), it limits the amount of CPU time given to a VM to not exceed the cap, i.e., NWC (Non-Work-Conserving) mode. By default the credits of all runnable VMs are recalculated in intervals of 30 ms in proportion to each VM's weight parameter, and the scheduling time slice is 10 ms, i.e., the credit of the running virtual CPU is decreased every 10 ms.

In the SEDF scheduler, each domain can specify a lower bound on the CPU reservations that it requests by specifying a tuple of (slice, period), so that the VM will receive at least slice time units in each period time units. A Boolean flag indicates whether the VM is eligible to receive extra CPU time. If true, then it is WC (WorkConserving) mode, and any available slack time is distributed in a fair manner after all the runnable VMs have received their specified slices. Unlike the Credit Scheduler, SEDF is a partitioned scheduling algorithm that does not allow VM migration across multiple cores, hence there is no global workload balancing on multicore processors.

Masrur et al. [28] presented improvements to Xen's SEDF scheduler so that a domain can utilize its whole budget (slice) within its period even if it blocks for I/O before using up its whole slice (in the original SEDF scheduler, the unused budget is lost once a task blocks ). In addition, certain critical domains can be designated as real-time domains and be given higher fixed-priority than other domains scheduled with SEDF. One limitation is that each real-time domain is constrained to contain a single real-time task. Masrur et al. [29] removed this limitation, and considered a hierarchical scheduling architecture in Xen, where both the Xen hypervisor and guest VMs adopt deadline-monotonic Fixed-Priority scheduling with a tuple of (period, slice) parameters (similar to SEDF, a VM is allowed to run for a maximum length of slice time units within each period), and proposed a method for selecting optimum time slices and periods for each VM in the system to achieve schedulability while minimizing the lengths of time slices.

The RT-Xen project [30,31] implemented a compositional and hierarchical scheduling architecture based on fixed-priority scheduling within Xen, and extensions of compositional scheduling framework [32] and periodic server design for fixed-priority scheduling. Similarly, Yoo et al. [33] implemented the Compositional Scheduling Framework [32] in Xen-ARM. Jeong et al. [34] developed PARFAIT, a hierarchical scheduling framework in Xen-ARM. At the bottom level (near the HW), SEDF is used to provide CPU bandwidth guarantees to Domain0 and real-time VMs; at the higher level, BVT (Borrowed Virtual Time) is used to schedule all non-realtime VMs to provide fair distribution of CPU time among them, by mapping all vCPUs in the non real-time VMs to a single abstract vCPU scheduled by the underlying SEDF scheduler. Lee et al. [30], Xi et al. [31], Yoo et al. [33], Jeong et al. [34] only addressed CPU scheduling issues, but did not consider I/O scheduling.

Xen has a split-driver architecture for handling I/O, where a special driver domain (Domain0) contains the backend driver, and user domains contain the frontend driver. Physical interrupts are first handled by the hypervisor, which then notifies the target guest domain with virtual interrupts, handled when the guest domain is scheduled by the hypervisor scheduler. Hong et al. [35] improved network I/O performance of Xen-ARM by performing dynamic load balancing of interrupts among the multiple cores by modifying the ARM11 MPCore interrupt distributor. In addition, each guest domain contains its own native device drivers, instead of putting all device drivers in Domain0. Yoo et al. [36] proposed several improvements to the Xen Credit Scheduler to improve interrupt response time, including: do not deschedule the driver domain when it disables virtual interrupts; exploit ARM processor support for FIQ, which has higher priority than regular IRQ, to support real-time I/O devices; ensure that the driver domain is always scheduled with the highest priority when it has pending interrupts.

Lee et al. [37] enhanced the soft real-time performance of the Xen Credit Scheduler. They defined a laxity value as the target scheduling latency that the workload desires, and preferentially schedule the vCPU with smallest laxity. Furthermore, they take cache-affinity into account for real time tasks when performing multicore load-balancing to prevent cache thrashing.

Yu et al. [38] presented real-time improvements to the Xen Credit Scheduler: real-time vCPUs are always given priority over non real-time vCPUs, and can preempt any non real-time vCPUs that may be running. When there are multiple real-time vCPUs, they are load-balanced across multiple cores to reduce their mutual interference. Wang et al. [39] proposed to insert a workload monitor in each guest VM to monitor and calculate both the CPU and GPU resource utilization of all active guest VMs, and give priority to guest VMs that are GPU-intensive in the Xen Credit Scheduler, since those are likely the interactive tasks that need the shortest response time.

Chen et al. [40] improved the Xen Credit Scheduler to have better audio-playing performance. The real-time vCPUs are assigned a shorter time slice, say 1 ms, while the non-real-time vCPUs keep the regular time slice of 30 ms. The real-time vCPUs are also allowed to stay in the BOOST state for longer periods of time, while the regular Credit Scheduler only allows a vCPU to stay in the BOOST state for one time slice before demoting it to UNDER state. Xen provides a mechanism to pin certain vCPUs on physical CPUs (pCPUs). Chen et al. [41] showed that when the number of vCPUs in a domain is greater than that of pinned pCPUs, the Xen Credit Scheduler may seriously impair the performance of I/O-intensive applications. To improve performance of pinned domains, they added a periodic runtime monitor in the VMM to monitor the length of time when each domain's vCPUs go into the BOOST state, as well as the bus transactions with the help of HW Performance Monitoring Unit, in order to distinguish between CPU-intensive and I/O intensive domains. The former are assigned larger time slices, and the latter are assigned smaller time slices to improve their responsiveness.

Gupta et al. [42] presented a set of techniques for enforcing performance isolation among multiple VMs in Xen: XenMon measures per-VM resource consumption, including work done on behalf of a particular VM in Xen's driver domains; a SEDF-DC (Debt Collector) scheduler periodically receives feedback from XenMon about the CPU consumed by driver domains for I/O processing on behalf of guest domains, and charges guest domains for the time spent in the driver domain on their behalf when allocating CPU time; ShareGuard limits the total amount of resources consumed in driver domains based on administrator-specified limits.

Ongaro et al. [43] studied impact of the Xen VMM scheduler on performance using multiple guest VMs concurrently running different types of application workloads, i.e., different combinations of CPU-intensive, I/Ointensive, and latency-sensitive applications. Several optimizations are proposed, including disabling preemption for the privileged driver domain, and optimizing the Credit Scheduler by sorting VMs in run queue based on remaining credits to give priority to short-running I/O VMs.

Govindan et al. [44] presented a communication-aware CPU scheduling algorithm and a CPU usage accounting mechanism for Xen. They modified the Xen SEDF scheduler by preferentially scheduling I/O-intensive VMs over their CPU-intensive VMs, by counting the number of packets flowing into or out of each VM, and selecting the VM with the highest count that has not yet consumed its entire slice during the current period.

Hu et al. [45] proposed a method for improving I/O performance of Xen on a multicore processor. The cores in the system are divided into 3 subsets, including the driver core hosting the single driver domain, hence it does not need VMM scheduling; fast-tick cores for handling I/O events, which employs preemptive scheduling with small time slices to ensure fast response to I/O events; and general cores for computation-intensive workloads, which use the default Xen Credit Scheduler for fair CPU sharing.

Lee et al. [46] improved performance of multimedia applications in Xen by assigning higher fixed-priorities to Domain0 and other real-time domains than non-realtime domains, which are scheduled by the default credit scheduler.

# 4. KVM-BASED SOLUTIONS

KVM is a Type-2 virtualization solution that uses Linux as the host OS, hence any real-time improvements to the Linux host OS kernel directly translate into real-time improvements to the KVM VMM. For example, realtime kernel patches like Ingo Milnar's PREEMPT_RT patch, can be applied to improve the real-time performance and predictability of the Linux host OS.

Kiszka [4] presented some real-time improvements to KVM. Real-time guest VM threads are given real-time priorities, including the main I/O thread and one or more vCPU threads, at the expense of giving lower priorities to threads in the host Linux kernel for various system-wide services. A paravirtualized scheduling interface was introduced to allow task-grain scheduling by introducing two hypercalls for the guest VM to inform the host VMM about priority of the currently running task in the VM, as well as when an interrupt handler is finished execution in the VM. Introduction of these hypercalls implies that the resulting system is no longer a strict fullvirtualization system as the conventional KVM. Zhang et al. [47] presented two real-time improvements to KVM with coexisting RTOS and GPOS guests: giving the guest RTOS vCPUs higher priority than GPOS vCPUs; use CPU shielding to dedicate one CPU core to the RTOS guest and shield it from GPOS interrupts, by setting the CPU affinity parameter of both host OS processes and interrupts. Experimental results indicate that the RTOS interrupt response latencies are reduced. Based on the work of [47], Zuo et al. [48] presented additional improvements by adding two hypercalls that enable the guest OS to boost priority of its vCPU when a high- priority task is started, e.g., like an interrupt handler, and deboost it when the high-priority task is finished.

Cucinotta et al. [49] presented the IRMOS scheduler, which implements a hard reservation variant of CBS (Constant Bandwidth Server) on top of the EDF scheduler in Linux by extending the Linux CGroup interface. When applied in the context of KVM, inter-VM scheduling is CBS/EDF, while intra-VM task scheduling is Fixed-Priority. While Cucinotta et al. [49] only addressed CPU scheduling, Cucinotta et al. [50] addressed I/O and networking issues by grouping both guest VM threads and interrupt handler threads in the KVM host OS kernel into the same CBS reservation, and over-provisioning the CPU budget assigned to each VM by an amount that is dependent on the overall networking traffic performed by VMs hosted on the same system. Cucinotta et al. [51] improved the CBS scheduler in the KVM host OS for a mixed workload of both compute-intensive and networkintensive workloads. In addition to the regular CPU CBS reservation of (Q, P), where the VM is guaranteed to receive budget Q time units of CPU time out of every P time units, a spare CPU reservation of ($Q_S$, $P_S$) is attached to the VM and dynamically activated upon a new packet arrival. The spare reservation ($Q_S$, $P_S$) has much smaller budget and period than the regular reservation (Q, P) to provide fast networking response time. Checconi et al. [52] addressed real-time issues in live migration of KVM virtual machines by using a probabilistic model of the migration process to select an appropriate policy for memory page migration, either based on a simple LRU (Least-Recently Used) order, or a more complex one based on observed page access frequencies in the past VM history.

RESCH (REal-time SCHeduler framework) [53] is an approach to implementing new scheduling algorithms within Linux without modifying the kernel. In contrast to typical user-level schedulers [54], RESCH consists of a loadable kernel module called RESCH core, and a user library called RESCH library. In addition to the built-in Fixed-Priority (FP) scheduling algorithm in Linux, 4 new real-time FP-based scheduling algorithms have been implemented with RESCH, including: FP-FF (partitioned scheduling with First-Fit heuristic for mapping tasks to processors), FP-PM (when a task cannot be assigned to any CPU by first-fit allocation, the task can migrate across multiple CPUs with highest priority on its allocated CPU), G-FP (Global FP scheduling, where tasks can freely migrate among different processors, and the task with globally highest priority is executed), FP-US (global FP scheduling, where tasks are classified into heavy tasks and light tasks, based on their utilizations factors. If the CPU utilization of a task is greater than or equal to $m/(3m-2)$, where m is the number of processors, it is a heavy task. Otherwise, it is a light task. All heavy tasks are statically assigned the highest priorities, while light tasks have the original priorities). Other scheduling algorithms can also be implemented. Asberg et al. [55] applied RESCH to KVM to implement a real-time hierarchical scheduling framework in a uni-processor environment, where RESCH is used in both the host OS and guest OS to implement FP scheduling. Asberg et al. [56] used RESCH to implement 4 variants of multi-core global hierarchical scheduling algorithms in Linux.

Lin et al. [54] presented VSched, an user-space implementation of EDF-based scheduling algorithm in the host OS of a Type-2 virtualization system VMware GSX Server. The scheduler is a user-level process with highest priority, and Linux SIGSTOP/SIGCONT signals are used to implement (optional) hard resource reservations, hence it does not require kernel modification, but carries large runtime overhead due to excessive context-switches between the scheduler process and application processes compared to RESCH. (Although VSched is not implemented on KVM, we place it here due to its similarity to RESCH.)

# 5. MICROKERNEL-BASED SOLUTIONS

L4 is a representative microkernel operating system, extended to be a Type-1 virtualization architecture. There are multiple active variants of L4. **Figure 1** shows the evolution lineage of L4 variants.

Authors from Avaya Labs [57] implemented a paravirtualized Android kernel, and ran it alongside a paravirtualized Linux kernel from OK Labs, L4Linux, on an ARM processor. Iqbal et al. [58] presented a detailed comparison study between microkernel-based approach, represented by L4, and hypervisor-based approach, represented by Xen, to embedded virtualization, and concluded that L4-based approaches have better performance and security properties. Gernot Heiser [59], founder of OKL4, argued for microkernel-based virtualization for embedded systems. Performance evaluation of OKL4 hypervisor on Beagle Board based on 500 MHz Cortex A8 ARMv7 processor, running netperf benchmark shows that the TCP and UDP throughput degradation due to virtualization is only 3% - 4%. Bruns et al. [60] and Lackorzynski et al. [61] performed performance evaluation of L4Linux. Using L4/Fiasco as the hypervisor, L4Linux as the guest OS, an ARM-based Infineon XGOLD618 processor for mobile phones, Bruns et al. [60] compared thread context-switching times and interrupt latencies of L4Linux to those of a stand-alone RTOS (FreeRTOS), and demonstrated that L4-based system has relatively small runtime overhead, but requires significantly more cache resources than an RTOS, with cache contention as the main culprit for performance degradations.

One important application area of L4 is mobile phone virtualization. A typical usage scenario is co-existence of multiple OSes on the same HW platform, e.g., have a "rich" OS like Android or Windows for handling user interface and other control-intensive tasks, and a "simple" real-time OS for handling performance and timingcritical tasks like baseband signal processing. Another goal is to save on hardware bill-of-material costs by having a single core instead of two processor cores. Open Kernel Labs implemented the first commercial virtualized phone in

2009 named the Motorola Evoke QA4, which runs two VMs on top of L4 hypervisor, one is Linux for handling user interface tasks, and the other is BREW (Binary Runtime Environment for Wireless) for handling baseband signal processing tasks on a single ARM processor.

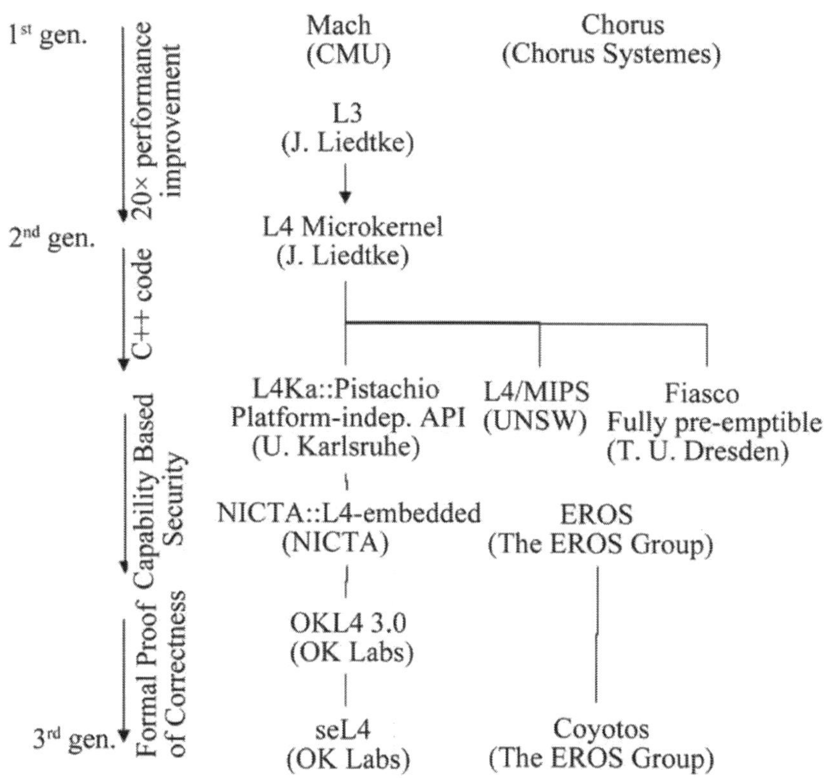


**Figure 1**. L4 evolution lineage (from Acharya et al. [57]).

The company SysGo AG developed PikeOS, which evolved from a L4-microkernel, designed for safetycritical applications. Kaiser et al. [62] described the scheduling algorithm in PikeOS, which is a combination of priority-based, time-driven and proportional share scheduling. Each real-time VM is assigned a fixed-priority decided by the designer, hence a time-driven VM can have lower or higher priority values than an event-driven VM. Non real-time VMs execute in the background when real-time VMs are not active. Yang et al. [63] developed a two-level

Compositional Scheduling Architecture (CSA), using the L4/Fiasco microkernel as a VMM and L4Linux as a VM.

The NOVA Hypervisor [64] from Technical University of Dresden is a Type-1 hypervisor focusing on security issues that shares many similarities with L4, but it is a full-virtualization solution based on processor HW support that does not require modification of the guest OS.

# 6. OTHER VIRTUALIZATION FRAMEWORKS FOR EMBEDDED SYSTEMS

Authors from Motorola [65] argued for the use of Type-1 hypervisors as opposed to Type-2 hypervisors for mobile phone virtualization for their security benefits due to a small TCB (Trusted Computing Base). Representative mobile virtualization solutions include MVP (Mobile Virtualization Platform) from VMWare [3,66], VLX from Red Bend [67,68], Xen-ARM from Samsung [69], etc. L4, VLX and Xen-ARM are all Type-1 hypervisors. VMWare MVP is a Type-2 virtualization solution with Linux as both host and guest OSes implemented on ARMv7 processor. It adopts a lightweight para-virtualization approach: 1) the entire guest OS is run in CPU user-mode; most privileged instructions are handled via trap-and-emulate, e.g., privileged coprocessor access instructions mcr and mrc; other sensitive instructions are replaced with hypercalls; 2) all devices are para-virtualized; especially, the paravirtualized TCP/IP is different from traditional para-virtualized networking by operating at the socket system call level instead of at the device interface level: When a guest VM calls a syscall to open a socket, the request is made directly to the offload engine in the host OS, which opens a socket and performs TCP/IP protocol processing within the host OS kernel.

SPUMONE (Software Processing Unit, Multiplexing ONE into two or more) [70,71] is a lightweight Type-1 virtualization software implemented on a SH-4A processor with the goal of running a GPOS (General-Purpose OS) like Linux and an RTOS like TOPPERS (an open source implementation of the ITRON RTOS standard [72]) on the same HW processor. It can either use fixedpriority scheduling, and always assign the RTOS higher priority than GPOS, or adopt task-grain scheduling [73], where each task can be assigned a different priority to allow more fine-grained control, e.g., an important task in the GPOS can be assigned a higher priority than a less important task in the RTOS. Inter-OS communication is achieved with IPI (Inter-Processor Interrupts) and shared memory. Aalto [74] developed DynOS SPUMONE, an extension to SPUMONE to enable runtime migration of guest OSes to different cores on a 4-core RP1 processor from Renesas. Lin et al. [75] presented a redesign of SPUMONE as a multikernel architecture. (Multikernel means that a separate copy of the kernel or VMM runs on each core on a multicore processor.) Each processor core has its private local memory. To achieve better fault isolation, the VMM runs in the local memory, while the guest OSes run in the global shared main memory; both run in kernel mode. To enhance security, Li et al. [76] added a small trusted OS called xv6 to run a monitoring service to detect any integrity violations of the large and untrusted Linux OS. Upon detection of such integrity violations, the monitoring service invokes a recovery procedure to recover the integrity of the data structures, and if that fails, reboot Linux.

SIGMA System [77] assigns a dedicated CPU core to each OS, to build a multi-OS environment with native performance. Since there is no virtualization layer, guest OSes cannot share devices and interrupts among them, hence all interrupts are bound and directly delivered to their target OSes, e.g., for the Intel multiprocessor architecture, APIC (Advanced Peripheral Interrupt Controller) can be used to distribute I/O interrupts among processors by interrupt numbers.

Gandalf [78,79] is a lightweight Type-1 VMM designed for resource-constrained embedded systems. It is called meso-virtualization, which is more lightweight and requires less modification to the guest OS than typical para-virtualization solutions. Similar to SIGMA, interrupts are not virtualized, but instead delivered to each guest OS directly.

Yoo et al. [80] developed MobiVMM, a lightweight virtualization solution for mobile phones. It uses preemptive fixed-priority scheduling and assigns the highest priority to the real-time VM (only a single real-time VM is supported), and uses pseudo-polling to provide lowlatency interrupt processing. Physical interrupts are stored temporarily inside the VMM, and delivered to the target guest VM when it is scheduled to run. Real-time schedulability test is used to determine if certain interrupts should be discarded to prevent overload. Yoo et al. [81] improved I/O performance of MobiVMM, by letting the non-real-time VM preempt the real-time VM whenever a device interrupt occurs targeting the non real-time VM.

Li et al. [82] developed Quest-V, a virtualized multikernel for high-confidence systems. Memory virtualization with shadow paging is used for fault isolation. It does not virtualize any other resources like CPU or I/O, i.e., processing or I/O handling are performed within the kernels or user-spaces on each core without intervention from the VMM. vCPUs are the fundamental kernel abstraction for scheduling and temporal isolation. A hierarchical approach is adopted where vCPUs are scheduled on pCPUs and threads are scheduled on vCPUs [83] Quest-V defines two classes of vCPUs: Main vCPUs, configured as sporadic servers by default, are used to schedule and track the pCPU usage of conventional software threads, while I/O vCPUs are used to account for, and schedule the execution of, interrupt handlers for I/O devices. Each device is assigned a separate I/O vCPU, which may be shared among multiple main vCPUs. I/O vCPUs are scheduled with a Priority-Inheritance Bandwidth-Preserving (PIBS) server algorithm, where each shared I/O vCPU inherits its priority from the main vCPUs of tasks responsible for I/O requests, and is assigned a certain CPU bandwidth share that should not be exceeded.

# 7. OS VIRTUALIZATION

OS virtualization, also called container-based virtualization, allows to partition an OS environment into multiple domains with independent name spaces to achieve a certain level of security and protection between different domains. Examples include FreeBSD Jails [84], OpenVZ

[85], Linux VServer [86], Linux Containers LXC and Solaris Zones. The key difference between OS virtualization and system-level virtualization is that the former only has a single copy of OS kernel at runtime shared among multiple domains, while the latter has multiple OS kernels at runtime. As a result, OS virtualization is more lightweight, but can only run a single OS, e.g., Linux. Commercial products that incorporate OS virtualization technology include: Parallels Virtuozzo Containers [87] is a commercial version of the open-source OpenVZ software; the MontaVista Automotive Technology Platform [88] adopts Linux Containers in combination with SELinux (Security Enhanced Linux) to run multiple Linux or Android OSes on top of MontaVista Linux host OS.

Resource control and isolation in OS virtualization are often achieved with the Linux kernel mechanism CGroup. For example, Linux VServer [86] enforces CPU isolation by overlaying a token bucket filter (TBF) on top of the standard O(1) Linux CPU scheduler. Each VM has a token bucket that accumulates incoming tokens at a specified rate; every timer tick, the VM that owns the running process is charged one token. The authors modified the TBF to provide fair sharing and/or work-conserving CPU reservations. CPU capacity is effectively partitioned between two classes of VMs: VMs with reservations get what they have reserved, and VMs with shares split the unreserved CPU capacity proportionally. For network I/O, the Hierarchical Token Bucket (HTB) queuing discipline of the Linux Traffic Control facility is used to provide network bandwidth reservations and fair service among VMs. Disk I/O is managed using the standard Linux CFQ (Completely-Fair Queuing) I/O scheduler, which attempts to divide the bandwidth of each block device fairly among the VMs performing I/O to that device.

OS virtualization has been traditionally applied in server virtualization, since it is essentially a name-space separation technique, but has limited support for I/O device virtualization (typically only disk and network devices). Recently, Andrus et al. [89] developed Cells, an OS virtualization architecture for enabling multiple virtual Android smart phones to run simultaneously on the same physical cell phone in an isolated, secure manner. The main technical challenges is to develop kernel-level and user-level device virtualization techniques for a variety of handset devices like GPU, touch screen, GPS, etc.

# 8. TASK-GRAIN SCHEDULING

Conventional VMM schedulers view each guest VM as an opaque blackbox and unaware of individual tasks within each VM. This is true for both full-virtualization solutions like KVM and para-virtualization solutions like Xen. This opacity is beneficial for system modularity, but can sometimes be a impediment to optimal performance. Some authors have implemented task-grain scheduling schemes, where the VMM scheduler has visibility into the internal task-grain details within each VM. This work can be further divided into two types: one approach is to modify the guest OS to inform the VMM about its internal tasks via hypercalls in a paravirtualization architecture; another approach is to let the VMM infer the task-grain information transparently without guest OS modification in a full-virtualization architecture.

## 8.1. Approaches That Require Modifying the Guest OS

Augier et al. [90] implemented task-grain scheduling algorithm within VirtualLogix VLX, by removing the scheduler from each guest OS and letting the hypervisor handle scheduling of all tasks.

KimD et al. [91] presented a guest-aware, task-grain scheduling algorithm in Xen by selecting the next VM to be scheduled based on the highest-priority task within each VM and the I/O behavior of the guest VMs via inspecting the I/O pending status.

Kiszka [4] developed a para-virtualized scheduling interface for KVM. Two hypercalls are added: one for letting the guest OS inform the VMM about the priority of currently running task in the guest OS, and the VMM schedules the guest VMs based on task priority information; another for the guest OS to inform the VMM that it has just finished handling an interrupt, and its priority should be lowered to its nominal priority.

Xia et al. [92] presented PaS (Preemption-aware Scheduling) with two interfaces: one to register VM preemption conditions, the other to check if a VM is preempting. VMs with incoming pending I/O events are given higher priorities and allowed to preempt the currently running VM scheduled by the Credit Scheduler. Instead of adding hypercalls, the PaS interface is implemented by adding two fields in a data structure which is shared between the hypervisor and guest VM.

Wang et al. [93] implemented task-grain scheduling within Xen by adding a hypercall to inform the VMM about the timing attributes of a task at its creation time, and using either fixed-priority or EDF to schedule the tasks directly, bypassing the guest VM scheduler.

Kim et al. [94] presented a feedback control architecture for adaptive scheduling in Xen, by adding two hypercalls for the guest VMs to increase or decrease the CPU budget (slice size) requested per period based on CPU utilization and deadline miss ratios in the guest VMs.

## 8.2. Approaches That Do Not Require Modifying the Guest OS

To avoid modifying the guest OS, the VMM attempts to infer graybox knowledge about a VM by monitoring certain HW events. Kim et al. [95] presented task-aware virtual machine scheduling for I/O Performance by introducing a partial boosting mechanism into the Xen Credit Scheduler, which enables the VMM to boost the priority of a vCPU that contains an inferred I/O-bound task in response to an incoming event. The correlation mechanism for block and network I/O events is besteffort and lightweight. It works by monitoring the CR3 register on x86 CPU for addressing the MMU, in order to capture process context-switching events, which are classified into disjoint classes: positive evidence, negative evidence, and ambiguity, to determine a degree of belief on the I/O boundedness of tasks. Kim et al. [96] presented an improved credit scheduler that transparently estimates multimedia quality by inferring frame rates from low-level hardware events, and dynamically adjusts CPU allocation based on the estimates as feedback to keep the video frame rate around a set point Desired Frame Rate. For memory-mapped display, the hypervisor monitors the frequency of frame buffer writes in order to estimate the frame rates; for GPU-accelerated display, the hypervisor monitors the rate of interrupts raised by a video device, which is shown to exhibit good linear correlation with frame rate.

Tadokoro et al. [97] implemented the Monarch scheduler in the Xen VMM, which works by monitoring and manipulating the run queue and the process data structure in guest VMs without modifying guest OSes, using Virtual Machine Intraspection (VMI) to monitor process execution in the guest VMs, and Direct Kernel Object Manipulation (DKOM) to modify the scheduler queue data structure in the guest VMs.

# 9. THE LOCK-HOLDER PREEMPTION PROBLEM

Spinlocks are used extensively in the Linux kernel for synchronizing access to shared data. When one thread is in its critical section holding a spinlock, another thread trying to acquire the same spinlock to enter the critical section will busy-wait (spin in a polling loop and continuously check the locking condition) until the lockholding thread releases the spinlock. Since the typical critical sections protected by the spinlocks are kept very short, the waiting times are acceptable for today's Linux kernels, especially with real-time enhancements like the PREEMPT_RT patch. However, in a virtualized environment, Lock Holder Preemption (LHP) may cause excessively long waiting times for guest OSes configured with SMP support with multiple vCPUs in the same guest VM. A VM is called overcommitted when its number of vCPUs exceeds the available number of physical cores. Since the VMM scheduler is not aware of any spinlocks held within the guest OSes, when thread A in a guest OS holding a spinlock being waited for by another thread B on a different vCPU in the same guest OS is preempted by the VMM scheduler to run another vCPU, possibly in a different guest OS, Thread B will busy-wait for a long time until the VMM scheduler switches back to this guest OS to allow thread A to continue execution and release the spinlock. When LHP occurs, the waiting times can be tens of milliseconds instead of the typical tens of microseconds in the Linux kernel without virtualization.

There are two general approaches to addressing the LHP problem: preventing it from occurring, or mitigating it after detecting that it has occurred.

Pause Loop Exit (PLE) is an HW mechanism built-in the latest Intel processors for detecting guest spin-lock. It can be used by the VMM software to mitigate LHP after detection. It enables the VMM to detect spin-lock by monitoring the execution of PAUSE instructions in the VM through the PLE_Gap and PLE_Window values. PLE_Gap denotes upper bound on the amount of time between two successive executions of PAUSE in a loop. PLE_Window denotes upper bound on the amount of time a guest is allowed to execute in a PAUSE loop. If the amount of time between this execution of PAUSE and previous one exceeds the PLE_Gap, then processor consider this PAUSE belongs to a new loop. Otherwise, processor determines the total execution time of this loop (since 1st PAUSE in this loop), and triggers a VM exit if total time exceeds PLE_Window. According to KVM's source code, PLE_Gap is set to 41 and PLE_Window is 4096 by default, which means that this approach can detect a spinning loop that lasts around 55 microseconds on a 3GHz CPU. AMD processors has similar HW support called Pause-Filter-Count. (Since these HW mechanisms are relatively new, the techniques discussed below generally do not make use of them.)

Uhlig et al. [98] presented techniques to address LHP for both fully virtualized and para-virtualized environments. In the paravirtualization case, the guest OS is modified to add a delayed preemption mechanism:

before acquiring a spinlock, the guest OS invokes a hypercall to indicate to the VMM that it should not be preempted for the next n microseconds, where n is a configurable parameter depending how long the guest OS expects to be holding a lock. After releasing the lock, the guest OS indicates its willingness to be preempted again. In the full virtualization case where the guest OS cannot be modified, the VMM transparently monitors guest OS switches between user space and kernel space execution, and prevents a vCPU from being preempted when it is running in kernel space and may be holding kernel spinlocks. (The case when a user-level application is holding a spinlock is not handled, and it is assumed that the application itself is responsible for handling this case.) The implementation is based on a L4-ka microkernel-based virtualization system with a paravirtualized Linux as guest OS, although their techniques do not depend on the specific virtualization software.

Friebel [99] extended the spinlock waiting code in the guest OS to issue a yield() hypercall when a vCPU has been waiting longer than a certain threshold of $2^{16}$ cycles. Upon receiving the hypercall, the VMM schedules another VCPU of the same guest VM, giving preference to vCPUs preempted in kernel mode because they are likely to be preempted lock-holders.

Coscheduling, also called Gang Scheduling, is a common technique for preventing the LHP problem, where all vCPUs of a VM are simultaneously scheduled on physical processors (PCPUs) for an equal time slice. Strict co-scheduling may lead to performance degradation due to fragmentation of processor availability. To improve runtime efficiency, VMWare ESX 4.x implements relaxed co-scheduling to allow vCPUs to be co-scheduled with slight skews. It maintain synchronous progress of vCPU siblings by deferring the advanced vCPUs until the slower ones catch up. Several authors developed various versions of relaxed co-scheduling, as we discuss next.

Jiang et al. [100] presented several optimizations to the CFS (Completely Fair Scheduler) in KVM to help prevent or mitigate LHP. Three techniques were proposed for LHP prevention: 1) add two hypercalls that enable the guest VM to inform the host VMM that one of its vCPU threads is currently holding a spinlock or just released a spinlock. The host VMM will not de-schedule a vCPU that is currently holding a spinlock; 2) add two hypercalls for one vCPU thread to boost its priority when acquiring a spinlock, and resume its nominal priority when releasing it; 3) implement approximate co-scheduling by temporarily changing a VM's scheduling policy from SCHED_OTHER (default CFS scheduling class) to SCHED_RR (real-time scheduling class) when the VM has high degree of internal concurrency, and changing it back a short period of time later. Two techniques were proposed for LHP mitigation after it occurs: 1) Add a hypercall yield() in the vCPU thread source code to let it give up the CPU when it has been spin-waiting for a spinlock for too long, by adding a counter in the source code to record the spin-waiting time; 2) implement codescheduling by slowing down or stopping all other vCPUs of the same VM if one of its vCPUs is descheduled, since if a vCPU thread requires a spinlock, it is possible for the other vCPUs to require the same spinlock later.

Weng et al. [101] presented a hybrid scheduling framework in Xen by distinguishing between two types of VMs: the high-throughput type and the concurrent type. A VM is set as the concurrent type when the majority of its workload is concurrent applications in order to reduce the cost of synchronization, and otherwise set as the high-throughput type by default. Weng et al. [102] implemented dynamic co-scheduling by adding vCPU Related Degree (VCRD) to reflect the degree of relatedness of vCPUs in a VM. When long waiting times occur in a VM due to spinlocks, the VCRD of the VM is set as HIGH, and all vCPUs should be co-scheduled; otherwise, the VCRD of the VM is set as LOW, and vCPUs can be scheduled asynchronously. A monitoring module is added in each VM to detect long waiting times due to spinlocks, and uses a hypercall to inform the host VMM about the VCRD values of the guest VM.

Bai et al. [103] presented a task-aware co-scheduling method, where the VMM infers gray-box knowledge about the concurrency and synchronization of tasks within guest VMs. By tracking the states of tasks within guest VMs and combining this information with states of vCPUs, they are able to infer occurrence of spinlock waiting without modifying the guest OS.

Yu et al. [104] presented two approaches: Partial Coscheduling and Boost Co-scheduling, both implemented within the Xen credit scheduler. Partial Co-scheduling allows multiple VMs to be co-scheduled concurrently, but only raises co-scheduling signals to the CPUs whose run-queues contain the corresponding co-scheduled VCPUs, while other CPUs remain undisturbed; Boost Co-scheduling promotes the priorities of vCPUs to be co-scheduled, instead of using co-scheduling signals to force them to be co-scheduled. They performed performance comparisons with hybrid co-scheduling [101] and co-de-scheduling [100] and showed clear advantages.

Sukwong et al. [105] presented a balance scheduling algorithm which attempts to balance vCPU siblings in the same VM on different physical CPUs without forcing the vCPUs to be scheduled simultaneously by dynamically setting CPU affinity of vCPUs so that no two vCPU siblings are in the same CPU run-queue. Balance scheduling is shown to significantly improve application performance without the complexity and drawbacks found in co-scheduling (CPU fragmentation, priority inversion and execution delay). Balance scheduling is similar to relaxed co-scheduling in VMWare ESX 4.x [106], but it never delays execution of a vCPU to wait for another vCPU in order to maintain synchronous progress of vCPU siblings. It differs from the approximate co-scheduling algorithm in [100] in that it does not change vCPU scheduling class or priorities.

SPUMONE [71] adopts a unique runtime migration approach to address the LHP (Lock-Holder Preemption) problem by migrating a vCPU away from a core where LHP may occur with another co-located vCPU: if vCPUs of a GPOS and an RTOS share the same pCPU core on a multicore processor, and the thread running on the vCPU of GPOS issues a system call, or when an interrupt is raised to the vCPU of GPOS, the vCPU of GPOS is immediately migrated away from to another core that does not host any RTOS vCPUs, thus achieving the effect of co-scheduling on different cores. This is a pessimistic approach, since the migration takes place even when there may not be any lock contention.

# 10. CONCLUSION

In this paper, we have presented a comprehensive survey on real-time issues in embedded systems virtualization. We hope this article can serve as a useful reference to researchers in this area.

# ACKNOWLEDGEMENTS

This work was supported by MoE-Intel Information Technology Special Research Fund under Grant Number MOE-INTEL-10-02; NSFC Project Grant #61070002; the Fundamental Research Funds for the Central Universities.

## REFERENCES

1. Y. Kinebuchi, H. Koshimae and T. Nakajima, "Constructing Machine Emulator on Portable Microkernel," Proceedings of the 2007 ACM Symposium on Applied Computing, 11-15 March 2007, Seoul, 2007, pp. 1197- 1198.

2. H. Schild, A. Lackorzynski and A. Warg, "Faithful Virtualization on a Realtime Operating System," 11th RealTime Linux Workshop, Dresden, 28-30 September 2009.

3. K. Barr, P. P. Bungale, S. Deasy, V. Gyuris, P. Hung, C. Newell, H. Tuch and B. Zoppis, "The VMware Mobile Virtualization Platform: Is That a Hypervisor in Your Pocket?" Operating Systems Review, Vol. 44, No. 4, 2101, pp. 124-135.

4. J. Kiszka, "Towards Linux as a Real-Time Hypervisor," 11th Real-Time Linux Workshop, Dresden, 28-30 September 2009.

5. Airlines Electronic Engineering Committee, "ARINC 653—Avionics Application Software Standard Interface," 2003

6. T. Gaska, B. Werner and D. Flagg, "Applying Virtualization to Avoinics Systems—The Integration Challenge," Proceedings of the 29th Digital Avionics Systems Conference of the IEEE/AIAA, Salt Lake City, 3-7 October 2010, pp. 1-19.

7. Wind River Hypervisor Product Overview. http://www.windriver.com/products/hypervisor

8. INTEGRITY Multivisor Datasheet. http://www.ghs.com

9. Real-Time Systems GmbH. http://www.real-time-systems.com

10. Tenasys eVM for Windows. http://www.tenasys.com/ products/evm.php

11. Quick Start Guide, NI Real-Time Hypervisor. http://www.ni.com/pdf/manuals/375174b.pdf.

12. OpenSynergy COQOS. http://www.opensynergy.com/en/ Products/ COQOS

13. Enea Hypervisor. http://www.enea.com/software/products/ hypervisor

14. SysGO GmbH. http://www.sysgo.com

15. S. H. VanderLeest, "ARINC 653 Hypervisor," Proceedings of 29th Digital Avionics Systems Conference of IEEE/AIAA, Salt Lake City, 3-7 October 2010, pp. 1-20.

16. M. Masmano, I. Ripoll, A. Crespo and J. J. Metge "XtratuM: A Hypervisor for Safety Critical Embedded Systems," Proceedings of Real-Time Linux Workshop, Dresden, 28-30 September 2009.

17. J. Zamorano and J. A. de la Puente, "Open Source Implementation of Hierarchical Scheduling for Integrated Modular Avionics," Proceedings of Real-Time Linux Workshop, Nairobi, 25-27 October 2010.

18. Á. Esquinas, J. Zamorano, J. Antonio de la Puente, M. Masmano, I. Ripoll and A. Crespo, "ORK+/XtratuM: An Open Partitioning Platform for Ada," Lecture Notes in Computer Science, Vol. 6652, pp. 160-173.

19. S. Campagna, M. Hussain and M. Violante, "Hypervisor-Based Virtual Hardware for Fault Tolerance in COTS Processors Targeting Space Applications," Proceedings of the 2010 IEEE 25th International Symposium on Defect and Fault Tolerance in VLSI Systems, Kyoto, 6-8 October 2010, pp. 44-51.

20. N. McGuire, A. Platschek and G. Schiesser, "OVERSEE—A Generic FLOSS Communication and Application Platform for Vehicles," Proceedings of 12th RealTime Linux Workshop, Nairobi, 25-27 October 2010.

21. Platschek and G. Schiesser, "Migrating a OSEK Runtime environment to the OVERSEE Platform," Proceedings of 13th Real-Time Linux Workshop, Prague, 22-22 October 2011.

22. S. Han and H. W. Jin, "Full Virtualization Based ARINC 653 Partitioning," Proceedings of the 30th Digital Avionics Systems (DASC) Conference of the IEEE/AIAA, Seattle, 16-20 October 2011, pp. 1-11.

23. S. Ghaisas, G. Karmakar, D. Shenai, S. Tirodkar and K. Ramamritham, "SParK: Safety Partition Kernel for Integrated Real-Time Systems," Lecture Notes in Computer Science, Vol. 6462, 2010, pp. 159-174.

24. M. Lemerre, E. Ohayon, D. Chabrol, M. Jan and M.-B. Jacques, "Method and Tools for Mixed-Criticality RealTime Applications within PharOS," Proceedings of IEEE International Symposium on Object/Component/Service-Oriented Real-Time Distributed Computing Workshops, Newport Beach, 28-31 March 2011, pp. 41-48.

25. Aguiar and F. Hessel, "Virtual Hellfire Hypervisor: Extending Hellfire Framework for Embedded Virtualization Support," Proceedings of the 12th International Symposium on Quality Electronic Design (ISQED), Santa Clara, 14-16 March 2011, pp. 129-203.

26. F. Moraes, N. Calazans, A. Mello, L. Möller and L. Ost, "HERMES: An Infrastructure for Low Area Overhead Packet-Switching Networks on Chip," Integration, the VLSI Journal, Vol. 38, No. 1, 2004, pp. 69-93.

27. L. Cherkasova, D. Gupta and A. Vahdat, "Comparison of the Three CPU Schedulers in Xen," ACM SIGMETRICS Performance Evaluation Review, Vol. 35, No. 2, 2007, pp. 42-51.

28. Masrur, S. Drössler, T. Pfeuffer and S. Chakraborty, "VM-Based Real-Time Services for Automotive Control Applications," Proceedings of the 2010 IEEE 16th International Conference on Embedded and Real-Time Computing Systems and Applications, Macau, 23-25 August 2010, pp. 218-223.

29. Masrur, T. Pfeuffer, M. Geier, S. Drössler and S. Chakraborty, "Designing VM Schedulers for Embedded Real-Time Applications,"

Proceedings of the 7th IEEE/ACM/IFIP International Conference on Hardware/Software Codesign and System Synthesis, Taipei, 9-14 October 2011, pp. 29-38.

30. J. Lee, S. S. Xi, S. J. Chen, L. T. X. Phan, C. Gill, I. Lee, C. Y. Lu and O. Sokolsky, "Realizing Compositional Scheduling through Virtualization," Technical Report, University of Pennsylvania, Philadelphia, 2011.

31. S. S. Xi, J. Wilson, C. Y. Lu and C. Gill, "RT-Xen: Towards Real-Time Hypervisor Scheduling in Xen," Proceedings of the 2011 International Conference on Embedded Software, Taipei, 9-14 October 2011, pp. 39-48.

32. Shin and I. Lee, "Compositional Real-Time Scheduling Framework with Periodic Model," ACM Transactions on Embedded Computing Systems, Vol. 7, No. 3, 2008.

33. S. Yoo, Y.-P. Kim and C. Yoo, "Real-time Scheduling in a Virtualized CE Device," Proceedings of 2010 Digest of Technical Papers International Conference on Consumer Electronics (ICCE), Las Vegas, 9-13 January 2010, pp. 261-262.

34. J.-W. Jeong, S. Yoo and C. Yoo, "PARFAIT: A New Scheduler Framework Supporting Heterogeneous Xen-ARM Schedulers," Proceedings of 2011 Consumer Communications and Networking Conference of the IEEE CCNC, Las Vegas, 9-12 January 2011, pp. 1192-1196.

35. C.-H. Hong, M. Park, S. Yoo, C. Yoo and H. D. Considering, "Hypervisor Design Considering Network Performance for Multi-Core CE Devices," Proceedings of 2010 Digest of Technical Papers International Conference on Consumer Electronics of the IEEE ICCE, Las Vegas, 9-13 January 2010, pp. 263-264.

36. S. Yoo, K.-H. Kwak, J.-H. Jo and C. Yoo, "Toward Under-Millisecond I/O Latency in Xen-ARM," The 2nd ACM SIGOPS Asia-Pacific Workshop on Systems, Shanghai, 11-12 July 2011, p. 14.

37. M. Lee, A. S. Krishnakumar, P. Krishnan, N. Singh and S. Yajnik, "Supporting Soft Real-Time Tasks in the Xen Hypervisor," Proceedings of the 6th ACM SIGPLAN/SIGOPS International Conference on Virtual Execution Environments, Pittsburgh, March 2010, pp. 97-108.

38. P. J. Yu, M. Y. Xia, Q. Lin, M. Zhu, S. Gao, Z. W. Qi, K. Chen and H. B. Guan, "Real-Time Enhancement for Xen Hypervisor," Proceedings of the 8th International Conference on Embedded and Ubiquitous Computing of the IEEE/IFIP, Hong Kong, 11-13 December 2010, pp. 23-30.

39. Y. X. Wang, X. G. Wang and H. Guo, "An Optimized Scheduling Strategy Based on Task Type In Xen," Lecture Notes in Electrical Engineering, Vol. 123, 2011, pp. 515-522.

40. H. C. Chen, H. Jin, K. Hu and M. H. Yuan, "Adaptive Audio-Aware Scheduling in Xen Virtual Environment," Proceedings of the International Conference on Computer Systems and Applications (AICCSA) of the IEEE/ACS, Hammamet, 16-19 May 2010, pp. 1-8.

41. H. C. Chen, H. Jin and K. Hu, "Affinity-Aware Proportional Share Scheduling for Virtual Machine System," Proceedings of the 9th International Conference on Grid and Cooperative Computing (GCC), Nanjing, 1-5 November 2010, pp. 75-80.

42. D. Gupta, L. Cherkasova, R. Gardner and A. Vahdat, "Enforcing Performance Isolation across Virtual Machines in Xen," Proceedings of the ACM/IFIP/USENIX 2006 International Conference on Middleware, Melbourne, 27 November-1 December 2006, pp. 342-362.

43. D. Ongaro, A. L. Cox and S. Rixner, "Scheduling I/O in Virtual Machine Monitors," Proceedings of the 4th ACM SIGPLAN/SIGOPS International Conference on Virtual Execution Environments, Seattle, 5-7 March 2008, pp. 1- 10.

44. S. Govindan, J. Choi, A. R. Nath, A. Das, B. Urgaonkar, and A. Sivasubramaniam, "Xen and Co.: Communication-Aware CPU Management in Consolidated XenBased Hosting Platforms," IEEE Transactions on Computers, Vol. 58, No. 8, 2009, pp. 1111-1125.

45. Y. Y. Hu, X. Long, J. Zhang, J. He and L. Xia, "I/O Scheduling Model of Virtual Machine Based on MultiCore Dynamic Partitioning," Proceedings of the 19th ACM International Symposium on High Performance Distributed Computing, Chicago, 21-25 June 2010, pp. 142- 154.

46. G. Lee, K. W. Hur and Y. W. Ko, "Minimizing Scheduling Delay for Multimedia in Xen Hypervisor," Communications in Computer and Information Science, Vol. 199, 2011, pp. 96-108.

47. Zhang, K. Chen, B. J. Zuo, R. H. Ma, Y. Z. Dong and H. B. Guan, "Performance Analysis towards a KVMBased Embedded Real-Time Virtualization Architecture," Proceedings of the 5th International Conference on Computer Sciences and Convergence Information Technology (ICCIT), Seoul, 30 November-2 December 2010, pp. 421-426.

48. J. Zuo, K. Chen, A. Liang, H. B. Guan, J. Zhang, R. H. Ma and H. B. Yang, "Performance Tuning towards a KVM-Based Low Latency Virtualization System," Proceedings of the 2nd International Conference on Information Engineering and Computer Science (ICIECS), Wuhan, 25-26 December 2010, pp. 1-4.

49. T. Cucinotta, G. Anastasi and L. Abeni, "Respecting Temporal Constraints in Virtualised Services," Proceedings of the 33rd Annual IEEE International Conference on Computer Software and Applications, Seattle, Washington DC, 20-24 July 2009. pp. 73-78.

50. T. Cucinotta, D. Giani, D. Faggioli and F. Checconi, "Providing Performance Guarantees to Virtual Machines Using Real-Time Scheduling," Proceedings of Euro-Par Workshops, Naples, 31 August-3 September 2010, pp. 657- 664.

51. T. Cucinotta, F. Checconi and D. Giani, "Improving Responsiveness for Virtualized Networking under Intensive Computing Workloads," Proceedings of the 13th Real-Time Linux Workshop, Prague, 20-22 October 2011.

52. F. Checconi, T. Cucinotta and M. Stein, "Real-Time Issues in Live Migration of Virtual Machines," Proceedings of Euro-Par Workshops, Delft, 29-28 August 2009, pp. 454- 466.

53. S. Kato, R. (Raj) Rajkumar and Y. Ishikawa, "A Loadable Real-Time Scheduler Framework for Multicore Platforms," Proceedings of the 6th IEEE International Conference on Embedded and Real-Time Computing Systems and Applications (RTCSA), Macau, 23-25 August 2010.

54. Lin and P. A. Dinda, "VSched: Mixing Batch And Interactive Virtual Machines Using Periodic Real-time Scheduling," Proceedings of the ACM/IEEE SC 2005 Conference Supercomputing, Seattle, 12-18 November 2005, p. 8.

55. Asberg, N. Forsberg, T. Nolte and S. Kato, "Towards Real-Time Scheduling of Virtual Machines without Kernel Modifications," Proceedings of the 2011 IEEE 16th Conference on Emerging Technologies & Factory Automation (ETFA), Toulouse, 5-9 September 2011, pp. 1-4.

56. Asberg, T. Nolte and S. Kato, "Towards Hierarchical Scheduling in Linux/Multi-Core Platform," Proceedings of the 2010 IEEE Conference on Emerging Technologies and Factory Automation (ETFA), Bilbao, 13-16 September 2010, pp. 1-4.

57. Acharya, J. Buford and V. Krishnaswamy, "Phone Virtualization Using a Microkernel Hypervisor," Proceedings of the 2009 IEEE International Conference on Internet Multimedia Services Architecture and Applications (IMSAA), Bangalore, 9-11 December 2009, pp. 1-6.

58. Iqbal, N. Sadeque and R. I. Mutia, "An Overview of Microkernel, Hypervisor and Microvisor Virtualization Approaches for Embedded Systems," Technical Report, Lund University, Lund, 2009.

59. G. Heiser, "Virtualizing Embedded Systems: Why Bother?" Proceedings of the 2011 48th ACM/EDAC/IEEE Conference on Design Automation, San Diego, 5-9 June 2011, pp. 901-905.

60. F. Bruns, S. Traboulsi, D. Szczesny, M. E. Gonzalez, Y. Xu and A. Bilgic, "An Evaluation of Microkernel-Based Virtualization for Embedded Real-Time Systems," Proceedings of the 22nd Euromicro Conference on Real-Time Systems (ECRTS), Dublin, 6-9 July 2010, pp. 57-65.

61. Lackorzynski, J. Danisevskis, J. Nordholz and M. Peter, "Real-Time Performance of L4Linux," Proceedings of the 13th Real-Time Linux Workshop, Prague, 20-22 October 2011.

62. R. Kaiser, "Alternatives for Scheduling Virtual Machines in Real-Time Embedded Systems," Proceedings of the 1st Workshop on Isolation and Integration in Embedded Systems, Glasgow, 1 April 2008, pp. 5-10.

63. J. Yang, H. Kim, S. Park, C. K. Hong and I. Shin, "Implementation of Compositional Scheduling Framework on Virtualization," SIGBED Review, Vol. 8, No. 1, 2011, pp. 30-37.

64. U. Steinberg and B. Kauer, "NOVA: A MicrohypervisorBased Secure Virtualization Architecture," Proceedings of the 5th European Conference on Computer Systems, Paris, 13-16 April 2010, pp. 209-222.

65. K. Gudeth, M. Pirretti, K. Hoeper and R. Buskey, "Delivering Secure Applications on Commercial Mobile Devices: The Case for Bare Metal Hypervisors," Proceedings of the 1st ACM Workshop on Security and Privacy in Smartphones and Mobile Devices, Chicago, 17-21 October 2011, pp. 33-38.

66. VMware MVP (Mobile Virtualization Platform) http://www.vmware.com/products/mobile

67. F. Armand and M. Gien, "A Practical Look at Micro-Kernels and Virtual Machine Monitors," Proceedings of the 6th IEEE Consumer Communications and Networking Conference, Las Vegas, 10-13 January 2009, pp. 1-7.

68. Red Bend VLX for Mobile Handsets. http://www.virtuallogix.com/products/vlx-for-mobile-handsets.html

69. J.-Y. Hwang, S.-B. Suh, S.-K. Heo, C.-J. Park, J.-M. Ryu, S.-Y. Park and C.-R. Kim, "Xen on ARM: System Virtualization Using Xen Hypervisor for ARM-Based Secure Mobile Phones," Proceedings of the 5th IEEE Consumer Communications and Networking Conference, Las Vegas, 10-12 January 2008, pp. 257-261.

70. W. Kanda, Y. Yumura, Y. Kinebuchi, K. Makijima and T. Nakajima, "SPUMONE: Lightweight CPU Virtualization Layer for Embedded Systems," Proceedings of the IEEE/IFIP International Conference on Embedded and Ubiquitous Computing, Shanghai, 17-20 December 2008, pp. 144-151.

71. H. Mitake, Y. Kinebuchi, A. Courbot and T. Nakajima, "Coexisting Real-Time OS and General Purpose OS on an Embedded Virtualization Layer for a Multicore Processor," Proceedings of the 2011 ACM Symposium on Applied Computing, Taichung, 21-24 March 2011, pp. 629- 630.

72. H. Tadokoro, K. Kourai and S. Chiba, "A Secure System-wide Process Scheduler across Virtual Machines," Proceedings of the 16th Pacific Rim International Symposium on Dependable Computing (PRDC), Tokyo, 13- 15 December 2010, pp. 27-36.

73. Y. Kinebuchi, M. Sugaya, S. Oikawa and T. Nakajima, "Task Grain Scheduling for Hypervisor-Based Embedded System," Proceedings of the 10th IEEE International Conference on High Performance

Computing and Communications, Dalian, 25-27 September 2008, pp. 190-197.

74. Aalto, "Dynamic Management of Multiple Operating Systems in an Embedded Multi-Core Environment," Master's Thesis, Aalto University, Finland, 2010.

75. T.-H. Lin, Y. Kinebuchi, H. Shimada, H. Mitake, C.-Y. Lee and T. Nakajima, "Hardware-Assisted Reliability Enhancement for Embedded Multi-Core Virtualization Design," Proceedings of the 17th International Conference on Embedded and Real-Time Computing Systems and Applications of the IEEE RTCSA, Toyama, 28-31 August 2011, pp. 241-249.

76. Li, Y. Kinebuchi and T. Nakajima, "Enhancing Security of Embedded Linux on a Multi-Core Processor," Proceedings of the 17th International Conference on Embedded and Real-Time Computing Systems and Applications of the IEEE RTCSA, Toyama, 28-31 August 2011, pp. 117-121.

77. W. Kanda, Y. Murata and T. Nakajima, "SIGMA System: A Multi-OS Environment for Embedded Systems," Journal Of Signal Processing Systems, Vol. 59, No. 1, 2010, pp. 33-43.

78. M. Ito and S. Oikawa, "Mesovirtualization: Lightweight Virtualization Technique for Embedded Systems," Sociedad Española de UitraSonidos, Vol. 4761, 2007, pp. 496- 505.

79. M. Ito and S. Oikawa, "Making a Virtual Machine Monitor Interruptible," Journal of Information Processing, Vol. 19, 2011, pp. 411-420.

80. S.-H. Yoo, Y. X. Liu, C.-H. Hong, C. Yoo and Y. G. Zhang, "MobiVMM: A Virtual Machine Monitor for Mobile Phones," Proceedings of the 1st Workshop on Virtualization in Mobile Computing, Breckenridge, 17 June 2008, pp. 1-5.

81. S. Yoo, M. Park and C. Yoo, "A Step to Support RealTime in Virtual Machine," Proceedings of the 6th International Conference on

Consumer Communications and Networking of the IEEE CCNC, Las Vegas, 10-13 January 2009, pp. 1-7.

82. Y. Li, M. Danish and R. West, "Quest-V: A Virtualized Multikernel for High-Confidence Systems," Technical Report, Boston University, Boston, 2011.

83. M. Danish, Y. Li and R. West, "Virtual-CPU Scheduling in the Quest Operating System," Proceedings of the 17th International Conference on Real-Time and Embedded Technology and Applications Symposium of the IEEE RTAS, Chicago, 11-14 April 2011, pp. 169-179.

84. P.-H. Kamp and R. N. M. Watson, "Jails: Confining the Omnipotent Root," Proceedings of the 2nd International System Administration and Networking Conference, Maastricht, 22-25 May 2000.

85. OpenVZ Linux Containers. http://wiki.openvz.org

86. S. Soltesz, H. Pötzl, M. E. Fiuczynski, A. C. Bavier and L. L. Peterson, "Container-Based Operating System Virtualization: A Scalable, High-Performance Alternative to Hypervisors," Proceedings of EuroSys 2007, Lisbon, 21-23 March 2007, pp. 275-287.

87. Parallels Virtuozzo Containers. http://www.parallels.com/products/pvc

88. MontaVista Automotive Technology Platform. http://mvista.com/sol_detail_ivi.php

89. J. Andrus, C. Dall, A. V. Hof, O. Laadan and J. Nieh, "Cells: A Virtual Mobile Smartphone Architecture," Columbia University Computer Science Technical Reports, Columbia University, Columbia, 2011, pp. 173-187.

90. Augier, "Real-Time Scheduling in a Virtual Machine Environment," Proceedings of Junior Researcher Workshop on Real-Time Computing (JRWRTC), Nancy, 29-30 March 2007.

91. Kim, H. Kim, M. Jeon, E. Seo and J. Lee, "GuestAware Priority-Based Virtual Machine Scheduling for Highly Consolidated Server," Proceedings of the 14th International Euro-Par Conference on Parallel Processing, Las Palmas de Gran Canaria, 26-29 August 2008, pp. 285-294.

92. Y. B. Xia, C. Yang and X. Cheng, "PaS: A PreemptionAware Scheduling Interface for Improving Interactive Performance in Consolidated Virtual Machine Environment," Proceedings of the 15th International Conference on Parallel and Distributed Systems (ICPADS), Shenzhen, 8-11 December 2009, pp. 340-347.

93. Y. D. Wang, J. Zhang, L. H. Shang, X. Long and H. H. Jin, "Research of Real-Time Task in Xen Virtualization Environment," Proceedings of the 2nd International Conference on Computer and Automation Engineering (ICCAE), Mumbai, 26-28 February 2010, pp. 496-500.

94. B. K. Kim, K. W. Hur, J. H. Jang and Y. W. Ko, "Feedback Scheduling for Realtime Task on Xen Virtual Machine," Communication and Networking, Vol. 266, 2011, pp. 283-291.

95. H. Kim, H. Lim, J. Jeong, H. Jo and J. Lee, "Task-Aware Virtual Machine Scheduling for I/O Performance," Proceedings of the 2009 ACM SIGPLAN/SIGOPS International Conference on Virtual Execution Environments, Washington DC, 11-13 March 2009, pp. 101-110.

96. H. Kim, J. Jeong, J. Hwang, J. Lee and S. Maeng, "Scheduler Support for Video-Oriented Multimedia on ClientSide Virtualization," Proceedings of the 3rd Multimedia Systems Conference, Orange County, 22 February 2012.

97. H. Tadokoro, K. Kourai and S. Chiba, "A Secure System-wide Process Scheduler across Virtual Machines," Proceedings of the 16th Pacific Rim International Symposium on Dependable Computing of the IEEE PRDC, Tokyo, 13-15 December 2010, pp. 27-36.

98. V. Uhlig, J. LeVasseur, E. Skoglund and U. Dannowski, "Towards Scalable Multiprocessor Virtual Machines," Proceedings of the 3rd

Conference on Virtual Machine Research and Technology Symposium, San Jose, 6-12 May 2004, pp. 43-56.

99. T. Friebel and S. Biemueller, "How to Deal with Lock Holder Preemption," Proceedings of the Xen Summit, Boston, 23-24 June 2008.

100. W. Jiang, Y. S. Zhou, Y. Cui, W. Feng, Y. Chen, Y. C. Shi and Q. B. Wu, "CFS Optimizations to KVM Threads on Multi-Core Environment," Proceedings of the 15th International Conference on Parallel and Distributed Systems of the IEEE ICPADS, Shenzhen, 8-11 December 2009, pp. 348-354.

101. L. Weng, Z. G. Wang, M. L. Li and X. D. Lu, "The Hybrid Scheduling Framework for Virtual Machine Systems," Proceedings of the 2009 ACM SIGPLAN/SIGOPS International Conference on Virtual Execution Environments, Washington DC, 11-13 March 2009, pp. 111-120.

102. L. Weng, Q. Liu, L. Yu and M. L. Li, "Dynamic Adaptive Scheduling for Virtual Machines," Proceedings of the 20th International Symposium on High Performance Distributed Computing, San Jose, 8-11 June 2011, pp. 239- 250.

103. Y. B. Bai, C. Xu and Z. Li, "Task-Aware Based CoScheduling for Virtual Machine System," Proceedings of the 2010 ACM Symposium on Applied Computing, Sierre, 22-26 March 2010, pp. 181-188.

104. Y. L. Yu, Y. X. Wang, H. Guo and X. B. He, "Hybrid Co-Scheduling Optimizations for Concurrent Applications in Virtualized Environments," Proceedings of the 6th IEEE International Conference on Networking, Architecture and Storage (NAS), Dalian, 28-30 July 2011, pp. 20-29.

105. Sukwong and H. S. Kim, "Is Co-Scheduling Too Expensive for SMP VMs?" Proceedings of EuroSys 2011, Salzburg, 10-13 April 2011, pp. 257-272.

106. VMWARE White Paper, Performance Tuning Best Practices for ESX Server, 2007. http://www.vmware.com/ pdf/vi_ performance_ tuning.pdf

5

# REAL TIME SYSTEMS WITH NONPREEMPTIVE PRIORITIES AND AMPLE MAINTENANCE FACILITIES

**Joseph Kreimer[1], Edward Ianovsky[2]**

[1]Department of Industrial Engineering and Management, Ben-Gurion University of the Negev, Beersheba, Israel

[2]RAVAL ACS Ltd., Beersheba, Israel

## ABSTRACT

We consider a real time data acquisition and processing multiserver system with identical servers (such as unmanned aerial vehicles, machine controllers, overhearing devices, medical monitoring devices, etc.) which can be maintained/programmed for different kinds of activities (e.g. passive or active). This system provides a service for real time tasks arriving via several channels (such as surveillance regions, assembly lines, communication channels, etc.) and involves maintenance. We focus on the worst case analysis of the system with ample maintenance facilities exponentially distributed time to failure and maintenance times. We consider two kinds of models (with and without nonpreemptive priorities) and provide balance equations for steady state probabilities and various performance measures, when both operation and maintenance times are exponentially distributed.

## KEYWORDS

Performance, Priority, Queueing, Real Time System, Unmanned Aerial Vehicles

## 1. INTRODUCTION

Real time systems (RTS) are imbedded in most modern technological structures, such as production control systems, robotic and telecommunications systems, radars, self-guided missiles, reconnaissance, aircraft and space stations, etc. These systems are widely used for the monitoring and control of physical processes.

The sustained demands of the environments in which RTS operate pose relatively rigid requirements (usually stated as time constraints) on their performance.

In RTS, a calculation that uses temporally invalid data or an action performed too early/late may be useless, and sometimes harmful—even if such a calculation or action is functionally correct. These systems are often associated with applications, in which human lives or expensive machinery may be at stake.

There exists a rich literature covering RTS and different scientific communities are treating various problems in this area. We will site only a small portion of it.

Liu and Layland in their famous work [1] presented analytic combinatorial analysis for multiprogram scheduling on a single processor. They suggested two preemptive priority driven algorithms.

Dhall and Liu [2] treated the problem of specifying an order in which the requests made by a set of periodic real-time jobs are to be executed by a multiprocessor computing system, with the goal of meeting all the deadlines with a minimum number of processors. Xio et al. in [3] presented a general cost model and an optimal solution algorithm achieving required performance objective (reliability and availability) for redundant RTS.

Several authors treated real-time Flexible Manufacturing Systems (FMS). Tawegoum et al. [4] introduced management functions in real-time monitoring of FMS. Chakravarty and Balakrishnan [5] presented the procedure for the real-time revision of production and inventory schedules in a capacitated FMS.

Efficient metaheuristic methods, such as Tabu Search (Glover and Laguna [6] ) and Greedy Randomized Adaptive Search Procedure (Feo et al. [7] ) were proposed during the last two decades of the previous century. A comprehensive survey on real-time decision problems in OR perspective is given in (Seguin et al. [8] ). Good survey on applications of Artificial Intelligence to RTS is given in (Strosnider and Paul [9] ).

We will focus on RTS with a zero deadline for the beginning of job processing. Queueing of jobs in such systems is impossible, since jobs are executed immediately upon arrival, conditional on system availability.

That part of the job which is not processed immediately is lost forever and cannot be served later.

The following works treated this kind of RTS. Kreimer and Mehrez ( [10] and [11] ) showed that the non-mix policy of never relieving an operative server maximizes the availability of a single channel RTS involving preventive maintenance and working in general regime with any arrival pattern under consideration and constant service and maintenance times. Kreimer and Mehrez [12] and Kreimer [13] treated muliserver and multichannel (with identical servers and channels) RTS (with unrestricted and restricted number of maintenance facilities respectively), working under maximum load regime (worst case) as finite source queues (Gross and Harris, [14] ). Kreimer [15] applied the two dimensional birth and death processes in worst case analysis of a multiserver RTS (with ample and limited maintenance facilities respectively) with two different channels, when both service and maintenance times were exponentially distributed. Ianovsky and Kreimer [16] obtained optimal assignment/ routing probabilities to maximize the availability of RTS with limited maintenance facilities, for large number of servers and two different channels. Kreimer [17] obtained the steady state probabilities for RTS with arbitrary number of different channels operating under a maximum load regime. Kreimer [18] considered multiserver and multichannel RTS working in general regime. Shimshi and Kreimer [19] and Kreimer [20] studied single-channel RTS with two different kinds of activities. In [21] we computed analytically (for exponentially distributed service times) and via Cross Entropy [22] - [24] simulation approach (for generally distributed service times) optimal routing probabilities for RTS with ample maintenance facilities. Bassan and Kreimer [25] treated RTS with preemptive priorities.

The work presented here is a generalization of results obtained by Shimshi and Kreimer [19] and Kreimer [20] for RTS with single channel and two kinds of activities. It deals with multiserver RTS, providing the service to the requests of real-time jobs arriving via several channels. Servers are identical, but may be maintained/pro- grammed for several (two or more) kinds of activities. We provide balance equations describing two models (with and without nonpreemptive priorities) operating under a maximum load regime and show how to compute various performance measures, when both operation and maintenance times are exponentially distributed.

The paper is organized as follows: In Section 2, the description of the model is presented. Section 3 provides balance equations for RTS with nonpreemptive priorities. Section 4 provides balance equations for RTS without priorities. Section 5 is devoted to computation of various performance characteristics. Finally, Section 6 contains conclusions.

## 2. DESCRIPTION OF THE MODEL

The most important characteristics of RTS with a zero deadline for the beginning of job processing are summarized in Kreimer and Mehrez [24] as follows:

1) Jobs/data acquisition and execution are as fast as the data arrival rate.

2) Jobs are executed immediately upon arrival, conditional on system availability. Between jobs arrival and their execution, delays are negligible.

3) That part of the job which is not executed in real time is lost forever. Storage of non-completed jobs or their parts is impossible. Thus, queues of jobs do not exist in such an RTS.

Nevertheless, some important elements of queueing theory can be successfully applied in analysis of these RTS.

We consider a multiserver multichannel RTS consisting of N identical servers (e.g. unmanned aerial vehicles- UAV, machine controllers, overhearing devices, medical monitoring devices, etc.) that provide service for the requests of real time jobs, arriving via r identical channels (e.g. surveillance regions, assembly lines, communication channels, hospital patients, etc.).

Each server can serve different channels, but not simultaneously. There is exactly one request in each channel at any instant (there are no additional job arrivals, while the channel is busy), and therefore one server at most is used (with others being on stand-by or in maintenance or providing the service to another channel) to process the job of this channel at any given time. Thus, the total number of jobs in the system is r (is equal to a number of channels). Different parts of the same job can be served by different servers. Any part of the job that is not processed immediately is lost.

It is assumed that there are ample identical maintenance teams available to repair (with repair times $R_i$ being independent identically distributed random variables—i.i.d.r.v.) all N servers simultaneously, if needed. Thus, each broken server enters maintenance facilities without delay. A fixed server may be of one of m kinds (e.g. of activity or quality) with probabilities $p_i$, $i = 1,\cdots,m$ respectively. These probabilities can be used sometimes as control parameters. Only after the maintenance is completed, the type of fixed server can be determined. The fixed server of i-th type is operative for a period of time $S_i$ before requiring $R_i$ hours of repair. Both $S_i$ and $R_i$ are independent exponentially distributed random values with parameters $\mu_i$ $(i = 1,\cdots,m)$ and $\lambda$ respectively. The duration $R_i$ of maintenance does not depend on the server's type (neither before nor after the maintenance). After maintenance is completed, the fixed server will either be on stand-by or providing service to one of channels.

The system works under a maximum load (worst case) of nonstop data arrival, which is equivalent to the case of a unique job of infinite duration in each one of r channels. This kind of operation is typical in high performance data acquisition and control systems. Decisions based on the nonstop data flow arriving via all r channels must be made extremely fast—in real time. If, during some period of time of length T, there is no available server to serve one of the channels, it means that the part of the job of length T is lost forever.

Our purpose is to provide balance equations for steady-state probabilities of this system, its availability and other performance characteristics. We will consider two policies/models: 1) nonpreemptive priority; 2) random choice of the fixed server.

# 3. MODEL WITH NONPREEMPTIVE PRIORITY

First we will provide the list of various terms, which are used in our equations.

## 3.1. Equations

We suppose that servers of first activity type have the highest priority, servers of the second activity type are after them, and so on, finally, servers of the m-th activity type have the lowest priority (Figure 1). Operating server is not interrupted, independently of its priority. When the operating server must be repaired, the fixed server with highest priority takes its place.

We denote $\{(n_1,k_1),\cdots,(n_m,k_m)\}$ the state of the system, where $n_i$ $(i=1,\cdots,m)$ is the total number of fixed servers of i-th activity type and $k_i$ $(i=1,\cdots,m)$ is the number of operating (providing service) fixed servers of i-th activity type respectively, and $p\{(n_1,k_1),\cdots,(n_m,k_m)\}$ the corresponding steady state probability. It is clear that $n_1+\cdots+n_m \le N,\ n_i \ge k_i \ge 0, \sum_{i=1}^{m} k_i = \min\left[r, \sum_{i=1}^{m} n_i\right]$.

Theorem 1. Steady state probabilities for the model with nonpreemptive priorities can be found from the fol- lowing system of balance equations:

$$\left[\sum_{i=1}^{m}k_i\mu_i+\left(N-\sum_{j=1}^{m}n_j\right)\lambda\right]p\{(n_1,k_1),(n_2,k_2),\cdots,(n_m,k_m)\}=\min\left(r-\sum_{i=1}^{m}k_i,1\right)$$
$$\times\sum_{j=1}^{m}(k_j+1)\mu_j p\{(n_1,k_1),\cdots,(n_{j-1},k_{j-1}),(n_j+1,k_j+1),(n_{j+1},k_{j+1}),\cdots,(n_m,k_m)\}$$
$$+\left(1-\min\left(r-\sum_{i=1}^{m}k_i,\ 1\right)\right)\sum_{j=1}^{m}\sum_{i=1}^{m}(k_j+1-\delta_{ij})\mu_j\left(1-\min\left(\sum_{s=1}^{i-1}(n_s-k_s),\ 1\right)\right)$$
$$\times p\{(n_1,k_1),\cdots,(n_{i-1},k_{i-1}),(n_i+\delta_{ij},k_i-1+\delta_{ij}),(n_{i+1},k_{i+1}),\cdots,(n_{j-1},k_{j-1}),$$
$$(n_j+1,k_j+1-\delta_{ij}),(n_{j+1},k_{j+1}),\cdots,(n_m,k_m)\}$$
$$+\left(1-\min\left(\sum_{i=1}^{m}(n_i-k_i),1\right)\right)\sum_{j=1}^{m}\left(N-\sum_{i=1}^{m}n_i+1\right)\lambda p_j$$
$$\times p\{(n_1,k_1),\cdots,(n_{j-1},k_{j-1}),(n_j-1,k_j-1),(n_{j+1},k_{j+1}),\cdots,(n_m,k_m)\}$$
$$+\min\left(\sum_{i=1}^{m}(n_i-k_i),1\right)\sum_{j=1}^{m}\left(N-\sum_{i=1}^{m}n_i+1\right)\lambda p_j$$
$$\times p\{(n_1,k_1),\cdots,(n_{j-1},k_{j-1}),(n_j-1,k_j),(n_{j+1},k_{j+1}),\cdots,(n_m,k_m)\},\qquad (1)$$

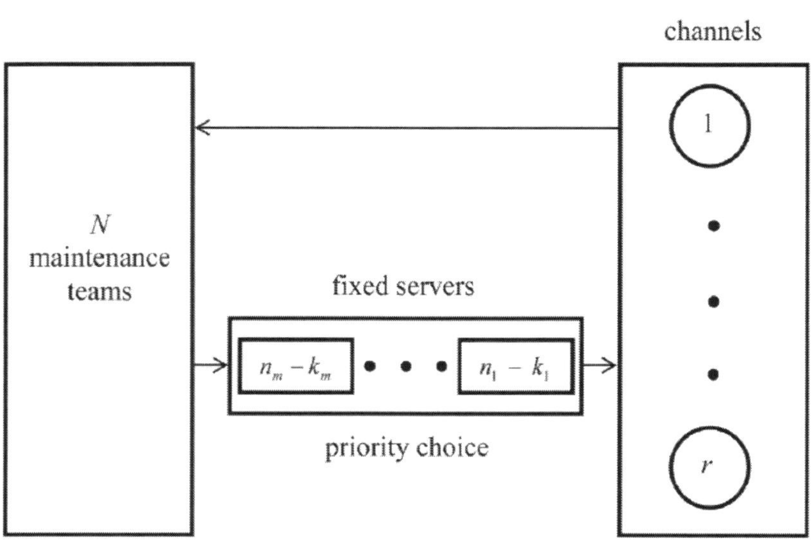


**Figure 1**. Model with priorities.

where $\{(n_1,k_1),\cdots,(n_m,k_m)\}$ is any feasible state of the system, $\delta_{ij}=\begin{cases}0, \text{ if } i\neq j\\ 1, \text{ if } i=j\end{cases}$.

And

$$\sum_{\{(n_1,k_1),\cdots,(n_m,k_m)\}\in E} p\{(n_1,k_1),\cdots,(n_m,k_m)\}=1 \tag{2}$$

where

$$E=\left\{\{(n_1,k_1),\cdots,(n_m,k_m)\}:0\le k_i\le n_i,\ i=\overline{1,m},\ \sum_{i=1}^{m}n_i\le N,\ \sum_{i=1}^{m}k_i=\min\left(r,\sum_{j=1}^{m}n_j\right)\right\}$$

is the set of all feasible states of the system.

Proof:

1) First we consider the case $r\ge N$. Then it is clear that $n_i=k_i$, $i=\overline{1,m}$, i.e. all fixed servers must be operative and priorities do not work in this case (each server coming from maintenance immediately start to work independently of its priority class). We have therefore [26]

$$N\lambda\cdot p\{(0,0),(0,0),\cdots,(0,0)\}=\sum_{j=1}^{m}\mu_j p\{(0,0),\cdots,(0,0),(n_j=1,k_j=1),(0,0),\cdots,(0,0)\} \tag{3}$$

for the state $\{(0,0),\cdots,(0,0)\}$, i.e. $n_i=k_i=0$, $i=\overline{1,m}$;

$$\left[\sum_{j=1}^{s}k_{i_j}\mu_{i_j}+\left(N-\sum_{l=1}^{s}k_{i_l}\right)\lambda\right]p\{(k_1,k_1),(k_2,k_2),\cdots,(k_m,k_m)\}$$
$$=\sum_{j=1}^{m}(k_j+1)\mu_j p\{(k_1,k_1),\cdots,(k_{j-1},k_{j-1}),(k_j+1,k_j+1),(k_{j+1},k_{j+1}),\cdots,(k_m,k_m)\}$$
$$+\sum_{j=1}^{s}\left(N-\sum_{l=1}^{s}k_{i_l}+1\right)\lambda p_{i_j}*p\{(k_1,k_1),\cdots,(k_{i_j-1},k_{i_j-1}),(k_{i_j}-1,k_{i_j}-1),(k_{i_j+1},k_{i_j+1}),\cdots,(k_m,k_m)\}, \tag{4}$$

for the states $n_i = k_i$, $i=\overline{1,m}$, $k_{i_j} > 0$, $j=\overline{1,s}$, $k_{i_j} = 0$, $j=\overline{s+1,m}$, $0<s<m$, $\sum_{j=1}^{s} n_{i_j} = \sum_{j=1}^{s} k_{i_j} < N$;

$$\left[\sum_{j=1}^{s} k_{i_j}\mu_{i_j}\right] p\{(k_1,k_1),(k_2,k_2),\cdots,(k_m,k_m)\}$$
$$=\sum_{j=1}^{s}\lambda p_{i_j} p\{(k_1,k_1),\cdots,(k_{i_j-1},k_{i_j-1}),(k_{i_j}-1,k_{i_j}-1),(k_{i_j+1},k_{i_j+1}),\cdots,(k_m,k_m)\},$$

(5)

for the states $n_i = k_i$, $i=\overline{1,m}$, $k_{i_j} > 0$, $j=\overline{1,s}$, $k_{i_j} = 0$, $j=\overline{s+1,m}$, $0<s<m$, $\sum_{j=1}^{s} n_{i_j} = \sum_{j=1}^{s} k_{i_j} = N$;

$$\left[\sum_{i=1}^{m} k_i\mu_i + \left(N-\sum_{j=1}^{m} k_j\right)\lambda\right] p\{(k_1,k_1),(k_2,k_2),\cdots,(k_m,k_m)\}$$
$$=\sum_{j=1}^{m}(k_j+1)\mu_j p\{(k_1,k_1),\cdots,(k_{j-1},k_{j-1}),(k_j+1,k_j+1),(k_{j+1},k_{j+1}),\cdots,(k_m,k_m)\}$$
$$+\sum_{j=1}^{m}\left(N-\sum_{i=1}^{m} k_i+1\right)\lambda p_j * p\{(k_1,k_1),\cdots,(k_{j-1},k_{j-1}),(k_j-1,k_j-1),(k_{j+1},k_{j+1}),\cdots,(k_m,k_m)\},$$

(6)

for the states $n_i = k_i > 0$, $i=\overline{1,m}$, $\sum_{i=1}^{m} n_i = \sum_{i=1}^{m} k_i < N$;

$$\left[\sum_{i=1}^{m} k_i\mu_i\right] p\{(k_1,k_1),(k_2,k_2),\cdots,(k_m,k_m)\}$$
$$=\sum_{j=1}^{m}\lambda p_j p\{(k_1,k_1),\cdots,(k_{j-1},k_{j-1}),(k_j-1,k_j-1),(k_{j+1},k_{j+1}),\cdots,(k_m,k_m)\},$$

(7)

for the states $n_i = k_i > 0$, $i=\overline{1,m}$, $\sum_{i=1}^{m} n_i = \sum_{i=1}^{m} k_i = N$;

Now Equation (1) follows from Equations (3)-(7).

2) Next, we consider the case $r < N$. Then we have:

Equation (3) again for the state $\{(0,0),\cdots,(0,0)\}$, i.e. $n_i = k_i = 0$, $i = \overline{1, m}$;

Equation (4) for the states $n_i = k_i$, $i = \overline{1,m}$, $k_{i_j} > 0$, $j = \overline{1,s}$, $k_{i_j} = 0$, $j = \overline{s+1,m}$, $0 < s < m$, $\sum_{j=1}^{s} n_{i_j} = \sum_{j=1}^{s} k_{i_j} < r$;

Equation (6) for the states $n_i = k_i > 0$, $i = \overline{1,m}$, $\sum_{i=1}^{m} n_i = \sum_{i=1}^{m} k_i < r$;

$$\left[\sum_{j=1}^{s} k_{i_j}\mu_{i_j} + (N-r)\lambda\right] p\{(k_1,k_1),\,(k_2,k_2),\,\ldots,\,(k_m,k_m)\}$$
$$= \sum_{j=1}^{s} k_{i_j}\mu_{i_j} p\{(k_1,k_1),\,\ldots,\,(k_{i_j-1},k_{i_j-1}),\,(k_{i_j}+1,k_{i_j}),\,(k_{i_j+1},k_{i_j+1}),\,\ldots,\,(k_m,k_m)\}$$
$$+ \sum_{j=1}^{m}\sum_{\substack{l=1 \\ i_l \neq j}}^{s} (k_j+1)\mu_j p\{(k_1,k_1),\,\ldots,\,(k_{i_l-1},k_{i_l-1}),\,(k_{i_l},k_{i_l}-1),\,(k_{i_l+1},k_{i_l+1}),\,\ldots,\,(k_{j-1},k_{j-1}),$$
$$(k_j+1,\,k_j+1),\,(k_{j+1},k_{j+1}),\,\ldots,\,(k_m,k_m)\} + \sum_{j=1}^{s}(N-r+1)\lambda p_{i_j}$$
$$\times p\{(k_1,k_1),\,\ldots,\,(k_{i_j-1},k_{i_j-1}),\,(k_{i_j}-1,\,k_{i_j}-1),\,(k_{i_j+1},k_{i_j+1}),\,\ldots,\,(k_m,k_m)\}$$

(8)

for the states $n_i = k_i$, $i = \overline{1,m}$, $k_{i_j} > 0$, $j = \overline{1,s}$, $k_{i_j} = 0$, $j = \overline{s+1,m}$, $0 < s < m$, $\sum_{j=1}^{s} n_{i_j} = \sum_{j=1}^{s} k_{i_j} = r$;

$$\left[\sum_{i=1}^{m} k_i\mu_i + (N-r)\lambda\right] p\{(k_1,k_1),(k_2,k_2),\cdots,(k_m,k_m)\}$$
$$= \sum_{j=1}^{m}\sum_{i=1}^{m} (k_j + 1 - \delta_{ij})\mu_j + \sum_{j=1}^{m}(N-r+1)\lambda p_j$$
$$* p\{(k_1,k_1),\cdots,(k_{j-1},k_{j-1}),(k_j-1,k_j-1),(k_{j+1},k_{j+1}),\cdots,(k_m,k_m)\},$$

(9)

for the states $n_i = k_i > 0$, $i = \overline{1,m}$, $\sum_{i=1}^{m} n_i = \sum_{i=1}^{m} k_i = r$;

$$\left[\sum_{i=1}^{m} k_i\mu_i + \left(N-\sum_{j=1}^{m} n_j\right)\lambda\right] p\{(n_1,k_1),(n_2,k_2),\cdots,(n_m,k_m)\}$$
$$=\sum_{j=1}^{m} k_j\mu_j\left(1-\min\left(\sum_{s=1}^{j-1}(n_s-k_s),\ 1\right)\right)$$
$$*\,p\{(n_1,k_1),\cdots,(n_{j-1},k_{j-1}),(n_j+1,k_j),(n_{j+1},k_{j+1}),\cdots,(n_m,k_m)\}$$
$$+\sum_{j=1}^{m}\sum_{\substack{l=1\\ i_l\neq j}}^{t}(k_j+1)\mu_j\left(1-\min\left(\sum_{s=1}^{i_l-1}(n_s-k_s),1\right)\right)$$
$$*\,p\{(n_1,k_1),\cdots,(n_{i_l-1},k_{i_l-1}),(n_{i_l},k_{i_l}-1),(n_{i_l+1},k_{i_l+1}),\cdots,(n_{j-1},k_{j-1}),$$
$$(n_j+1,k_j+1),(n_{j+1},k_{j+1}),\cdots,(n_m,k_m)\}+\sum_{j=1}^{s}\left(N-\sum_{i=1}^{m} n_i+1\right)\lambda p_{i_j}$$
$$*\,p\{(n_1,k_1),\cdots,(n_{i_j-1},k_{i_j-1}),(n_{i_j}-1,k_{i_j}),(n_{i_j+1},k_{i_j+1}),\cdots,(n_m,k_m)\},$$

(10)

for the states $k_{i_l}>0$, $l=\overline{1,t}$, $k_{i_l}=0$, $l=\overline{t+1,m}$, $0<t<m$, $n_{i_j}>k_{i_j}$, $j=\overline{1,s}$, $n_{i_j}=k_{i_j}$, $j=\overline{s+1,m}$, $0<s<m$, $\sum_{l=1}^{t}k_{i_l}=r$, $\sum_{i=1}^{m}n_i<N$;

$$\left[\sum_{i=1}^{m} k_i\mu_i + \left(N-\sum_{j=1}^{m} n_j\right)\lambda\right] p\{(n_1,k_1),(n_2,k_2),\cdots,(n_m,k_m)\}$$
$$=\sum_{j=1}^{m} k_j\mu_j\left(1-\min\left(\sum_{s=1}^{j-1}(n_s-k_s),1\right)\right)$$
$$*\,p\{(n_1,k_1),\cdots,(n_{j-1},k_{j-1}),(n_j+1,k_j),(n_{j+1},k_{j+1}),\cdots,(n_m,k_m)\}$$
$$+\sum_{j=1}^{m}\sum_{\substack{i=1\\ i\neq j}}^{m}(k_j+1)\mu_j\left(1-\min\left(\sum_{s=1}^{i-1}(n_s-k_s),1\right)\right)$$
$$*\,p\{(n_1,\ k_1),\cdots,(n_{i-1},k_{i-1}),(n_i,k_i-1),(n_{i+1},k_{i+1}),\cdots,(n_{j-1},k_{j-1}),$$
$$(n_j+1,k_j+1),(n_{j+1},k_{j+1}),\cdots,(n_m,k_m)\}+\sum_{j=1}^{s}\left(N-\sum_{i=1}^{m} n_i+1\right)\lambda p_{i_j}$$
$$*\,p\{(n_1,\ k_1),\cdots,(n_{i_j-1},k_{i_j-1}),(n_{i_j}-1,k_{i_j}),(n_{i_j+1},k_{i_j+1}),\cdots,(n_m,k_m)\},$$

(11)

for the states $k_i > 0$, $i = \overline{1,m}$, $n_{i_j} > k_{i_j}$, $j = \overline{1,s}$, $n_{i_j} = k_{i_j}$, $j = \overline{s+1,m}$, $0 < s < m$, $\sum_{i=1}^{m} k_i = r$, $\sum_{i=1}^{m} n_i < N$;

$$\left[\sum_{i=1}^{m} k_i\mu_i + \left(N - \sum_{j=1}^{m} n_j\right)\lambda\right] p\{(n_1,k_1),(n_2,k_2),\cdots,(n_m,k_m)\}$$
$$= \sum_{j=1}^{m} k_j\mu_j \left(1 - \min\left(\sum_{s=1}^{j-1}(n_s - k_s),1\right)\right)$$
$$* p\{(n_1,k_1),\cdots,(n_{j-1},k_{j-1}),(n_j+1,k_j),(n_{j+1},k_{j+1}),\cdots,(n_m,k_m)\}$$
$$+ \sum_{j=1}^{m}\sum_{\substack{l=1 \\ i_l \neq j}}^{t} (k_j+1)\mu_j \left(1 - \min\left(\sum_{s=1}^{i_l-1}(n_s - k_s),1\right)\right)$$
$$* p\{(n_1,k_1),\cdots,(n_{i_l-1},k_{i_l-1}),(n_{i_l},k_{i_l}-1),(n_{i_l+1},k_{i_l+1}),\cdots,(n_{j-1},k_{j-1}),$$
$$(n_j+1,k_j+1),(n_{j+1},k_{j+1}),\cdots,(n_m,k_m)\} + \sum_{j=1}^{m}\left(N - \sum_{i=1}^{m} n_i + 1\right)\lambda p_j$$
$$* p\{(n_1,k_1),\cdots,(n_{j-1},k_{j-1}),(n_j-1,k_j),(n_{j+1},k_{j+1}),\cdots,(n_m,k_m)\},$$

(12)

for the states $k_i < n_i$, $i = \overline{1,m}$, $k_{i_l} > 0$, $l = \overline{1,t}$, $k_{i_l} = 0$, $l = \overline{t+1,m}$, $0 < t < m$, $\sum_{l=1}^{t} k_{i_l} = r$, $\sum_{i=1}^{m} n_i < N$;

$$\left[\sum_{i=1}^{m} k_i\mu_i + \left(N - \sum_{j=1}^{m} n_j\right)\lambda\right] p\{(n_1,k_1),(n_2,k_2),\cdots,(n_m,k_m)\}$$
$$= \sum_{j=1}^{m}\sum_{i=1}^{m} (k_j + 1 - \delta_{ij})\mu_j \left(1 - \min\left(\sum_{s=1}^{i-1}(n_s - k_s),1\right)\right)$$
$$* p\{(n_1,k_1),\cdots,(n_{i-1},k_{i-1}),(n_i+\delta_{ij},k_i-1+\delta_{ij}),(n_{i+1},k_{i+1}),\cdots,(n_{j-1},k_{j-1}),$$
$$(n_j+1,k_j+1-\delta_{ij}),(n_{j+1},k_{j+1}),\cdots,(n_m,k_m)\} + \sum_{j=1}^{m}\left(N - \sum_{i=1}^{m} n_i + 1\right)\lambda p_j$$
$$* p\{(n_1,k_1),\cdots,(n_{j-1},k_{j-1}),(n_j-1,k_j),(n_{j+1},k_{j+1}),\cdots,(n_m,k_m)\},$$

(13)

for the states $0 < k_i < n_i$, $i = \overline{1,m}$, $\sum_{i=1}^{m} k_i = r$, $\sum_{i=1}^{m} n_i < N$;

$$\left[\sum_{i=1}^{m} k_i \mu_i\right] p\{(n_1,k_1),(n_2,k_2),\cdots,(n_m,k_m)\}$$
$$= \sum_{j=1}^{s} \lambda p_{i_j} p\left\{(n_1,k_1),\cdots,\left(n_{i_j-1},k_{i_j-1}\right),\left(n_{i_j}-1,k_{i_j}\right),\left(n_{i_j+1},k_{i_j+1}\right),\cdots,(n_m,k_m)\right\},$$

(14)

for the states $k_i \geq 0$, $i = \overline{1,m}$, $n_{i_j} > k_{i_j}$, $j = \overline{1,s}$, $n_{i_j} = k_{i_j}$, $j = \overline{s+1,m}$, $0 < s < m$, $\sum_{i=1}^{m} k_i = r$, $\sum_{i=1}^{m} n_i = N$;

$$\left[\sum_{i=1}^{m} k_i \mu_i\right] p\{(n_1,k_1),(n_2,k_2),\cdots,(n_m,k_m)\}$$
$$= \sum_{j=1}^{m} \lambda p_j p\left\{(n_1,k_1),\cdots,(n_{j-1},k_{j-1}),(n_j-1,k_j),(n_{j+1},k_{j+1}),\cdots,(n_m,k_m)\right\},$$

(15)

for the states $0 \leq k_i < n_i$, $i = \overline{1,m}$, $\sum_{i=1}^{m} k_i = r$, $\sum_{i=1}^{m} n_i = N$;

Now, Equation (1) follows from Equations (3), (4), (6), (8)-(15).

Q.E.D.

## 4. MODEL WITHOUT PRIORITIES

We suppose that when the operating server must go to maintenance, the server which takes its place is chosen among the fixed servers in a random way (Figure 2). Namely, if there are $n_i - k_i$ fixed servers of the i-th activity type $(i = 1,\cdots,m)$ on stand-by, then it is chosen for operation with probability $\left(n_i - k_i\right) \Big/ \sum_{u=1}^{m}\left(n_u - k_u\right)$. Denoting the state of the system $\left\{\left(n_1,k_1\right),\cdots,\left(n_m,k_m\right)\right\}$ and the corresponding steady state probability $p\left\{\left(n_1,k_1\right),\cdots,\left(n_m,k_m\right)\right\}$ as in previous Section, we obtain

Theorem 2. Steady state probabilities for the model without priorities can be found from the following system of balance equations:

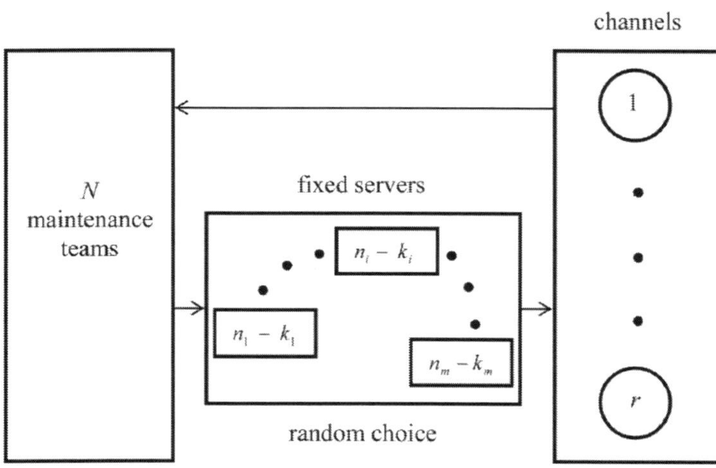


**Figure 2**. Model without priorities.

$$\begin{aligned}
&\left[\sum_{i=1}^{m} k_i\mu_i + \left(N - \sum_{j=1}^{m} n_j\right)\lambda\right] p\left\{\left(n_1,k_1\right),\left(n_2,k_2\right),\cdots,\left(n_m,k_m\right)\right\} = \min\left(r - \sum_{i=1}^{m} k_i, 1\right) \\
&* \sum_{j=1}^{m}\left(k_j+1\right)\mu_j p\left\{\left(n_1,k_1\right),\cdots,\left(n_{j-1}, k_{j-1}\right),\left(n_j+1,k_j+1\right),\left(n_{j+1},k_{j+1}\right),\cdots,\left(n_m,k_m\right)\right\} \\
&+\left(1-\min\left(r-\sum_{i=1}^{m} k_i,1\right)\right)\sum_{j=1}^{m}\sum_{i=1}^{m}\left(k_j+1-\delta_{ij}\right)\mu_j \frac{n_i-k_i+1}{\sum_{s=1}^{m}\left(n_s-k_s\right)+1} * p\left\{\left(n_1,k_1\right),\cdots,\left(n_{i-1},k_{i-1}\right),\right. \\
&\left.\left(n_i+\delta_{ij},k_i-1+\delta_{ij}\right),\left(n_{i+1},k_{i+1}\right),\cdots,\left(n_{j-1},k_{j-1}\right),\left(n_j+1,k_j+1-\delta_{ij}\right),\left(n_{j+1},k_{j+1}\right),\cdots,\left(n_m,k_m\right)\right\} \\
&+\left(1-\min\left(\sum_{i=1}^{m}\left(n_i-k_i\right),1\right)\right) * \sum_{j=1}^{m}\left(N-\sum_{i=1}^{m} n_i+1\right)\lambda p_j * p\left\{\left(n_1,k_1\right),\cdots,\left(n_{j-1},k_{j-1}\right),\left(n_j-1,k_j-1\right),\right. \\
&\left.\left(n_{j+1},k_{j+1}\right),\cdots,\left(n_m,k_m\right)\right\} + \min\left(\sum_{i=1}^{m}\left(n_i-k_i\right),1\right)\sum_{j=1}^{m}\left(N-\sum_{i=1}^{m} n_i+1\right)\lambda p_j \\
&* p\left\{\left(n_1,k_1\right),\cdots,\left(n_{j-1},k_{j-1}\right),\left(n_j-1,k_j\right),\left(n_{j+1},k_{j+1}\right),\cdots,\left(n_m,k_m\right)\right\},
\end{aligned} \tag{16}$$

where $\{(n_1,k_1),\cdots,(n_m,k_m)\}$ is any feasible state of the system, $\delta_{ij}=\begin{cases}0, & \text{if } i\neq j\\ 1, & \text{if } i=j\end{cases}$.

And

$$\sum_{\{(n_1,k_1),\cdots,(n_m,k_m)\}\in E} p\{(n_1,k_1),\cdots,(n_m,k_m)\}=1 \tag{17}$$

where

$$E=\left\{\{(n_1,k_1),\cdots,(n_m,k_m)\}:0\le k_i\le n_i,\ i=\overline{1,m},\ \sum_{i=1}^{m}n_i\le N,\ \sum_{i=1}^{m}k_i=\min\left(r,\sum_{j=1}^{m}n_j\right)\right\}$$

is the set of all feasible states of the system.

**Proof:**

1) First, we consider the case $r\ge N$. Then, it is clear that there are no fixed servers on stand-by, i.e. all fixed servers are operative. Each server coming back from maintenance immediately starts to work. We, therefore, have the same situation (and Equations (3)-(7)) as in Theorem 1 of the previous section.

2) Next, we consider the case $r<N$. Then equations of previous Section do not change for the following types of states:

Equation (3) for the state $\{(0,0),\cdots,(0,0)\}$, i.e. $n_i=k_i=0$, $i=\overline{1,m}$;

Equation (4) for the states $n_i=k_i$, $i=\overline{1,m}$, $k_{i_j}>0$, $j=\overline{1,s}$, $k_{i_j}=0$, $j=\overline{s+1,m}$, $0<s<m$, $\sum_{j=1}^{s}n_{i_j}=\sum_{j=1}^{s}k_{i_j}<r$;

Equation (6) for the states $n_i=k_i>0$, $i=\overline{1,m}$, $\sum_{i=1}^{m}n_i=\sum_{i=1}^{m}k_i<r$;

Equation (8) for the states $n_i=k_i$, $i=\overline{1,m}$, $k_{i_j}>0$, $j=\overline{1,s}$, $k_{i_j}=0$, $j=\overline{s+1,m}$, $0<s<m$, $\sum_{j=1}^{s}n_{i_j}=\sum_{j=1}^{s}k_{i_j}=r$;

Equation (9) for the states $n_i = k_i > 0$, $i = \overline{1,m}$, $\sum_{i=1}^{m} n_i = \sum_{i=1}^{m} k_i = r$;

Equation (14) for the states $k_i \geq 0$, $i = \overline{1,m}$, $n_{i_j} > k_{i_j}$, $j = \overline{1,s}$, $n_{i_j} = k_{i_j}$, $j = \overline{s+1,m}$, $0 < s < m$, $\sum_{i=1}^{m} k_i = r$, $\sum_{i=1}^{m} n_i = N$;

And Equation (15) for the states $0 \leq k_i < n_i$, $i = \overline{1,m}$, $\sum_{i=1}^{m} k_i = r$, $\sum_{i=1}^{m} n_i = N$.

For the states below, we will have following new equations:

$$\left[\sum_{i=1}^{m} k_i \mu_i + \left(N - \sum_{j=1}^{m} n_j\right)\lambda\right] p\{(n_1,k_1),(n_2,k_2),\cdots,(n_m,k_m)\}$$
$$= \sum_{j=1}^{m} k_j \mu_j \frac{n_j - k_j + 1}{\sum_{s=1}^{m}(n_s - k_s) + 1} \times p\{(n_1,k_1),\cdots,(n_{j-1},k_{j-1}),(n_j+1,k_j),(n_{j+1},k_{j+1}),\cdots,(n_m,k_m)\}$$
$$+ \sum_{j=1}^{m} \sum_{\substack{l=1 \\ i_l \neq j}}^{t} (k_j+1)\mu_j \frac{n_{i_l} - k_{i_l} + 1}{\sum_{s=1}^{m}(n_s - k_s) + 1} \times p\{(n_1,k_1),\cdots,(n_{i_l-1},k_{i_l-1}),(n_{i_l},k_{i_l}-1),$$
$$(n_{i_l+1},k_{i_l+1}),\cdots,(n_{j-1},k_{j-1}),(n_j+1,k_j+1),(n_{j+1},k_{j+1}),\cdots,(n_m,k_m)\}$$
$$+ \sum_{j=1}^{s}\left(N - \sum_{i=1}^{m} n_i + 1\right)\lambda p_{i_j} * p\{(n_1,k_1),\cdots,(n_{i_j-1},k_{i_j-1}),(n_{i_j}-1,k_{i_j}),(n_{i_j+1},k_{i_j+1}),\cdots,(n_m,k_m)\}, \tag{18}$$

for the states $k_{i_l} > 0$, $l = \overline{1,t}$, $k_{i_l} = 0$, $l = \overline{t+1,m}$, $0 < t < m$, $n_{i_j} > k_{i_j}$, $j = \overline{1,s}$, $n_{i_j} = k_{i_j}$, $j = \overline{s+1,m}$, $0 < s < m$, $\sum_{l=1}^{t} k_{i_l} = r$, $\sum_{i=1}^{m} n_i < N$;

$$\left[\sum_{i=1}^{m}k_i\mu_i+\left(N-\sum_{j=1}^{m}n_j\right)\lambda\right]p\{(n_1,k_1),(n_2,k_2),\cdots,(n_m,k_m)\}$$
$$=\sum_{j=1}^{m}k_j\mu_j\frac{n_j-k_j+1}{\sum_{s=1}^{m}(n_s-k_s)+1}\times p\{(n_1,k_1),\cdots,(n_{j-1},k_{j-1}),(n_j+1,k_j),(n_{j+1},k_{j+1}),\cdots,(n_m,k_m)\}$$
$$+\sum_{j=1}^{m}\sum_{\substack{i=1\\i\neq j}}^{m}(k_j+1)\mu_j\frac{n_i-k_i+1}{\sum_{s=1}^{m}(n_s-k_s)+1}\times p\{(n_1,k_1),\cdots,(n_{i-1},k_{i-1}),(n_i,k_i-1),$$
$$(n_{i+1},k_{i+1}),\cdots,(n_{j-1},k_{j-1}),(n_j+1,k_j+1),(n_{j+1},k_{j+1}),\cdots,(n_m,k_m)\}$$
$$+\sum_{j=1}^{s}\left(N-\sum_{i=1}^{m}n_i+1\right)\lambda p_{i_j}*p\{(n_1,k_1),\cdots,(n_{i_j-1},k_{i_j-1}),(n_{i_j}-1,k_{i_j}),(n_{i_j+1},k_{i_j+1}),\cdots,(n_m,k_m)\},$$

(19)

for the states $k_i>0$, $i=\overline{1,m}$, $n_{i_j}>k_{i_j}$, $j=\overline{1,s}$, $n_{i_j}=k_{i_j}$, $j=\overline{s+1,m}$, $0<s<m$, $\sum_{i=1}^{m}k_i=r$, $\sum_{i=1}^{m}n_i<N$;

$$\left[\sum_{i=1}^{m}k_i\mu_i+\left(N-\sum_{j=1}^{m}n_j\right)\lambda\right]p\{(n_1,k_1),(n_2,k_2),\cdots,(n_m,k_m)\}$$
$$=\sum_{j=1}^{m}k_j\mu_j\frac{n_j-k_j+1}{\sum_{s=1}^{m}(n_s-k_s)+1}\times p\{(n_1,k_1),\cdots,(n_{j-1},k_{j-1}),(n_j+1,k_j),(n_{j+1},k_{j+1}),\cdots,(n_m,k_m)\}$$
$$+\sum_{j=1}^{m}\sum_{\substack{l=1\\i_l\neq j}}^{t}(k_j+1)\mu_j\frac{n_{i_l}-k_{i_l}+1}{\sum_{s=1}^{m}(n_s-k_s)+1}\times p\{(n_1,k_1),\cdots,(n_{i_l-1},k_{i_l-1}),(n_{i_l},k_{i_l}-1),$$
$$(n_{i_l+1},k_{i_l+1}),\cdots,(n_{j-1},k_{j-1}),(n_j+1,k_j+1),(n_{j+1},k_{j+1}),\cdots,(n_m,k_m)\}$$
$$+\sum_{j=1}^{m}\left(N-\sum_{i=1}^{m}n_i+1\right)\lambda p_j*p\{(n_1,k_1),\cdots,(n_{j-1},k_{j-1}),(n_j-1,k_j),(n_{j+1},k_{j+1}),\cdots,(n_m,k_m)\},$$

(20)

for the states $k_i<n_i$, $i=\overline{1,m}$, $k_{i_l}>0$, $l=\overline{1,t}$, $k_{i_l}=0$, $l=\overline{t+1,m}$, $0<t<m$, $\sum_{l=1}^{t}k_{i_l}=r$, $\sum_{i=1}^{m}n_i<N$;

$$\left[\sum_{i=1}^{m} k_i\mu_i + \left(N-\sum_{j=1}^{m} n_j\right)\lambda\right] p\{(n_1,k_1),(n_2,k_2),\cdots,(n_m,k_m)\}$$
$$=\sum_{j=1}^{m}\sum_{i=1}^{m}(k_j+1-\delta_{ij})\mu_j \frac{n_i-k_i+1}{\sum_{s=1}^{m}(n_s-k_s)+1}$$
$$\times p\{(n_1,k_1),\cdots,(n_{i-1},k_{i-1}),(n_i+\delta_{ij},k_i-1+\delta_{ij}),(n_{i+1},k_{i+1}),\cdots,(n_{j-1},k_{j-1}),$$
$$(n_j+1,k_j+1-\delta_{ij}),(n_{j+1},k_{j+1}),\cdots,(n_m,k_m)\} + \sum_{j=1}^{m}\left(N-\sum_{i=1}^{m} n_i+1\right)\lambda p_j$$
$$\times p\{(n_1,k_1),\cdots,(n_{j-1},k_{j-1}),(n_j-1,k_j),(n_{j+1},k_{j+1}),\cdots,(n_m,k_m)\},$$

(21)

for the states $0<k_i<n_i$, $i=\overline{1,m}$, $\sum_{i=1}^{m} k_i = r$, $\sum_{i=1}^{m} n_i < N$;

Now, Equations (16) follows from Equations (3), (4), (6), (8), (9), (14), (15), (18)-(21).

Q.E.D.

# 5. PERFORMANCE CHARACTERISTICS

In this section, we shall show how to compute some useful performance characteristics of the RTS under consideration.

Each server can be in one of following positions:

a) Busy (operating);

b) Out of order (in maintenance);

c) On stand-by;

Each channel can be in one of two positions:

a) In service;

b) Out of service.

Keeping in mind that, the state of the system is represented by the vector $\{(n_1,k_1),\cdots,(n_m,k_m)\}$, where $n_i$ $(i=1,\cdots,m)$ is the total number of fixed servers of i-th activity type and $k_i$ $(i=1,\cdots,m)$ is the number of operating fixed servers of i-th activity type, we can represent the number of servers and channels in different positions in terms of $n_i$ and $k_i$, namely:

Number of fixed servers is $\sum_{i=1}^{m} n_i$;

Number of operating fixed servers (the number of channels in service) is $\sum_{i=1}^{m} k_i$;

Number of fixed servers of i-th activity type being on stand-by is $n_i - k_i$;

Number of all fixed servers being on stand-by is $\sum_{i=1}^{m} (n_i - k_i)$;

Number of broken servers is $N - \sum_{i=1}^{m} n_i$;

Number of channels out of service is $r - \sum_{i=1}^{m} k_i$;

Now we can obtain corresponding average values, using steady state probabilities, namely:

$L_i = E[n_i]$—average number of fixed servers of i-th activity type $\left(i=\overline{1,m}\right)$;

$L = \sum_{i=1}^{m} L_i$—average number of all fixed servers;

$N-L$—average number of broken servers (also the average number of servers in maintenance);

$E[k_i]$—average number of operating servers of i-th activity type $\left(i=\overline{1,m}\right)$;

$\sum_{i=1}^{m} E[k_i]$ —average number of all operating servers (as well as the average number of channels in service);

$r - \sum_{i=1}^{m} E[k_i]$ —average number of non-executed real-time jobs;

$L_{i,sb} = E[n_i - k_i]$ —average number of i-th type fixed servers on stand-by $(i = \overline{1,m})$;

$L_{sb} = \sum_{i=1}^{m} L_{i,sb}$ —average number of all fixed servers on stand-by;

$\lambda_{av} = \lambda(N - L)$ —average rate of servers arriving from maintenance;

$\lambda_{av,i} = \lambda p_i (N - L)$ —average rate of i-th type servers arriving from maintenance $(i = \overline{1,m})$;

$W_{i,sb} = L_{i,sb} / \lambda_{av,i}$ —average time spent on stand-by by the i-th type server $(i = \overline{1,m})$ -Little Theorem;

$W_i = W_{i,sb} + 1/\mu_i$ —average time of the i-th type server being fixed $(i = \overline{1,m})$ -Little Theorem.

The use of RTS relies on the principle of availability, which can be given in our case by the following formula $Av = \frac{1}{r} \sum_{i=1}^{m} E[k_i]$.

Another important performance measure is the average cost of system operation during time unit. Denote $C_i$ $(i = 1, \cdots, m)$ the cost of time unit activity of the i-th type server, and D the penalty paid for the time unit during which one of channels was not served. Then the average cost is defined as follows

$$TC = \sum_{i=1}^{m} C_i E[k_i] + D\left( r - \sum_{i=1}^{m} E[k_i] \right) = Dr - \sum_{i=1}^{m} (D - C_i) E[k_i]$$

# 6. CONCLUSIONS

In this paper, we provided equations for steady-state probabilities, as well as formulas for availability, average cost function and other performance characteristics of multiserver and multichannel RTS with different activity types and ample maintenance facilities. We have examined models with nonpreemptive priorities and without them. Practitioners and researchers can submit their parameters in equations for steady state probabilities and performance characteristics and to make their choice between two models in order to solve real life problems. Further research should address following problems:

- RTS with preemptive priorities;
- RTS in which each server needs more than one kind of maintenance;
- Optimization of RTS involving costs and penalties;
- Multilevel RTS;
- RTS with shortage of maintenance teams.

The use of queueing theory methodology will have significant benefits in analysis of these systems.

# REFERENCES

1. Liu, C.L. and Layland, J.W. (1973) Scheduling Algorithms for Multiprogramming in a Hard-Real-Time Environment. The Journal of the ACM, 20, 46-61.

2. Dhal, S.K. and Liu, C.L. (1978) On a Real-Time Scheduling Problem. Operations Research, 26, 127-140.

3. Xie, M., Dai, Y.S., Poh, K.L. and Lai, C.D. (2004) Optimal Number of Hosts in a Distributed System Based on Cost Criteria. International Journal of Systems Science, 35, 343-353.

4. Tawegoum, R., Castelain, E. and Gentina, J.C. (1994) Real-Time Piloting of Flexible Manufacturing Systems. European Journal of Operational Research, 78, 252-261.

5. Chakravarty, A.K. and Balakrishnan, N. (1998) Reacting in Real-Time to Production Contingencies in a Capacitated Flexible Cell. European Journal of Operational Research, 110, 1-19.

6. Glover, F.W. and Laguna, M. (1997) Tabu Search. Kluwer Academic Publishers, Dordrecht.

7. Feo, T.A., Venkatraman, K. and Bard, J.F. (1991) A GRASP for a Difficult Single Scheduling Problem. Computers and Operations Research, 18, 635-643.

8. Seguin, R., Potvin, J.-Y., Gendreau, M., Crainic, T.G. and Marcotte, P (1997) Real-Time Decision Problems: An Operational Research Perspective. Journal of the Operational Research Society, 48, 162-174

9. Strosnider, J.K. and Paul, C.J. (1993) A Structured View of Real-Time Problem Solving. AI Magazine, 14, 45-66.

10. Kreimer, J. and Mehrez, A. (1993) An Optimal Operation Policy for Real-Time N-Server Stand-By System Involving Preventive Maintenance. European Journal of Operational Research, 69, 50-54.

11. Kreimer, J. and Mehrez, A. (1994) Optimal Real-Time Data Acquisition and Processing by a Multiserver Stand-By System. Operations Research, 42, 24-30.

12. Kreimer, J. and Mehrez, A. (1998) Computation of Availability of a Real-Time System Using Queueing Theory Methodology. Journal of the Operational Research Society, 49, 1095-1100.

13. Kreimer, J. (1999) Real-Time Multiserver and Multichannel Systems with Shortage of Maintenance Crews. Mathematical and Computer Modelling, 30, 169-176.

14. Gross, D. and Harris, C.M. (1998) Fundamentals of Queueing Theory. John Wiley, New York.

15. Kreimer, J. (2000) Real-Time Multiserver System with Two Non-Identical Channels and Limited Maintenance Facilities. Mathematics and Computers in Simulation, 53, 85-94.

16. Ianovsky, E. and Kreimer, J. (2003) Optimization of Real-Time Multiserver System with Two Different Channels and Shortage of Maintenance Teams. Mathematics and Computers in Simulation, 63, 615-627.

17. Kreimer, J. (2002) Real-Time System with Homogeneous Servers and Nonidentical Channels in Steady State. Computers and Operations Research, 29, 1465-1473.

18. Kreimer, J. (2002) Effectiveness Analysis of Real-Time Data Acquisition and Processing Multichannel Systems. IEEE Transactions on Reliability, 51, 91-99.

19. Shimshi, Y. and Kreimer, J. (2000) Real-Time Multiserver System with Different kinds of Activities. Proceedings of the 11th Conference on Industrial Engineering and Management, IE&M'2000, Beer-Sheva, May 2000, 17-21.

20. Kreimer, J. (2003) Multiserver Single-Channel Real-Time System with Different Kinds of Activities. Communications in Dependability and Quality Management, 6, 91-100.

21. Ianovsky, E. and Kreimer, J. (2011) An Optimal Routing Policy for Unmanned Aerial Vehicles (Analytical and Cross- Entropy Simulation Approach). Annals of Operations Research, 189, 215-253.

22. Rubinstein, R.Y. and Kroese, D.P. (2008) Simulation and the Monte Carlo Method. 2nd Edition, John Wiley & Sons, New York.

23. Rubinstein, R.Y., Ridder, A. and Vaisman, R. (2014) Fast Sequential Monte Carlo Methods for Counting and Optimization. John Wiley & Sons, New York.

24. Kroese, D.P., Taimre, T. and Botev, Z.I. (2011) Handbook of Monte Carlo Methods, John Wiley & Sons, New York.

25. Bassan, E. and Kreimer, J. (2008) Multiserver and Multichannel Real-Time Systems with Separate Queues and Pre- emptive priorities. Computer Modelling and New Technologies, 42, 7-15.

26. Ianovsky, E. (2005) Analysis and Optimization of Real-Time Systems. PhD Thesis, Ben-Gurion Univer-sity of the Negev, Beer-Sheva.

6

# ON THE EFFECTIVENESS OF CACHE PARTITIONING IN HARD REAL-TIME SYSTEMS

**Sebastian Altmeyer , Roeland Douma, Will Lunniss, Robert I. Davis**

University of Amsterdam, Amsterdam, The Netherlands

## ABSTRACT

In hard real-time systems, cache partitioning is often suggested as a means of increasing the predictability of caches in pre-emptively scheduled systems: when a task is assigned its own cache partition, inter-task cache eviction is avoided, and timing verification is reduced to the standard worst-case execution time analysis used in non-pre-emptive systems. The downside of cache partitioning is the potential increase in execution times. In this paper, we evaluate cache partitioning for hard real-time systems in terms of overall schedulability. To this end, we examine the sensitivity of (i) task execution times and (ii) pre-emption costs to the size of the cache partition allocated and present a cache partitioning algorithm that is optimal with respect to taskset schedulability. We also devise an alternative algorithm which primarily optimises schedulability but also minimises processor utilization. We evaluate the performance of cache partitioning compared to state-of-the-art pre-emption cost analysis based on benchmark code and on a large number of synthetic tasksets with both fixed priority and EDF scheduling. This allows us to derive general conclusions about the usability of cache partitioning and identify taskset and system parameters that influence the relative effectiveness of cache partitioning. We also examine the improvement in processor utilization obtained using an alternative cache partitioning algorithm, and the tradeoff in terms of increased analysis time.

## KEYWORDS

Timing verification, Cache partitioning, WCET analysis, Real-time scheduling

## 1. EXTENDED VERSION

This paper builds upon and extends the ECRTS 2014 paper on *Evaluation of Cache Partitioning for Hard Real-Time Systems* (Altmeyer et al. 2014) as follows:

- The evaluation now covers both fixed priority and EDF scheduling.
- We examined how the schedulability of a group of tasks sharing a partition depends upon partition size.
- We present an alternative cache partitioning algorithm which both optimises schedulability and minimises processor utilization. We examine the improvement in processor utilization obtained using this algorithm as compared to the original cache partitioning algorithm, and the tradeoff in terms of increased analysis time.

## 2. INTRODUCTION

Cache partitioning is often suggested as a means of increasing the predictability of caches in pre-emptively scheduled hard real-time systems. The rationale behind this argument is that when a task is assigned its own cache partition, inter-task cache eviction is avoided, and timing verification is reduced to the standard worst-case execution time (WCET) analysis used in non-pre-emptive systems. Cache partitioning comes at a cost. The reduced amount of cache available to each task potentially increases intra-task cache conflicts, trading an increase in (non-pre-emptive) execution times for reduced cache related pre-emption delays (CRPD).

Despite the wealth of publications on cache partitioning for real-time systems, little work has been done on the effectiveness of cache partitioning compared to systems where tasks make unconstrained use of the cache. Pre-emptive multi-tasking systems with unconstrained caches were considered unpredictable. Given recent advances in the analysis of cache related pre-emption delays, we consider this view outdated.

In this paper, we evaluate cache partitioning for hard real-time systems in terms of overall schedulability. To this end, we first determine the sensitivity of task execution times to the size of the available cache partition using application code from real-time benchmarks. Contrary to the implicit assumptions in prior work, the worst-case execution time of a task is not necessarily monotonic in the partition size. We show how the monotonicity property can be re-established using a monotonic upper bound function for the execution times. We then present a cache partitioning algorithm that aims at optimizing taskset schedulability. Under the assumption of monotonic execution times, the algorithm is optimal in the sense that it finds a schedulable cache partitioning whenever one exists. The algorithm is based on a branch-and-bound approach and is agnostic with respect to the schedulability test used, i.e., it is valid for any, *sustainable* schedulability test (Baruah and Burns 2006) and scheduling algorithm. Further, we introduce an alternative branch-and-bound algorithm which optimizes schedulability as its primary concern and minimizes processor utilization as a secondary concern. This algorithm is optimal under the same conditions, in the sense that it finds a schedulable cache partitioning with the minimum processor utilization whenever a schedulable partitioning exists.

We evaluate the performance of cache partitioning vs. a non-partitioned cache, using state-of-the-art pre-emption cost aware schedulability analysis, based on two different benchmark sets (PapaBench and Mälardalen Benchmark Suite) and on a large number of synthetic tasksets. The evaluation using synthetic tasksets enables us to derive results that are valid in general, and not just for a small selection of use-cases. In addition, we identify how different parameter settings affect the relative performance of the partitioned vs. non-partitioned approaches. We also evaluate the improvement in processor utilization obtained using the alternative cache partitioning algorithm as compared to the original cache partitioning algorithm, and the tradeoff in terms of increased analysis time. Finally, we quantify the error margin introduced by the assumption of monotonic execution times.

We focus on a completely analytical approach, where we compare the schedulability of real-time systems assuming pre-emptive scheduling under either a fixed priority or EDF scheduling policy, with a direct mapped cache. In both cases, partitioned and non-partitioned cache, we rely on bounds on the execution times obtained via WCET analysis, and in the non-partitioned case, also on analytical bounds on the CRPD.

The paper is structured as follows: In Sect. 2, we introduce the required terminology and notation and in Sect. 3 we present the schedulability tests for fixed priority and EDF scheduling. In Sect. 4, we review existing approaches to cache partitioning. Section 5 explains the sensitivity of the worst-case execution times of tasks with respect to the size of their allocated cache partitions. The optimal cache partitioning algorithms are presented in Sect. 6, the results of the case study in Sect. 7 and the evaluation based on synthetic tasksets in Sect. 8. Section 9 concludes with a summary and discussion of future work.

## 3. SYSTEM MODEL, TERMINOLOGY AND NOTATION

We consider both fixed priority pre-emptive scheduling and EDF (pre-emptive) scheduling of a set of sporadic tasks (or taskset) on a single processor. Each taskset $\Gamma$ comprises *n* tasks $\Gamma=\{\tau 1,\ldots,\tau n\}$, where *n* is a positive integer. We assume a discrete time model, where all task parameters are positive integers.

Each task $\tau i$ is characterized by its bounded worst-case execution time $Ci$ obtained assuming no pre-emption (i.e. not including any cache related pre-emption delays), minimum inter-arrival time or *period* $Ti$, and relative *deadline* $Di$. Each task $\tau i \tau i$ therefore gives rise to a potentially unbounded sequence of invocations or *jobs*, each of which has an execution time upper bounded by $Ci$, an arrival time at least $TiTi$after the arrival of its previous job, and an absolute deadline that is $Di$ after its arrival. In an *implicit-deadline* taskset, all tasks have $Di=TiDi=Ti$, in a *constrained-deadline* taskset, all tasks have $Di \leq Ti$ while in an *arbitrary-deadline* taskset, task deadlines are independent of their periods. In this paper, we assume constrained deadline tasksets. The tasks are assumed to be independent and so cannot block each other from executing by accessing mutually exclusive shared resources, with the exception of the processor. (We note that this restriction is only made to simplify comparisons between the different approaches, resource sharing can be accounted for by schedulability analysis that incorporates CRPD as shown by Altmeyer et al. 2011, 2012).

The utilization UiUi, of a task is given by its execution time divided by its period (Ui=Ci/Ti). The total utilization *U* of a taskset is the sum of the utilizations of all of its tasks, i.e.

$$U = \sum_{i} C_i / T_i. \tag{1}$$

## 3.1 Static timing analysis

The paper is set in the context of static timing analysis as used for many safety-critical hard real-time applications. This means that we derive the worst-case execution time CiCi of each task τiτi using a static analysis, in our case, the aiT Timing analyzer (Ferdinand and Heckmann 2004).

Static timing analyses offer higher reliability compared to measurement-based approaches, as exhaustive measurements are considered infeasible for modern architectures. The higher confidence in the correctness of the execution time estimates comes at the cost of system restrictions, which must be fulfilled in order to apply static timing analyses. Foremost the restriction to static instead of dynamic memory allocation and write-through data caches.

## 3.2 Pre-emption costs

We now extend the sporadic task model to include pre-emption costs. To this end, we need to explain how pre-emption costs can be derived. To simplify the following explanation and examples, we assume direct-mapped caches.

The additional execution time due to pre-emption is mainly caused by cache eviction: the pre-empting task evicts cache blocks of the pre-empted task that have to be reloaded after the pre-empted task resumes. The additional context switch costs due to the scheduler invocation and a possible pipeline-flush can be upper-bounded by a constant. We assume that these *constant* costs are already included in Ci. Hence, from here on, we use *pre-emption cost* to refer only to the cost of additional cache reloads due to pre-emption. This cache-related pre-emption delay (CRPD) is bounded by g×BRT where $g$ is an upper bound on the number of cache block reloads due to pre-emption and BRTBRT is an upper-bound on the time necessary to reload a memory block in the cache (block reload time).

To analyse the effect of pre-emption on a pre-empted task, Lee et al. (1998) introduced the concept of a useful cache block: A memory block $m$ is called a useful cache block (*UCB*) at program point PPPP, if (i) $m$may be cached at PPPP and (ii) $m$ may be reused at program point Q that may be reached from P without eviction of $m$ on this path. In the case of pre-emption at program point P, only the memory blocks that (i) are cached and (ii) will be reused, may cause additional reloads. Hence, the number of UCBs at program point P gives an upper bound on the number of additional reloads due to a pre-emption at P. The maximum possible pre-emption cost for a task is determined by the program point with the highest number of UCBs. Note that for each subsequent pre-emption, the program point with the next smaller number of UCBs can be considered. Thus, the $j$-th highest number of UCBs can be counted for the $j$-th pre-emption. A tighter definition is presented by Altmeyer and Burguière 2009; however, in this paper we need only the basic concept.

The worst-case impact of a pre-empting task is given by the number of cache blocks that the task may evict during its execution. Recall that we consider direct-mapped caches: in this case, loading one block into the cache may result in the eviction of at most one cache block. A memory block accessed during the execution of a pre-empting task is referred to as an evicting cache block (*ECB*). Accessing an ECB may evict a cache block of a pre-empted task.

In this paper, we represent the sets of ECBs and UCBs as sets of integers with the following meaning:

$$s \in \text{UCB}_i \Leftrightarrow \tau_i \text{ has a useful cache block in cache-set } s$$

$$s \in \text{ECB}_i \Leftrightarrow \tau_i \text{ may evict a cache block in cache-set } s$$

Separate computation of the pre-emption cost is restricted to architectures without timing anomalies (Lundqvist and Stenström 1999) but is independent of the type of cache used, i.e. data, instruction or unified cache.

In the case of set-associative LRU caches1, a single cache-set may contain several useful cache blocks. For instance, UCB1={1,2,2,2,3,4} means that task τ1 contains 3 UCBs in cache-set 2 and one UCB in each of the cache sets 1, 3 and 4. As one ECB suffices to evict all UCBs of the same cache-set (Burguière et al. 2009), multiple accesses to the same set by the pre-empting task does not need to appear in the set of ECBs. Hence, we keep the set of ECBs as used for direct-mapped caches. A bound on the CRPD in the case of LRU caches due to task τiτi directly pre-empting τjτj is thus given by the intersection UCBj∩′ECBi={m|m∈UCBj:m∈ECBi}UCBj∩′ECBi={m|m∈UCBj:m∈ECBi}, where the result is also a multiset that contains each element from UCBjUCBj if it is also in ECBiECBi. A precise computation of the CRPD in the case of LRU caches is given by Altmeyer et al. (2010). In this paper, we assume direct-mapped caches. Note that all equations provided within this paper are for direct-mapped caches, they are also valid for set-associative LRU caches with the above adaptation to the set-intersection.

# 4. SCHEDULABILITY TESTS

In this section, we present schedulability tests for fixed-priority scheduling using response time analysis and for EDF scheduling using processor demand analysis. Both analyses are *sustainable* (Baruah and Burns2006) in the sense that any taskset that was deemed schedulable by the test remains schedulable if the parameters "improve", e.g., if the execution times decrease or periods increase.

## 4.1 Fixed priority pre-emptive scheduling

We now recapitulate the exact (sufficient and necessary) schedulability test for fixed priority pre-emptive scheduling of constrained-deadline tasksets based on *response time analysis* (Audsley et al. 1993; Joseph and Pandya 1986; Davis et al. 2008). Subsequent work on integrating cache related pre-emption delays into schedulability analysis for fixed priority pre-emptive systems is based on this analysis. The basic form given below assumes that pre-emption costs are zero.

We assume that the index *i* of task τi represents its priority, hence τ1 has the highest priority, and τnτn the lowest. We use the notation *hp*(*i*) (and *lp*(*i*)) to mean the set of tasks with priorities higher than (and lower than) *i*, and the notation *hep*(*i*) (and *lep*(*i*)) to mean the set of tasks with priorities higher than or equal to (lower than or equal to) *i*.

The worst-case response time RiRi of a task τiτi is given by the longest possible time from release of a job of the task until it completes execution. Thus task τiτi is schedulable if and only if Ri≤Di , and a taskset is schedulable if and only if all of its tasks are schedulable.

The response time Ri of a task necessarily contains its execution time CiCi, and in addition, τiτi may suffer interference and be pre-empted by tasks with higher priority than *i*. Let τjτj be such a task. Within the response time Ri of τiτi, task τjτj executes at most $\left\lceil \frac{R_i}{T_j} \right\rceil$ times, each time for at most CjCj. Hence, the response time RiRi of task τiτi is given by:

$$R_i = C_i + \sum_{\forall j \in \mathrm{hp}(i)} \left\lceil \frac{R_i}{T_j} \right\rceil C_j \tag{2}$$

where hp(i) denotes the set of tasks with higher priority than *i*. The response time Ri of task τi appears on both the left-hand side and the right-hand side of (2). As the right-hand side is a monotonically non-decreasing function of Ri , then a solution may be found via fixed-point iteration:

$$R_i^{x+1} = C_i + \sum_{\forall j \in \mathrm{hp}(i)} \left\lceil \frac{R_i^x}{T_j} \right\rceil C_j \tag{3}$$

Iteration starts with an initial value, typically $R_i^0 = C_i$, and ends when either $R_i^{x+1}$ >Di in which case the task is unschedulable, or when $R_i^{x+1} = R_i^x$, in which case the task is schedulable, with a worst-case response time $R_i^{x+1}$. We note that convergence may be speeded up using the techniques described by Davis et al. (2008).

### 4.1.1 Pre-emption cost aware schedulability test

To integrate pre-emption costs into response time analysis, Busquets-Mataix et al. (1996) extended (2) by adding a term γi,jγi,j representing the pre-emption cost of a job of task τjτj executing during the response time of task τi (with j∈hp(i):

$$R_i = C_i + \sum_{\forall j \in \mathrm{hp}(i)} \left\lceil \frac{R_i}{T_j} \right\rceil (C_j + \gamma_{i,j}) \qquad (4)$$

An alternative approach was taken by Petters and Farber (2001) and later Staschulat et al. (2005), who based their analyses on the following equation:

$$R_i = C_i + \sum_{\forall j \in \mathrm{hp}(i)} \left( \left\lceil \frac{R_i}{T_j} \right\rceil C_j + \hat{\gamma}_{i,j} \right) \qquad (5)$$

The value $\hat{\gamma}_{i,j}$ denotes the pre-emption cost of *all* jobs of task τj executing during the response time of taskτiτi (again with j∈hp(i)). It is given by the $\left\lceil \frac{R_i}{T_j} \right\rceil$ -highest pre-emption costs of a job of task τj executing during RiRi. Although the difference with respect to (4) is subtle, more precise analysis can be obtained by using $\hat{\gamma}_{i,j}$ as a bound on the *overall impact* of all jobs of τj on the response time RiRi instead of a bound on the impact of *just one* job of τj.

We note that when pre-emption costs are considered explicitly, the worst-case scenario is not necessarily given by a synchronous release of all higher priority tasks (Meumeu Yomsi and Sorel 2007) and hence (4) and (5) provide sufficient, but not exact schedulability tests.

### 4.1.2 Pre-emption cost computation

The value γi,jγi,j can be computed in a number of different ways, which are described in detail by Altmeyer et al. (2012), here, we restrict our explanations to the two dominant approaches: ECB-Union and UCB-Union.

*UCB-Union* Tan and Mooney (2007) analysed the pre-emption cost via an upper bound on the number of useful cache blocks (of all pre-empted tasks) that a pre-empting task τjτj may evict. As it is only the eviction of useful cache blocks belonging to tasks with equal or higher priority than task τiτi that may increase the response time of task τiτi, only tasks with intermediate priorities in the set aff $(i, j) = \mathrm{hep}(i) \cap lp(j)$, need be considered.

$$\gamma_{i,j}^{\text{UCB-U}} = \text{BRT} \cdot \left| \left( \bigcup_{k \in \text{aff}(i,j)} \text{UCB}_k \right) \cap \text{ECB}_j \right| \tag{6}$$

Here, $\gamma_{i,j}^{\text{UCB-U}}$ represents the worst-case impact a job of task τj can have on all (useful cache blocks of) tasks with lower priority than task τj down to task τi . We refer to this approach as UCB-Union.

*ECB-Union* Instead of considering the precise set of ECBs of a pre-empting task and bounding all possibly affected UCBs (as UCB-Union does), ECB-Union (Altmeyer et al. 2011, 2012) considers the precise number of UCBs of the pre-empted task. It then assumes that the pre-empting task τj has itself already been pre-empted by *all* tasks with higher priority. This nested pre-emption of the pre-empting task is represented by the union of the ECBs of all tasks with higher or equal priority than task τjτj:

$$\gamma_{i,j}^{\text{ECB-U}} = \max_{\forall k \in \text{aff}(i,j)} \left\{ \left| \text{UCB}_k \cap \left( \bigcup_{h \in \text{hep}(j)} \text{ECB}_h \right) \right| \right\} \tag{7}$$

The UCB-Union and ECB-Union approaches are *incomparable* in that there are tasks that may be deemed schedulable using one approach but not the other and vice-versa.

*Multiset approaches* The UCB-Union and ECB-Union can be lifted to the so-called Multiset approaches to be used within Eq. (5) to account for the $\left\lceil \frac{R_i}{T_j} \right\rceil$ -highest pre-emption costs of a job of task τj executing during Ri instead of accounting for the highest pre-emption costs of a job $\left\lceil \frac{R_i}{T_j} \right\rceil$ times. To simplify our equations, we introduce $E_k(R_i)$ to denote the maximum number of jobs of task τkτk that can execute during response time Ri, i.e.:

$$E_k(R_i) = \left\lceil \frac{R_i}{T_k} \right\rceil$$

The pre-emption cost $\gamma_{i,j}^{\text{ECB-M}}$ is then computed as follows, recognising the fact that task τj can pre-empt each intermediate task τk at most $E_j(R_k)E_k(R_i)$ times during the response time of task τiτi. We form a multiset *M* that contains the cost

$$\left| \mathrm{UCB}_k \cap \left( \bigcup_{h \in \mathrm{hp}(j) \cup \{j\}} \mathrm{ECB}_h \right) \right| \tag{8}$$

of τj pre-empting task $\tau_k$ $E_j(R_k)E_k(R_i)$ times, for each task $\tau_k \in \mathrm{aff}(i, j)$.. Hence:

$$M = \bigcup_{k \in \mathrm{aff}(i,j)} \left( \bigcup_{E_j(R_k)E_k(R_i)} \left| \mathrm{UCB}_k \cap \left( \bigcup_{h \in \mathrm{hp}(j) \cup \{j\}} \mathrm{ECB}_h \right) \right| \right) \tag{9}$$

$\gamma_{i,j}^{\mathrm{ECB-M}}$ is then given by the $E_j(R_i)$ largest values in M.

$$\gamma_{i,j}^{\mathrm{ECB-M}} = \mathrm{BRT} \cdot \sum_{l=1}^{E_j(R_i)} |M^l| \tag{10}$$

where Ml is the *l*-th largest value in *M*. We note that by construction, the ECB-Union Multiset approach dominates the ECB-Union approach.

The pre-emption cost $\gamma_{i,j}^{\mathrm{UCB-M}}$ is computed as follows; recognising the fact that task τj can pre-empt each intermediate task τk directly or indirectly at most $E_j(R_k)E_k(R_i)$ times during the response time of task τiτi. First, we form a multi-set $M_{i,j}^{\mathrm{ucb}}$ containing $E_j(R_k)E_k(R_i)$ copies of the UCBk of each task k∈aff(i,j). This multi-set reflects the fact that during the response time Ri of task τi , task τj cannot evict a UCB of task τk more than Ej(Rk)Ek(Ri) times. Hence:

$$M_{i,j}^{\mathrm{ucb}} = \bigcup_{k \in \mathrm{aff}(i,j)} \left( \bigcup_{E_j(R_k)E_k(R_i)} \mathrm{UCB}_k \right) \tag{11}$$

Next, we form a multi-set Mecbj containing Ej(Ri) copies of the ECBj of task τj. This multi-set reflects the fact that during the response time Ri of task τi, task τj can evict ECBs in the set ECBj at most Ej(Ri) times.

$$M_j^{\mathrm{ecb}} = \bigcup_{E_j(R_i)} (\mathrm{ECB}_j) \tag{12}$$

$\gamma_{i,j}^{\mathrm{UCB-M}}$ is then given by the size of the multi-set intersection of $M_j^{\mathrm{ecb}}$ and $M_{i,j}^{\mathrm{ucb}}$

$$\gamma_{i,j}^{\mathrm{UCB-M}} = \mathrm{BRT} \cdot \left| M_{i,j}^{\mathrm{ucb}} \cap M_j^{\mathrm{ecb}} \right| \tag{13}$$

We note that by construction, the UCB-Union Multiset approach dominates the UCB-Union approach.

The UCB-Union Multiset and the ECB-Union Multiset approach are *incomparable* in that there are tasks that may be deemed schedulable using one approach but not the other and vice-versa. More precise analysis can therefore be achieved by using a combination of both approaches as follows:

$$R_i = \min\left(R_i^{\mathrm{ECB-M}}, R_i^{\mathrm{UCB-M}}\right) \tag{14}$$

A detailed description of the pre-emption cost aware schedulability tests can be found in Altmeyer et al. (2012).

## 4.2 EDF scheduling

We now recapitulate the exact (sufficient and necessary) schedulability test for pre-emptive EDF scheduling of sporadic tasksets based on *processor demand analysis* (Baruah et al. 1990). Subsequent work on integrating cache related pre-emption delays into schedulability analysis for EDF scheduled systems is based on this analysis. The basic form given below assumes that pre-emption costs are zero. Pre-emptive EDF scheduling is optimal among all scheduling algorithms on a uniprocessor (Dertouzos 1974) under the assumption of negligible pre-emption overhead.

A necessary and sufficient schedulability test for EDF and implicit deadlines (Di=Ti) is given by the processor utilizations (Liu and Layland 1973): a task set is schedulable, iff

$$U = \sum_i \frac{C_i}{T_i} \leq 1 \tag{15}$$

This test is necessary, but not sufficient if Di≠Ti.

Baruah et al. (1990) introduced the processor demand function $h(t)$, which denotes the maximum execution time requirement of all tasks jobs which have both their arrival times and their deadlines in a contiguous interval of length $t$. Using this they showed that a taskset is schedulable iff $\forall t > 0, h(t) \leq t$ where $h(t)$ is defined as:

$$h(t) = \sum_{i=1} \max \left\{0, 1 + \left\lfloor \frac{t - D_i}{T_i} \right\rfloor \right\} C_i \tag{16}$$

As $h(t)$ can only change when $t$ is equal to an absolute deadline, we can restrict the number of values of $t$that need to be checked. To place an upper bound on $t$, and so on the number of calculations of $h(t)$, the minimum interval in which it can be guaranteed that an unschedulable taskset will be shown to be unschedulable must be found. For a general taskset with arbitrary deadlines $t$ can be bounded by La (George et al. 1996):

$$L_a = \max \left\{ D_i, \ldots, D_n, \frac{\sum_{i+1}^{n} (T_i = D_i) U_i}{1 - U} \right\} \tag{17}$$

And an alternative bound, Lb given by the length of the synchronous busy period can be used (Ripoll et al.1996), where Lb is computed using the following equation using fixed point iteration:

$$w^{\alpha+1} = \sum_{i=1}^{n} \left\lceil \frac{w^{\alpha}}{T_i} \right\rceil C_i \tag{18}$$

There is no direct relationship between LaLa and LbLb, which enables $t$ to be bounded by L=min(La,Lb). Combined with the knowledge that $h(t)$ can only change at an absolute deadline, a taskset is therefore schedulable under EDF iff U≤ and:

$$\forall t \in Q, h(t) \leq t \tag{19}$$

Where $Q$ is defined as

$$Q = \{d_k | d_k = kT_i + D_i \wedge d_k < \min(L_a, L_b), k \in \mathbb{N}\} \tag{20}$$

Zhang andBurns (2009) presented the Quick convergence Processor-demand Analysis (QPA) algorithm which exploits the monotonicity of $h(t)$ to reduce the number of required checks.

### 4.2.1 Pre-emption cost aware schedulability test

In order to account for CRPD using EDF scheduling, Lunniss et al. (2013) include a component γt,j which represents the CRPD associated with a pre-emption by a single job of task τj on jobs of other tasks that are both released and have their deadlines in an interval of length $t$. Note, unlike its counterpart in CRPD analysis for fixed priority scheduling, γt,j refers to the pre-empting task τj and $t$, rather than the pre-empting and pre-empted tasks. Including γt,j in (16) a revised equation for $h(t)$ is obtained:

$$h(t) = \sum_{i=1} \max\left\{0, 1 + \left\lfloor \frac{t - D_i}{T_i} \right\rfloor\right\} (C_i + \gamma_{t,j}) \tag{21}$$

The set of affected tasks for EDF is based on the relative deadlines of the tasks:

$$\text{aff}(t_j) = \{\forall \tau_i \,|\, t \geq D_i > D_j\} \tag{22}$$

Task τj can only pre-empt tasks with a larger relative deadline than Dj and only tasks with a relative deadline Di less than or equal to $t$ need to be accounted for when calculating $h(t)$

### 4.2.2 Pre-emption cost computation

The UCB-Union (see Eq. (23)) and ECB-Union (see Eq. (24)) approaches as used for fixed-priorities can be adapted as follows:

$$\gamma_{t,j}^{\text{UCB-U}} = \text{BRT} \cdot \left| \left( \bigcup_{k \in \text{aff}(t,j)} \text{UCB}_k \right) \cap \text{ECB}_j \right| \tag{23}$$

and

$$\gamma_{t,j}^{\mathrm{ECB-U}} = \max_{\forall k \in \mathrm{aff}(t,j)} \left\{ \left| \mathrm{UCB}_k \cap \left( \bigcup_{h \in \mathrm{hep}(j)} \mathrm{ECB}_h \right) \right| \right\} \tag{24}$$

The UCB-Union and ECB-Union approaches are *incomparable* in that there are tasks that may be deemed schedulable using one approach but not the other and vice-versa.

Similar to Eq. (5) that accounts for the highest *n* pre-emption costs of a job instead of the highest pre-emption costs of a job *n* times, we can adapt Eq. (21) as follows

$$h(t) = \sum_{i=1} \left( \max \left\{ 0, 1 + \left\lfloor \frac{t - D_i}{T_i} \right\rfloor \right\} C_i + \gamma_{t,j} \right) \tag{25}$$

and lift the UCB-Union and ECB-Union approaches to their multiset counterparts.

The ECB-Union multiset approach computes the union of all ECBs that may affect a pre-empted task during a pre-emption by task $\tau j$. It accounts for nested pre-emptions by assuming that task $\tau j$ has already been pre-empted by all other tasks that may pre-empt it. The first step is to form a multiset Mt,j that contains the cost of task $\tau j$ pre-empting task $\tau k$ repeated Pj(Dk)Ek(t) times, for each task $\tau k \in$aff(t,j), where Pj(Dk) denotes the maximum number of jobs of task $\tau j$ that can pre-empt a single job of task $\tau k$:

$$P_j(D_k) = \max\left(0, \left\lceil \frac{D_k - D_j}{T_j} \right\rceil\right)$$

and Ek(t) is defined as

$$E_k(t) = \max\left(0, \left\lfloor \frac{t - D_k}{T_k} \right\rfloor\right)$$

Hence:

$$M = \bigcup_{k \in \mathrm{aff}(t,j)} \left( \bigcup_{P_j(D_k)E_k(t)} \left| \mathrm{UCB}_k \cap \left( \bigcup_{h \in \mathrm{hp}(j) \cup \{j\}} \mathrm{ECB}_h \right) \right| \right) \tag{26}$$

$\gamma_{t,j}^{\text{ECB-M}}$ is then given by the Ej(t) largest values in M.

$$\gamma_{t,j}^{\text{ECB-M}} = \text{BRT} \cdot \sum_{l=1}^{E_j(t)} |M^l| \tag{27}$$

The pre-emption cost $\gamma_{t,i}^{\text{UCB-M}}$ for EDF scheduling is computed similarly to the UCB-Union Multiset approach for fixed-priority scheduling: Task τj can pre-empt each intermediate task τk directly or indirectly at most Pj(Dk)Ek(t) times within the deadline of task τiτi. First, we form a multi-set $M_{t,j}^{\text{ucb}}$ containing Pj(Dk)Ek(t) copies of the UCBk of each task k∈aff(t,j) reflecting the fact that within time *t*, task τj cannot evict a UCB of task τk more than Pj(Dk)Ek(t) times. Hence:

$$M_{t,j}^{\text{ucb}} = \bigcup_{k \in \text{aff}(t,j)} \left( \bigcup_{P_j(D_k)E_k(t)} \text{UCB}_k \right) \tag{28}$$

Next, we form a multi-set MecbjMjecb containing Ej(t) copies of the ECBj of task τj. This multi-set reflects the fact that during *t*, task τj can evict ECBs in the set ECBj at most Ej(t) times.

$$M_j^{\text{ecb}} = \bigcup_{E_j(t)} (\text{ECB}_j) \tag{29}$$

$\gamma_{i,j}^{\text{UCB-M}}$ is then given by the size of the multi-set intersection of $M_j^{\text{ecb}}$ and $M_{i,j}^{\text{ucb}}$

$$\gamma_{i,j}^{\text{UCB-M}} = \text{BRT} \cdot \left| M_{i,j}^{\text{ucb}} \cap M_j^{\text{ecb}} \right| \tag{30}$$

We note that the UCB-Union Multiset and the ECB-Union Multiset approach for EDF are also incomparable and hence, a combined approach can be defined as follows:

$$h(t) = \min\left( h(t)^{\text{ECB-M}}, h(t)^{\text{UCB-M}} \right) \tag{31}$$

As the multiset approaches effectively inflate the execution time of task $\tau j$ by the CRPD that it can cause in an interval of length $t$, the upper bound $L$, used for calculating the processor demand $h(t)$, must be adjusted. This is achieved by calculating an upper bound on the utilisation due to CRPD that is valid for all intervals of length greater than some value Lc. This CRPD utilisation value is then used to inflate the taskset utilisation and thus compute an upper bound Ld on the maximum length of the synchronous busy period. This upper bound is valid provided that it is greater than Lc, otherwise the actual maximum length of the busy period may lie somewhere in the interval [Ld,Lc], hence we can use max(Lc,Ld) as a bound. We refer the reader to (Lunniss et al. 2013) for a detailed explanation.

## 4.3 Optimal task layout

The precise cache mapping, i.e., the mapping of memory block to cache sets strongly influences the pre-emption costs. Consider for instance the extreme situation where all tasks are aligned to the first cache-set: Each task will definitely evict cache blocks of another task. If tasks' code is instead aligned sequentially in the cache, the pre-emption costs are very likely to be smaller. Lunniss et al. (2012) showed how to optimize the task layout with respect to the taskset schedulability and the pre-emption costs. The technique used determines the order in which the code for each task is placed sequentially in memory, without leaving any gaps. Optimizing the task layout does not require any changes to the source code or the compilation and is completely transparent to the user. Only the linker file is adapted. The optimzation changes the addresses of the code and data in the binary, but not the code/data itself, hence an appropriate layout can only improve performance.

# 5. REVIEW OF CACHE PARTITIONING FOR REAL-TIME SYSTEMS

Cache partitioning (Mueller 1995; Plazar et al. 2009) is a technique to reduce or even completely avoid cache-related pre-emption delays, aimed at increasing the predictability of real-time systems. Cache partitioning trades *inter-task* for *intra-task* cache conflicts, i.e. it trades off reduced cache-related pre-emption delays against potentially increased worst-case execution times. Partitioning techniques can be implemented either in hardware (Kirk and Strosnider 1990) or in software (Mueller 1995; Plazar et al. 2009). Modern common-off-the-shelf processors may provide native hardware support for partitioning, as for instance the *OMAP-L138* DSP from Texas Instruments.2 A native software-based solution can be implemented using page coloring (Ye et al. 2014) when virtual memory management is used. If no such support is available, the realization of cache partitioning is more compilcated: Mueller (1995) and later Plazar et al. (2009) proposed a partitioning-aware compiler, asserting that each task only accesses its own cache partition. This comes at the cost of often substantial changes to the code and data layout, which further increases task execution times; however, as no additional hardware is needed, the memory access delays remain unchanged. This is in contrast to hardware-based solutions where an additional mapping layer from code/data to main memory is needed.

Despite the wealth of publications on cache partitioning for real-time systems, little work has been done on evaluating the effects of cache partitioning, and in particular, its effectiveness compared to systems where tasks make unconstrained use of the cache. The previously cited papers either focus on the implementation of cache partitioning (Muller 1995; Plazar et al. 2009; Puaut and Decotigny 2002), or compare partitioned systems with systems without cache (Vera et al. 2007). The rationale behind this limited evaluation is the belief that pre-emptive systems that make unconstrained use of cache are unpredictable. Given recent advances in the analysis of cache related pre-emption delays, this view can now be considered somewhat outdated.

Studies on general usability of cache partitioning have been conducted by Busquets-Mataix and Wellings (1997) (to a limited extent), and more recently by Bui et al. (2008). Busquets-Mataix and Wellings based their evaluation on simplistic models of task execution times and pre-emption costs. The execution time variation was modelled according to Higbee (1990), favouring efficiency over precision, and only delivers rough estimates. The authors also assume that each evicting cache block causes an additional pre-emption cost, which is a very pessimistic assumption (Altmeyer et al. 2012).

Bui et al. (2008) based their evaluation on high-level execution time models (Wolf 1992) to estimate the execution time variation and pre-emption cost overhead. We rely on the results of state-of-the-art static timing analysis (both for the WCET bounds and the pre-emption costs) as used in safety-critical hard real-time systems, which provide firm guarantees.

Since finding an optimal cache partitioning is NP-hard (Bui et al. 2008), previous approaches employed heuristics either to minimize the number of cache misses, or to minimize the processor utilization (Kirk and Strosnider 1990; Busquets-Mataix and Wellings 1997; Bui et al. 2008; Plazar et al. 2009).

The research that we present in this paper differs in the following aspects: As schedulability is the key criterion in verifying the temporal correctness of hard real-time systems, we focus on taskset schedulability as opposed to utilization. A cache partitioning may be schedulable even though the task utilization is not the minimum that could be obtained. Similarly, minimizing the utilization does not necessarily optimize schedulability. We present partitioning algorithms which are optimal under the assumption that the worst-case execution time of each task is monotonic in the size of the partition allocated to that task. We aim at deriving general statements about the usability and efficiency of cache partitioning compared to a non-partitioned cache analysed using state-of-the-art pre-emption cost analyses.

# 6. PARTITION-SIZE SENSITIVITY

## 6.1 Partition-size sensitivity (task level)

In this section, we evaluate the sensitivity of the worst-case execution times of tasks with respect to the size of their allocated cache partitions. The aim of this sensitivity analysis is to form simple yet accurate execution time functions that are parametric in the size of the cache partition allocated to the task. These functions provide the information required by the optimal partitioning algorithm described in Sect. 6.

We perform sensitivity analysis by computing WCET bounds for varying cache partition sizes using static analysis. Based on these values, we can deduce typical variations in execution time depending on the code size of the task and the size of the cache partition allocated to it. The rationale behind this empirical evaluation is twofold: First, we are interested in the behaviour of a set of real examples, and second, we want to use realistic models of execution-time as a function of cache partition size to determine an effective partitioning of the cache between tasks. We note that with hardware support for cache partitioning, partitions are typically restricted to being a power of 2 in size e.g. 8,16,32 cache sets etc.; whereas software methods (Mueller 1995) can support cache partitions of any arbitrary number of sets. In the remainder of the paper, we assume that the number of cache sets in a partition may take any arbitrary value; however, we note that the techniques introduced are easily adapted to the case were partition sizes come from a restricted set of hardware-supported values.

The target architecture is an ARM7 processor3 with direct-mapped cache of size 4 kB with a line size of 16 Bytes (and thus, 256 cache sets), a block reload time of 8 μμs and a clock rate of 100 MHz. The cache uses a write-through policy to enable a constant block reload time, required for the static timing analysis. The values are derived from an example configuration of the ARM7 as used in previous work (see Altmeyer et al. 2011). As benchmarks, we used PapaBench (Nemer et al. 2006) and the Mälardalen benchmark suite (Gustafsson et al. 2010). We used the aiT Timing analyzer (Ferdinand and Heckmann 2004) to compute WCET bounds, and evaluate the sensitivity of execution time with respect to cache partition size.

Figures 1 and 2 show the normalized WCET bounds for the benchmark tasks with varying cache partition sizes and cache types. Each line denotes the execution time for one benchmark. The y-axis depicts the normalized execution time with the value 1 representing the largest WCET bound (which typically corresponds to the smallest cache partition size i.e. zero). The x-axis depicts the normalized cache partition size with the value 1 representing the code-size/maximum memory usage of the task. Increasing the size of the cache partition beyond the code size/memory footprint does not improve the execution time any further. The graphs are best viewed online in colour.

A perfect data (or instruction) cache means that all data (or instruction) accesses are served instantaneously. Even though this assumption is unrealistic, it removes possible noise and and allows us to fully concentrate on the effects of pre-emption and partitioning. We have also performed experiments with*instruction cache but without data cache* and also with *data cache but without instruction cache*. The results are very similar to the evaluation shown for perfect caches, but less accentuated.

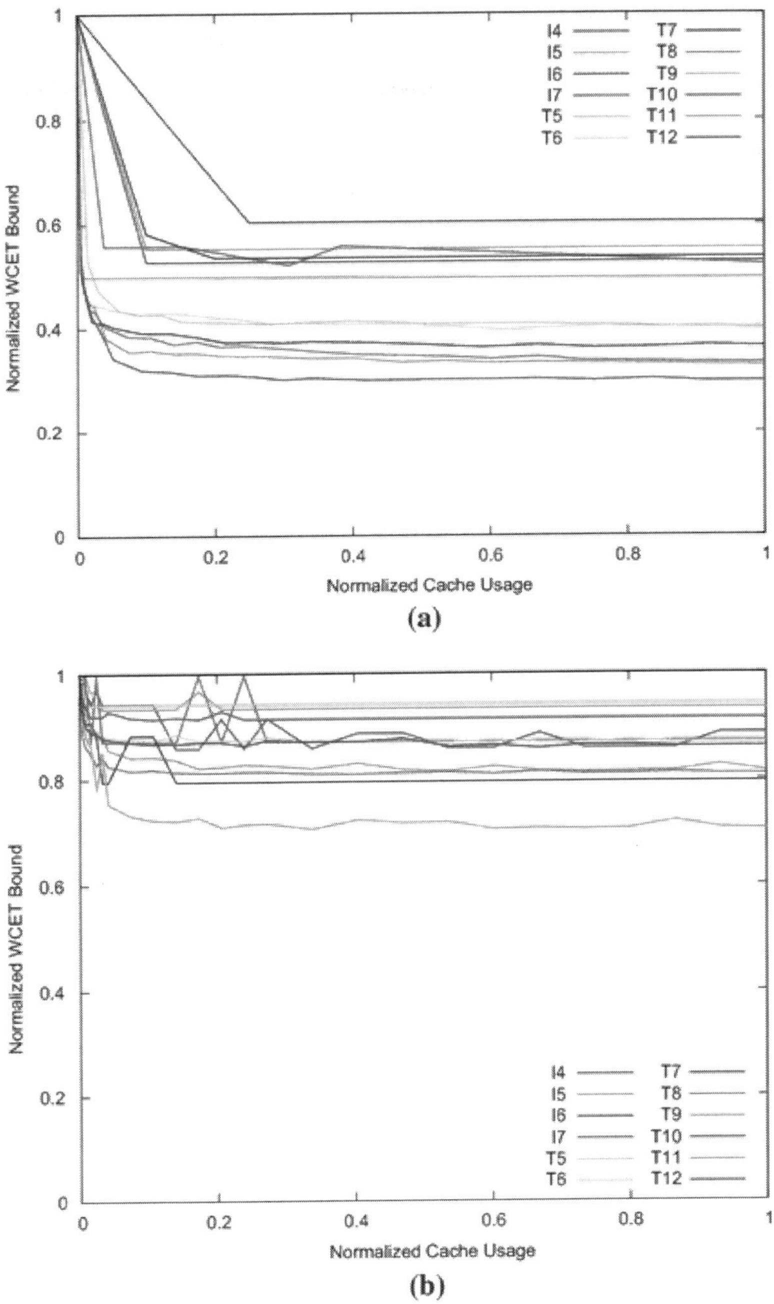


**Figure. 1** WCETs depending on the cache partition size (PapaBench, see Table 1). **a** Direct mapped instruction cache, perfect data cache. **b** Direct mapped data cache, perfect instruction cache

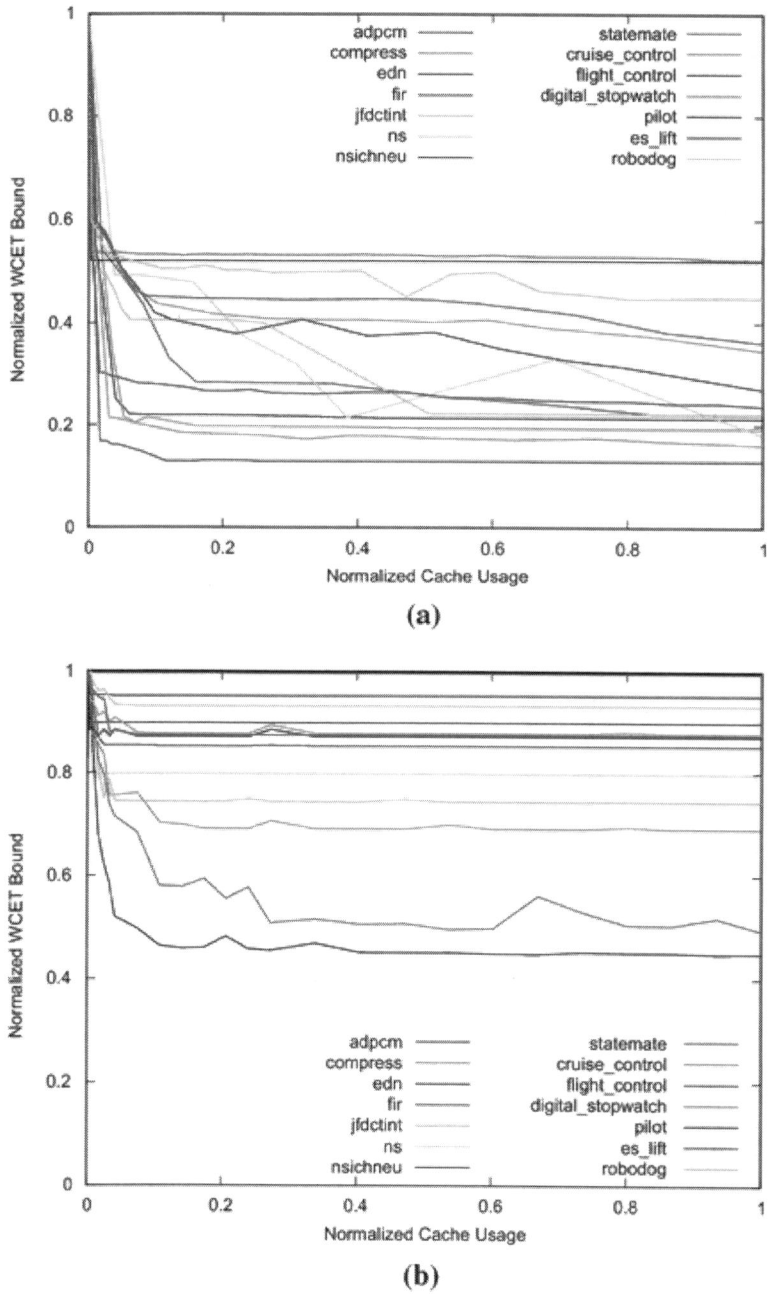


**Figure. 2** WCETs depending on the cache partition size (Mälardalen and SCADE Benchmarks, see Table 3). **a** direct mapped instruction cache, perfect data cache, **b** direct mapped data cache, perfect instruction cache

We can see that variation in the execution times is stronger in the case of instruction cache compared to data cache. This behaviour is as expected since each instruction results in an instruction cache access, but not necessarily in a data cache access. Similarly, the variation in the execution times is amplified by the assumption of a perfect data/instruction cache. Note we do not assume any implementation cost for cache partitioning. Additional delays to implement cache partitioning only occur if no native support for partitioning is available.

## 6.1.1 Monotonicity

We observe from Figs. 1 and 2 that the execution time bounds are not necessarily monotonic with respect to the cache partition size.

This counter-intuitive behaviour can be explained by differences in the mapping of memory blocks to the cache sets. Assuming a direct-mapped cache with a line size of 16 bytes and a task that exhibits the following access sequence 0x00030→0x00080→0x000300x00030→ 0x00080→ 0x00030

If we assign this task a cache partition of size 4, memory block 0*x*00030 maps to set 3 of this partition and 0*x*00080 maps to set 0. The last access to 0*x*00030 therefore results in a cache hit. In contrast, in a larger cache partition of size 5, memory blocks 0*x*00030 and 0*x*00080 both map to cache set 3 and the last access to 0*x*00030 is a cache miss. Hence, for this trivial example, the performance with 5 cache sets is worse than that for 4 cache sets.

We note that the assumption of monotonic execution time bounds is both common and often not explicitly stated in work on cache partitioning for real-time systems (Bui et al. 2008; Busquets-Mataix and Wellings1997; Kirk and Strosnider 1990; Mueller 1995; Plazar et al. 2009).

The impact of these effects is however limited, and so we can replace the actual execution time function with monotonic over/under-approximations without significant loss of precision, as shown in Fig. 3. Here, the basic function (black line) is non-monotonic, while the upper bound (blue line) and the lower bound (red line) are monotonically non-increasing functions of cache partition size. We thus establish monotonicity of the WCET with respect to the cache partition size and can use this property in our approach to partitioning the cache. In Sect. 8.5, we quantify the error introduced by this approximation.

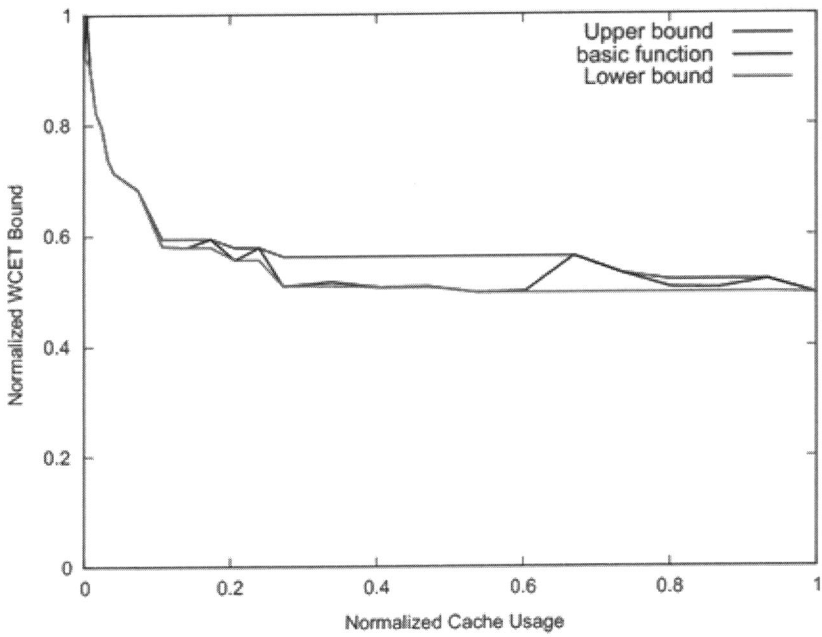


**Figure. 3** Over-/underapproximations of the WCET function (*statemate* benchmark, direct mapped data cache, perfect instruction cache)

## 6.2 Partition-size sensitivity (task group level)

In this section, we examine the sustainability of a group of tasks sharing a cache partition with respect to the partition size. The rational behind a shared cache partition is that a subset of the complete taskset can be grouped together, either to improve performance or to implement spatial isolation between several task groups for safety reasons—as often used in hierarchical scheduling. Optimality of the partitioning algorithm described in Sect. 6 can only be guaranteed for shared cache partitions, if the schedulability tests are sustainable with respect to the size of a cache partition.

In case of a shared cache partition, two opposing factors influence the system's performance: the execution time bounds and the pre-emption costs. Whereas the execution time bounds typically increase when the size of the assigned cache partition is reduced, the pre-emption costs decrease. A smaller cache results in a higher number of intra-task conflicts and hence, in fewer cache hits without pre-emption. Figure 4 depicts this behaviour. We note that a change in the maximum number of useful cache blocks always co-incides with a change in the execution time bound, whereas a change in the execution time bound does not necessarily imply a change in the maximum number of useful cache blocks. Furthermore under the hardware restrictions assumed in this paper (set-based partitioned, LRU or direct-mapped caches), the impact of the execution time limits the impact of the pre-emption costs: The pre-emption costs can only increase, if the number of cached and re-used memory blocks increases, which means that the execution time decreases. The decrease in the execution time always dominates the increase in the pre-emption costs. When the number of potentially evicted memory blocks increases, then the execution time decreases at least by the time to reload these additional memory blocks times how often these memory blocks need to be reloaded. A large number of pre-emptions will then at most cancel out the decrease in the execution time, but never exceed it.

However, the dominance relation between the execution time bound and the pre-emption costs is not necessarily reflected in these schedulability analyses: The terms γi,jγi,j in (4) and γi,jγi,j in (21) representing the pre-emption costs–and thus the number of UCBs—may contribute more often to the response time/demand bound than they actually occur in practice. Consequently, the schedulability tests presented in Sect. 3 are not sustainable for taskgroups, even under the assumption of monotonic execution times. This unsustainability of the schedulability tests means that the algorithms described in Sect. 6 would not retain their optimality if extended to the case where groups of tasks share partitions: False negatives are possible in the sense that no feasible shared cache partition is found although one may exist.

# 7. OPTIMAL CACHE PARTITIONING

In this section, we derive an optimal cache partitioning algorithm, which makes use of the monotonic upper bound execution time functions of cache partition size described in the previous section. We assume a direct-mapped cache of size *S*. A cache partitioning *P* is a tuple of non-negative integers describing for each task τi, the size pi of its allocated cache partition:

$$P = (p_1, p_2, \ldots, p_n) : \underbrace{\mathbb{N} \times \cdots \times \mathbb{N}}_{n} \tag{32}$$

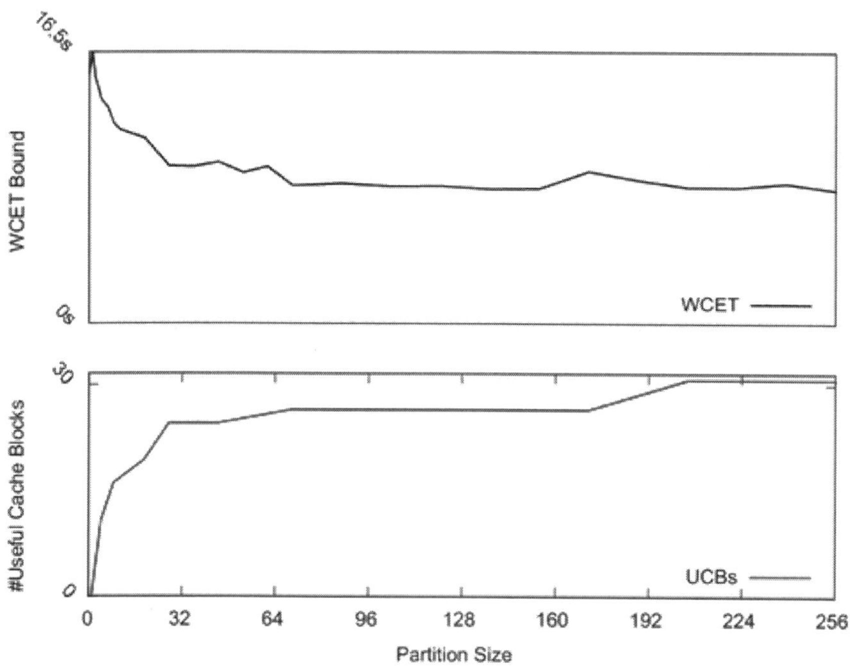


**Figure. 4** WCET and number of UCBs depending on the cache partition size (*statemate* benchmark, direct mapped data cache, perfect instruction cache)

We assume that each task has a dedicated cache partition which is not shared with any other tasks (we return to this point in Sect. 9). A cache partitioning is valid, if the total size of the cache partitions does not exceed the overall size *S* of the cache (i.e. if $\sum_i p_i \leq S$).

## 7.1 Schedulability

We are interested in the schedulability of a taskset, as this is the main optimization criterion for hard real-time systems. We therefore say that a cache partitioning algorithm is optimal, iff it finds a cache partitioning whereby the tasks are schedulable, whenever such a partitioning exists. Note that this is different from minimizing the utilization of a taskset, since taskset utilization is only a rough indicator of system schedulability.

To compute an optimal cache partitioning, we use a branch-and-bound approach (see Algorithm 1) which is certain, under the assumption of monotonic execution time functions, to find a feasible cache partitioning if one exists. To this end, we exploit the sustainability of the schedulability test with respect to execution times and the monotonicity of the execution time function with respect to the cache partition size to prune the search space.

The algorithm is implemented using a recursive function *checkPartition*. This function takes as its input the current task index *i*, a partially defined partitioning *P* and the remaining cache size *s*. The partitioning is defined up to index *i* and the remaining cache size *s* is given by *S* minus the sum of the sizes of the first *i*partitions i.e. $s = S - \sum_{i=1}^{i} p_i$.

The initial input to the function is the first task index 1, an arbitrary partitioning *P* and the overall cache size *S*. If the last task index is reached, the partitioning is fully defined and the result is determined by the function *isSchedulable*, which checks the schedulability of the taskset for the defined partitioning. Note, here we employ the basic schedulability tests without pre-emption costs (see Sect. 3) given by (2) and (16), as the cache partitioning prevents any cache-related pre-emption delays.

In the next step, the algorithm checks taskset schedulability under (a) the optimistic assumption that each not yet specified task partition is of size *s* and (b) under the pessimistic assumption that each not yet specified task partition is given an equal share of the remaining cache size, i.e., $\lfloor s/(n-i+1)\rfloor\lfloor s/(n-i+1)\rfloor$. This enables effective pruning of the search in the case where (a) schedulability is disproved for any extensions to the current partial partitioning, and early exit in the case (b) schedulability is proven assuming that all further tasks are schedulable with a cache partition of equal size.

**Algorithm 1** Optimal Cache Partitioning (Schedulability)

```
function CHECKPARTITION(int i, partition P, int s)
    if i = n then
        return isSchedulable(P)
    end if
    let P = (p_1, ..., p_n)
    if not isSchedulable((p_1, ..., p_{i-1}, s, ..., s)) then
        return false
    end if
    if isSchedulable((p_1, ..., p_{i-1}, ⌊s/(n-i+1)⌋, ..., ⌊s/(n-i+1)⌋)) then
        return true
    end if
    p_i = 0
    while p_i ≤ s do
        if checkPartition(i + 1, (p_1, ..., p_i, ..., p_n), s − p_i) then
            return true
        else
            p_i = nextStep(i,p_i)
        end if
    end while
    return false
end function
```

The last construct of the algorithm, the while loop, implements the branching. The partition size of cache partition pipi is varied from 0 up to the remaining cache size $s$ and each possible partitioning is evaluated using a recursive function call. This is done using the function *nextStep* which computes the next partition size for task τiτi. Due to the monotonicity of the execution time functions with respect to cache partition size,*nextStep* jumps directly to the next partition size where the execution time changes. All intermediate partition sizes with the same execution time can be safely ignored. In the worst-case, up to nS different cache partitionings must be evaluated, where $n$ is the number of tasks and $S$ the number of cache sets. In practice, the runtime is substantially lower due to early exits and the reduced number of partition sizes which give different execution times. We return to this point in the following section. Further, in the case where hardware support is provided for a limited number of partition sizes, the runtime is further reduced due to the restricted number of partition sizes supported.

## 7.2 Schedulability and minimal utilization

Algorithm 1 can be extended to find a schedulable cache partitioning with the minimum processor utilization (see Algorithm 2). Schedulability is usually the dominating criterion for hard real-time systems but a reduced processor utilization typically reduces the energy consumption and the response times and thus improves the overal performance of the system.

**Algorithm 2** Optimal Cache Partitioning (Minimal Processor Utilization)

```
float minUtil = 1.1
function CHECKPARTITION(int i, partition P, int s)
    if i = n then
        if not isSchedulable(P) then
            return false
        end if
        if Utilization(P) < minUtil then
            minUtil = Utilization(P)
        end if
        return true
    end if
    let P = (p_1, .., p_n)
    if not isSchedulable((p_1, .., p_{i-1}, s, .., s)) then
        return false
    end if
    if Utilization((p_1, .., p_{i-1}, s, .., s)) ≥ minUtil then
        return false
    end if
    p_i = 0
    bool result = false
    while p_i ≤ s do
        result = checkPartition(i + 1, (p_1, .., p_i, .., p_n), s − p_i) ∨ result
        p_i = nextStep(i, p_i)
    end while
    return result
end function
```

The global variable *minUtil* is initially set to 1.1 to indicate that no schedulable cache partitioning has been found yet. As soon as the algorithm encounters a schedulable partitioning, the utilization is computed and compared to *minUtil* (which is updated if necessary).

Algorithm 2 also differs in the abort conditions. We are no longer allowed to stop the algorithm once we have found a schedulable partitioning (see line 9 in Algorithm 1), as only one of the two optimization criteria has at that point been fulfilled. Instead, we can bound the search when the current value of *minUtil* is less than or equal to the utilization of the cache partitioning where each not yet specified task partition is given the complete remaining size *s* (see line 16). This step is valid as the processor utilization (1) is monotonically non-decreasing in the tasks' execution times. Due to the weaker abort-condition of Algorithm 2, a significantly higher number of cache partitionings must be evaluated when a schedulable partitioning exists. When no such partitioning exists, both algorithm consider exactly the same number of partitionings. We evaluate the difference in the average processor utilization and analysis time for the two algorithms in Sect. 7.3.

## 8. CASE STUDY

In this section, we evaluate the partitioning algorithms based on PapaBench (Nemer et al. 2006), the Mälardalen benchmark suite (Gustafsson et al. 2010) and a set of SCADE4 tasks (partially provided by SCADE, partially from our own SCADE models). Besides the effectiveness of the cache partitioning algorithms, we are interested in (i) the precision of the simplified execution time model, (ii) the runtime performance of the algorithms, and (iii) the difference between the two partitioning algorithms with respect to the minimum utilization obtained.

For the case study, the target architecture is an ARM7 processor (with a 4 kB direct-mapped write-through cache, line size of 16 Bytes, 256 cache sets, block reload time 8 μμs, clock rate of 100 MHz). The execution time bounds were derived using the aiT Timing analyzer (Ferdinand and Heckmann 2004). The values are derived from an example configuration of the ARM7 as used in previous work (see Altmeyer et al. 2011).

Papabench provides two different tasksets (*fbw* and *autopilot*) with deadlines and periods (except for the interrupts I4 to I7) (see Tables 1 and 2). With the initial processor frequency of 100 MHz, both tasksets are schedulable both with and without cache partitioning. The other benchmarks only provide code and do not form a meaningful taskset. We therefore randomly selected tasks from (i) Tables 1 and 2, and (ii) Table 3 and4 (together with execution times, the execution time variations, codes size and UCBs/ECBs).

The remaining task and taskset parameters used in our experiments were randomly generated as follows:

- The default taskset size was 10.
- Task utilizations were generated using the UUnifast (Bini and Buttazzo 2005) algorithm.
- Task periods were set based on the utilization and execution times: Ci=Ui·TiCi=Ui·Ti.
- Task deadlines were implicit,5 i.e., Di=TiDi=Ti.
- For fixed priority scheduling, priorities were assigned in Rate Monotonic priority order.

The tasks are indexed and processed by the partioning algorithms in decreasing priority order.

In each experiment the taskset utilization not including pre-emption cost was varied from 0.025 to 0.975 in steps of 0.025. For each utilization value, 1000 tasksets were generated and the schedulability of those tasksets was determined using the cache partitioning algorithms or pre-emption cost aware analysis with either sequential or optimal task layout (Lunniss et al. 2012). We thus compared the results for cache partitioning against those for (i) no partitioning with a sequential task layout, (ii) no partitioning with an optimized task layout, (iii) analysis ignoring pre-emption costs, but assuming that all the tasks shared the cache; (iv) naive cache partitioning with all tasks allocated the same size partition *S* / *n*; (v) no cache. The sequential task layout reflects the basic un-optimized cache mapping, i.e., where the code for each task is placed consecutively in memory. In case of unconstrained cache usage, we used the combined multiset approaches for fixed-priority (14) and for EDF scheduling (31) to compute the schedulability of the tasksets.

For fixed priority scheduling, we were able to compute the schedulability of all tasksets (42,000 tasksets per case study) in less than 10 min on a 2.6-GHz Quadcore processor—despite the exponential worst-case behaviour of the cache partitioning algorithm (Algorithm 1). For EDF scheduling, the computation for the same configurations took about 60 min. This shows a more than acceptable analysis time for the partitioning algorithm, with a strong dependency on the runtime of the schedulability test that it uses.

## 8.1 PapaBench

Most tasks from Tables 1 and 2 have rather short execution times, leading to relatively high pre-emption costs. These tasks are simple, short control tasks with limited computations and data accesses. Figure 5a and c for fixed priorities and Fig. 6a and c for dynamic priorities show the *success ratio*; the number of tasksets based on Papabench that were schedulable at the various levels of utilization. In the case of instruction caches (Figs. 5b and 6b), optimal partitioning has similar performance to sequential task layout with no partitioning, while optimal task layout with no partitioning results in improved performance. Optimal cache partitioning was only able to improve performance over sequential task layout with no partitioning in a few cases. In the case of data caches(Figs. 5d and 6d), optimal partitioning outperforms optimal task layout with no partitioning. The variation of the execution times in this case is rather low, while the number of UCBs is comparably high. We thus note that the two approaches are *incomparable*. Almost no tasksets were schedulable with no cache, except for the case of data cache with perfect instruction cache as the impact of the data cache alone is limited.

With respect to the scheduling policy, i.e. fixed priority vs. EDF, there was no significant difference in the relative performance of the various approaches. As expected, the schedulability tests for EDF deem consistently more tasksets schedulable (for all approaches) than those for fixed priority scheduling.

**Table 1** Execution times and number of UCBs and ECBs for the PapaBench benchmarks

| | Description | UCBs | ECBs | $WCET^1$ | $WCET^2$ | Period |
|---|---|---|---|---|---|---|
| I4 | Interrupt-modem | 2 | 10 | 303 µs | 520 µs | – |
| I5 | Interrupt-spi-1 | 1 | 10 | 251 µs | 447 µs | – |
| I6 | Interrupt-spi-2 | 1 | 4 | 151 µs | 228 µs | – |
| I7 | Interrupt-gps | 3 | 26 | 283 µs | 493 µs | – |
| T5 | Altitude-control | 20 | 66 | 1478 µs | 1660 µs | 250 ms |
| T6 | Climb-control | 1 | 210 | 5429 µs | 6241 µs | 250 ms |
| T7 | Link-fbw-send | 1 | 10 | 233 µs | 471 µs | 250 ms |
| T8 | Navigation | 1 | 256 | 44, 42 ms | 54, 35 ms | 50 ms |
| T9 | Radio-control | 0 | 256 | 15, 6 ms | 21, 1 ms | 50 ms |
| T10 | Receive-gps-data | 22 | 194 | 5987 µs | 6659 µs | 25 ms |
| T11 | Reporting | 2 | 256 | 12, 22 ms | 5 ms | 100 ms |
| T12 | Stabilization | 11 | 194 | 5681 µs | 6654 µs | 50 ms |

Data cache with perfect instruction cache ($WCET^1$) and without data cache ($WCET^2$)

**Table 2** Execution times and number of UCBs and ECBs for the PapaBench benchmarks

| | Description | UCBs | ECBs | WCET$^1$ | WCET$^2$ | Period |
|---|---|---|---|---|---|---|
| I4 | Interrupt-modem | 3 | 10 | 335 µs | 790 µs | – |
| I5 | Interrupt-spi-1 | 2 | 10 | 287 µs | 644 µs | – |
| I6 | Interrupt-spi-2 | 1 | 4 | 135 µs | 338 µs | – |
| I7 | Interrupt-gps | 3 | 26 | 278 µs | 712 µs | – |
| T5 | Altitude-control | 2 | 66 | 654 µs | 3860 µs | 250 ms |
| T6 | Climb-control | 5 | 210 | 2375 µs | 14, 21 µs | 250 ms |
| T7 | Link-fbw-send | 2 | 10 | 298 µs | 634 µs | 250 ms |
| T8 | Navigation | 10 | 256 | 23, 38 ms | 138 ms | 50 ms |
| T9 | Radio-control | 14 | 256 | 10, 2 ms | 51 ms | 50 ms |
| T10 | Receive-gps-data | 4 | 194 | 3058 µs | 20, 5 ms s | 25 ms |
| T11 | Reporting | 6 | 242 | 12, 8 ms | 32 ms | 100 ms |
| T12 | Stabilization | 6 | 194 | 2711 µs | 16, 1 ms s | 50 ms |

Data cache with perfect instruction cache ($WCET^1$) and without instruction cache ($WCET^2$)

**Table 3** Mälardalen benchmark suite (M) and SCADE benchmarks (S)

| | Description | UCBs | ECBs | $WCET^1$ | $WCET^2$ |
|---|---|---|---|---|---|
| M | Adpcm | 24 | 226 | 5541 s | 6521 s |
| M | Compress | 25 | 114 | 3664 s | 8426 s |
| M | Edn | 56 | 98 | 244, 8 ms | 458, 2 ms |
| M | Fir | 28 | 50 | 21, 52 ms | 497 ms |
| M | Jfdctinit | 40 | 162 | 13, 89 ms | 32, 98 ms |
| M | Ns | 17 | 26 | 73, 38 ms | 168 ms |
| M | Nsichneu | 53 | 256 | 77, 96 ms | 163 ms |
| M | Statemate | 3 | 256 | 9757 s | 20, 07 s |
| S | Cruise control system | 25 | 107 | 1959 s | 3548 s |
| S | Flight control system | 70 | 256 | 2138 s | 4083 s |
| S | Navigation system | 45 | 82 | 1409 s | 3712 s |
| S | Stopwatch | 58 | 130 | 3786 s | 5533 s |
| S | Elevator simulation | 40 | 114 | 1586 s | 2917 s |
| S | Robotics systems | 68 | 256 | 4311 s | 6377 s |

Data cache with perfect instruction cache ($WCET^1$) and without data cache ($WCET^2$)

## 8.2 Mälardalen and SCADE benchmarks

In contrast to the first case study, the execution times of the tasks from Tables 3 and 4 for the Mälardalen and SCADE Benchmarks are comparably high, and thus the pre-emption costs relatively low. These tasks exhibit a low locality of memory accesses but high amounts of computation. In this case, the low cache related pre-emption delays result in significantly better performance if the cache is not partitioned. Here, cache partitioning was unable to improve performance over the simple sequence task layout with no partitioning, as illustrated in Figs. 7a and 8a. Note that in this case there are no major differences for data and instruction caches, the results of the different approaches are just more (instruction caches) or less (data caches) accentuated.

## 8.3 Utilization versus analysis time

The first cache partitioning algorithm (Algorithm 1) only optimizes for schedulability and ignores the processor utilization. In this section, we evaluate the consequences of this simplified optimization: how much further can the processor utilization be reduced and what is the analysis time needed to compute a schedulable partitioning with minimum utilization. To this end, we compare the results and analysis times of both algorithms presented in Sect. 6, i.e. with and without optimizing minimum processor utilization as a secondary concern.

The results of this comparison are shown in Figs. 9 and 10 for the PapaBench benchmark suite and in Figs. 11 and 12 for the Mälardalen benchmark suite. Subfigures (a) show the average percentage increase in processor utilization (i.e. with the execution time overhead due to cache partitioning) of schedulable tasksets with respect to the nominal utilization (i.e. without execution time overhead due to cache partitioning). Subfigures (b) show the analysis time for all 1000 tasksets generated per utilization level. The blue line representes the optimal cache paritioning algorithm without optimized utilization (Algorithm 1) and the pink line with optimized utilization (Algorithm 2). We have omitted the results for data cache with perfect instruction cache as they resemble the results for instruction cache with perfect data cache, with a less significant difference.

**Table 4** Mälardalen benchmark suite (M) and SCADE benchmarks (S)

| | Description | UCBs | ECBs | WCET[1] | WCET[2] |
|---|---|---|---|---|---|
| M | Adpcm | 7 | 242 | 5856 s | 43, 17 s |
| M | Compress | 6 | 242 | 9740 s | 25, 26 s |
| M | Edn | 5 | 98 | 518, 9 ms | 1422 s |
| M | Fir | 5 | 50 | 42, 65 ms | 121 ms |
| M | Jfdctinit | 8 | 242 | 23, 2 ms | 73, 63 ms |
| M | Ns | 3 | 26 | 133, 7 ms | 466, 9 ms |
| M | Nsichneu | 8 | 242 | 66, 74 ms | 178, 3 ms |
| M | Statemate | 30 | 242 | 8143 s | 22, 45 s |
| S | Cruise control system | 15 | 98 | 1, 77 s | 6207 s |
| S | Flight control system | 12 | 242 | 3, 24 s | 11, 02 s |
| S | Navigation system | 3 | 82 | 2, 96 s | 7566 s |
| S | Stopwatch | 9 | 130 | 4417 s | 25, 03s |
| S | Elevator simulation | 4 | 114 | 1863 s | 5432 s |
| S | Robotics systems | 5 | 242 | 3427 s | 22, 45 s |

Data cache with perfect instruction cache ($WCET^1$) and without instruction cache ($WCET^2$)

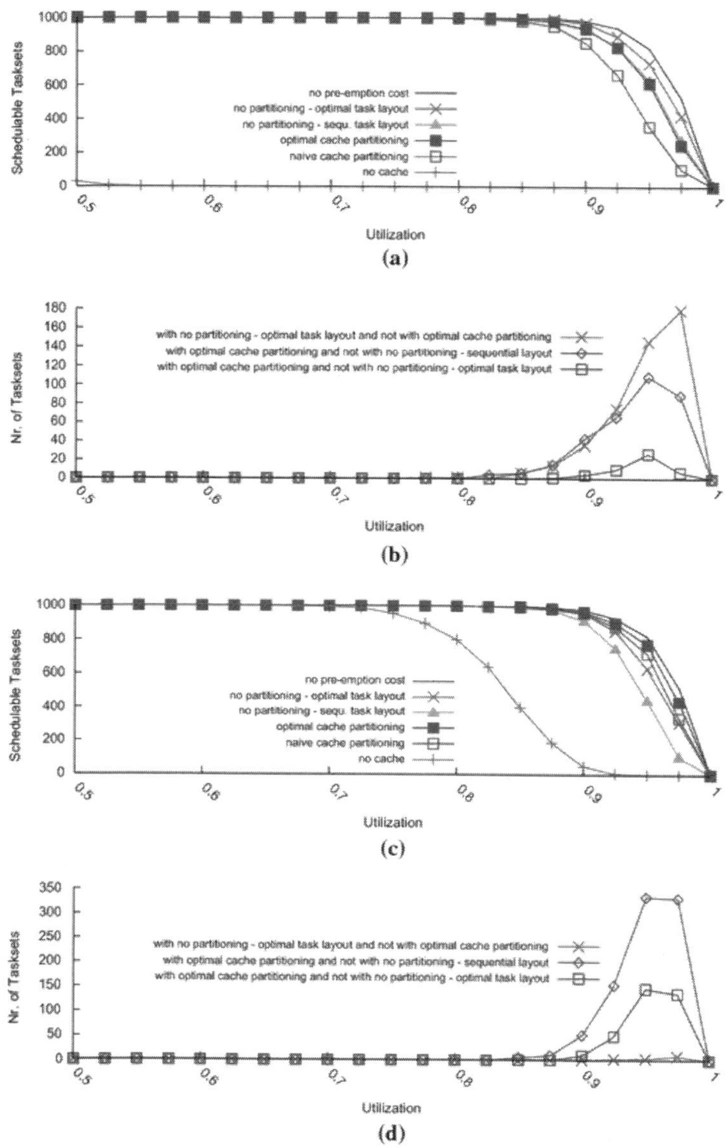


**Figure. 5** Evaluation of PapaBench benchmarks (fixed priority scheduling). **a** Number of tasksets deemed schedulable at the different total utilizations (instruction cache with perfect data cache), **b** number of tasksets deemed schedulable with one approach and not another (instruction cache with perfect data cache), **c** number of tasksets deemed schedulable at the different total utilizations (data cache with perfect instruction cache), **d**number of tasksets deemed schedulable with one approach and not another (data cache with perfect instruction cache)

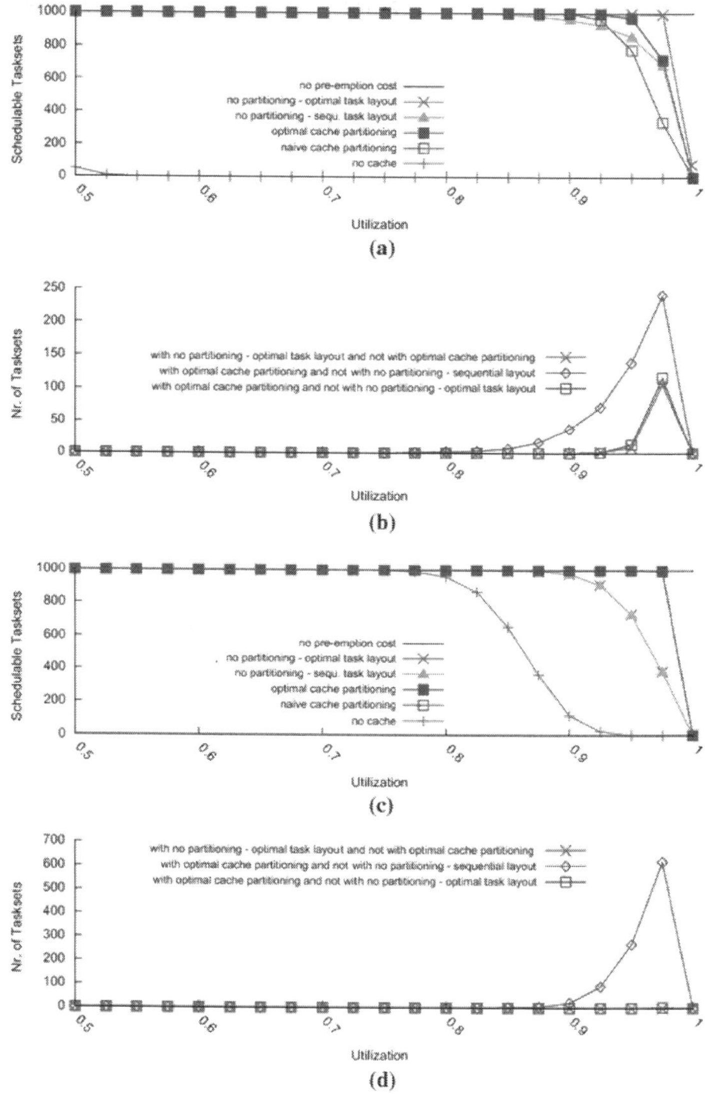


**Figure. 6** Evaluation of PapaBench benchmarks (EDF scheduling). **a** Number of tasksets deemed schedulable at the different total utilizations (instruction cache with perfect data cache), **b** number of tasksets deemed schedulable with one approach and not another (instruction cache with perfect data cache), **c** number of tasksets deemed schedulable at the different total utilizations (data cache with perfect instruction cache), **d**number of tasksets deemed schedulable with one approach and not another (data cache with perfect instruction cache)

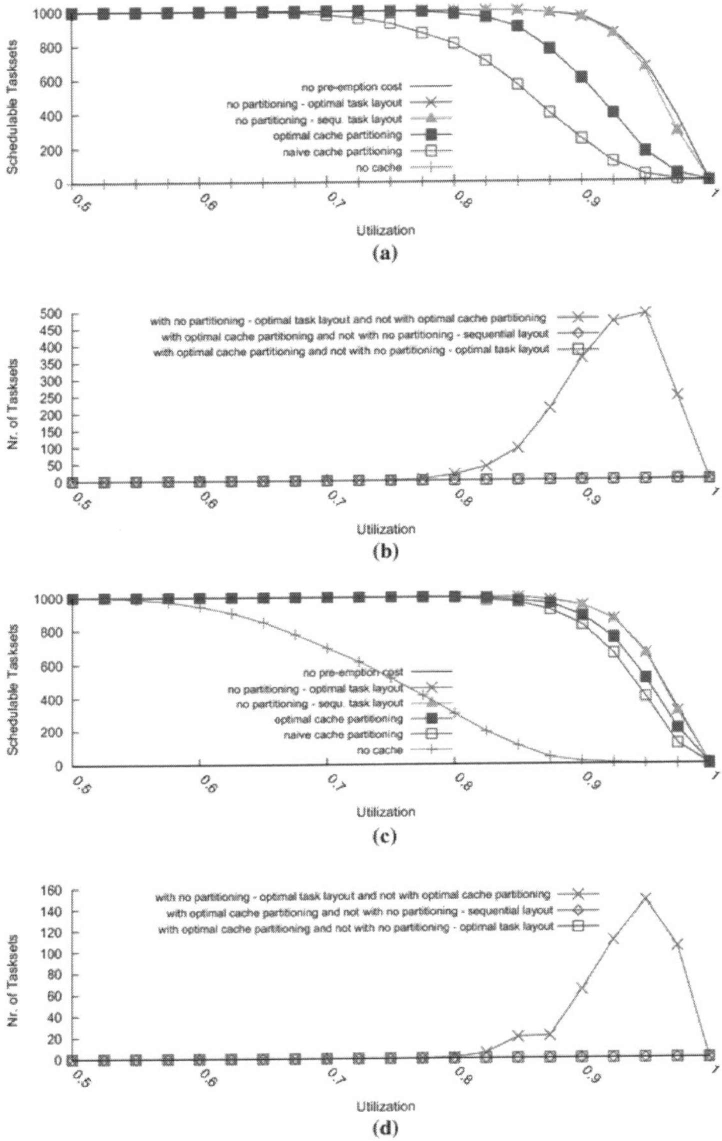


**Figure. 7** Evaluation of Mälardalen benchmarks (fixed priority scheduling). **a** Number of tasksets deemed schedulable at the different total utilizations (instruction cache with perfect data cache), **b** number of tasksets deemed schedulable with one approach and not another (instruction cache with perfect data cache), **c** number of tasksets deemed schedulable at the different total utilizations (data cache with perfect instruction cache), **d**number of tasksets deemed schedulable with one approach and not another (data cache with perfect instruction cache)

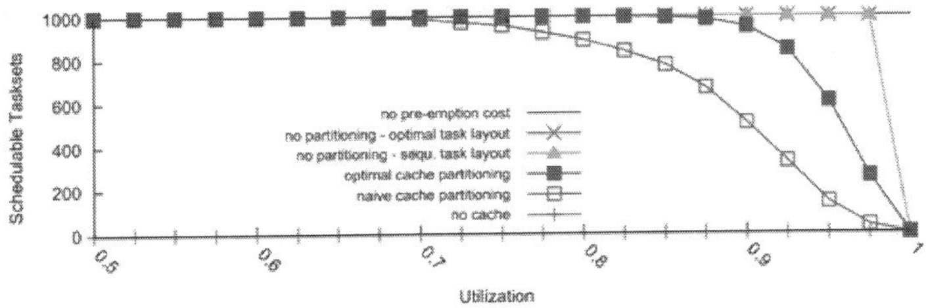


(a)

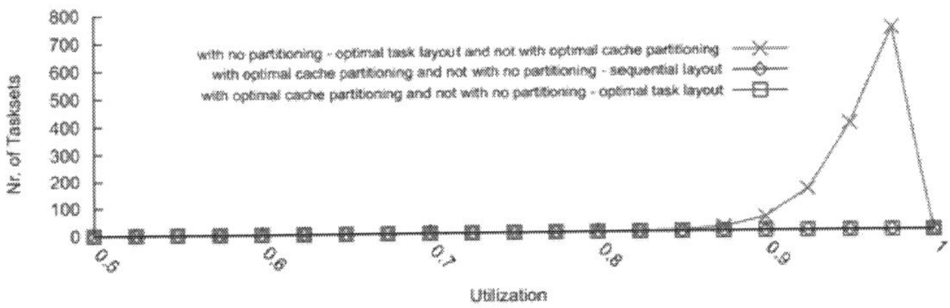


(b)

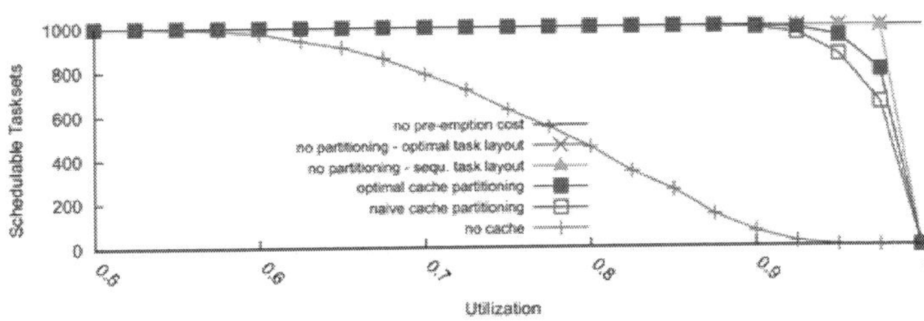


(c)

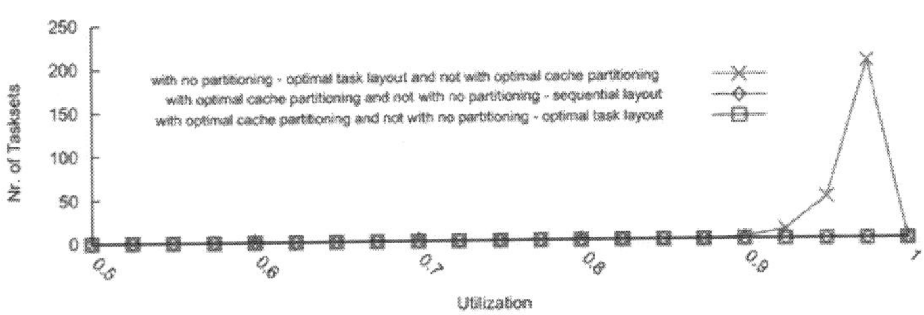


(d)

**Figure. 8** Evaluation of Mälardalen benchmarks (EDF scheduling). **a** Number of tasksets deemed schedulable at the different total utilizations (instruction cache with perfect data cache), **b** number of tasksets deemed schedulable with one approach and not another (instruction cache with perfect data cache), **c** number of tasksets deemed schedulable at the different total utilizations (data cache with perfect instruction cache), **d**number of tasksets deemed schedulable with one approach and not another (data cache with perfect instruction cache)

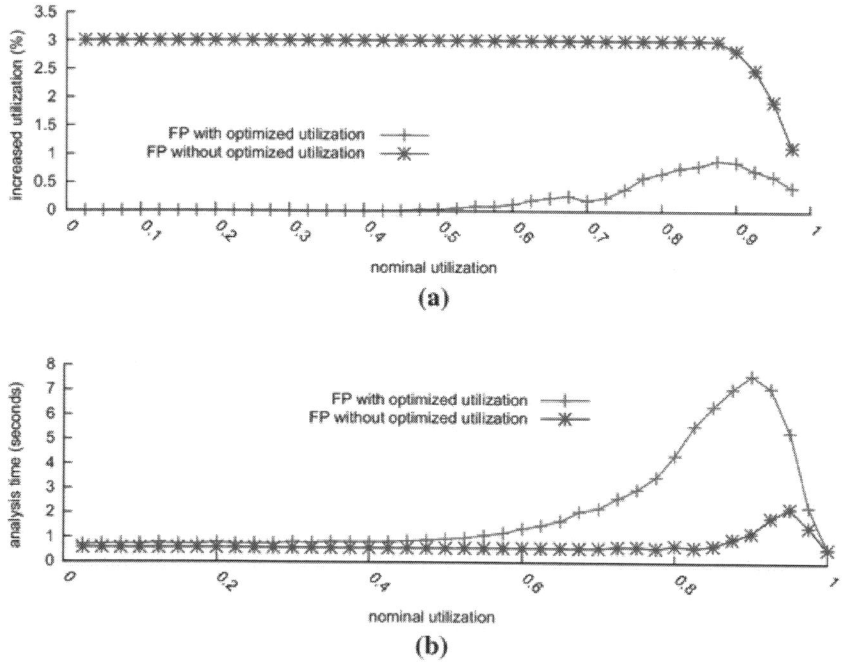


**Figure. 9** Evaluation of the average utilization PapaBench benchmarks (fixed priority scheduling, instruction cache with perfect data cache). **a** Average utilization of schedulable tasksets per nominal utilization, **b** total analysis time for 1000 tasksets

The minimum utilization of a schedulable cache partitioning is at most 1%1% above the nominal utilization. The average difference of the results of the two algorithms is also limited. Mälardalen benchmarks with instruction cache/perfect data cache—irrespective of the priority assignment—exhibits the largest relative difference in utilization of around 7%7% at a utilization level of 0.8, (i.e. an absolute difference in utilization of less than 0.056). In the case of data caches with perfect instruction cache, the difference is always below 2%2%.

In contrast to the processor utilization, the difference in the total analysis time is noticable in all cases, especially if the nominal processor utilization is above 0.8. This indicates that the algorithm to optimize the processor utilization requires a significant amount of time to either find an improved cache partitioning or to show the optimality of the current candidate. We conclude that a small but nevertheless useful improvement in utilization can be obtained using Algorithm 2; however, that this comes at a cost in terms of increased runtime of the analysis.

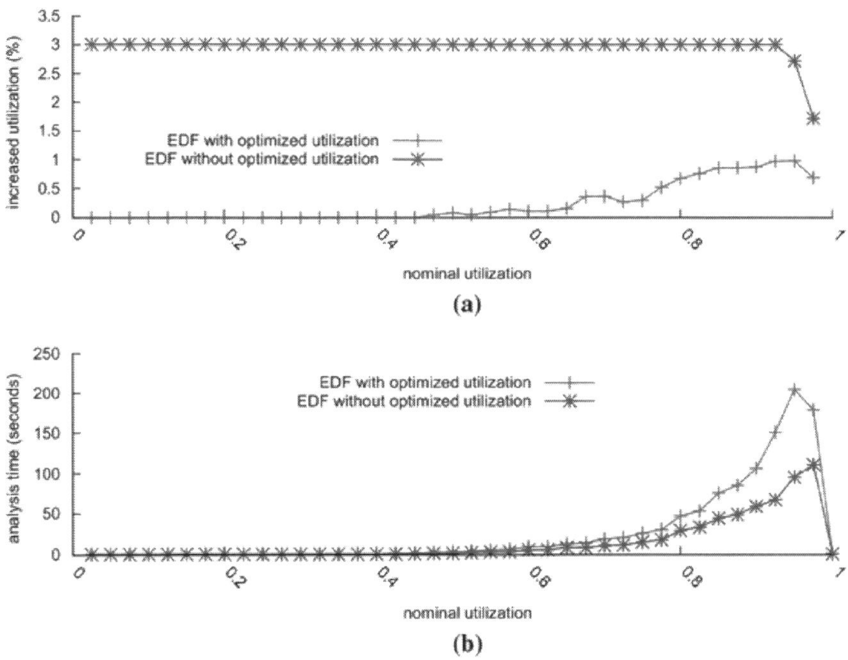


**Figure. 10** Evaluation of the average utilization PapaBench benchmarks (EDF scheduling, instruction cache with perfect data cache). **a** Average utilization of schedulable tasksets per nominal utilization, **b** total analysis time for 1000 tasksets

We note that the average increase in utilization which occurs using Algorithm 1 is similar for both fixed priority and EDF scheduling with the only difference beeing that the increase drops at a lower nominal utilization for fixed-priority scheduling (0.8) than for EDF scheduling (0.85). This is because EDF has a schedulable utilization bound of 1 (much higher than that for fixed priority scheduling), thus a careful tuning of the partition size to achieve a schedulable partitioning is only required at higher nominal utilizations. The reduced difference in the nominal utilization also coincides in both cases (fixed-priority and EDF) with an increase in the analysis time of Algorithm 1.

Note, as both algorithms behave similar in case no schedulable cache partitioning exists, the differences in the analysis time are only due to the optimization of *schedulable* partitionings.

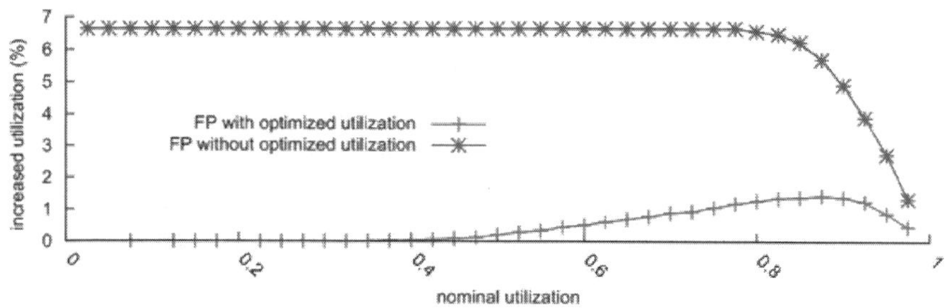


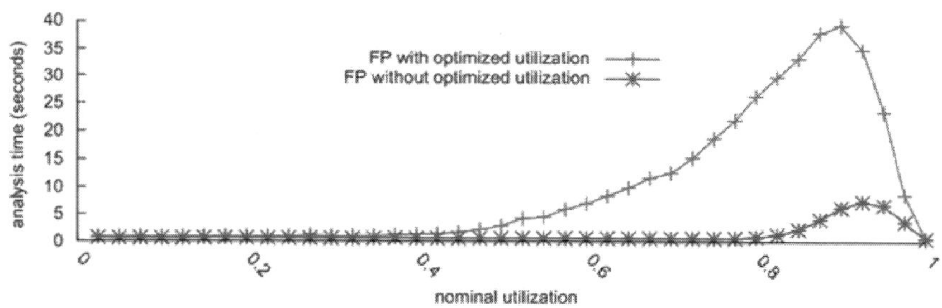


**Figure. 11** Evaluation of the average utilization of Mälardalen benchmarks (fixed priority scheduling, instruction cache with perfect data cache). **a** Average utilization of schedulable tasksets per nominal utilization, **b** total analysis time for 1000 tasksets

# 9. SYNTHETIC TASKSETS

We also evaluated the effectiveness of cache partitioning on a large number of synthetic tasksets with varying cache configurations and varying task parameters. Our aim here was to identify those parameters that have a significant influence on the relative effectiveness of cache partitioning versus a non-partitioned cache. The evaluation using randomly generated tasksets enables us to fully control all relevant parameters, which is not possible using the benchmark tasks directly.

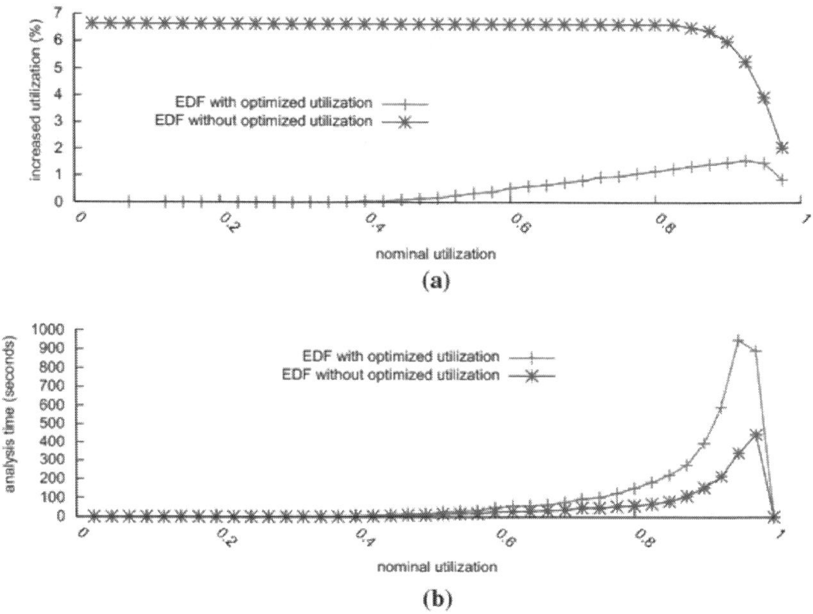


**Figure. 12** Evaluation of the average utilization of Mälardalen benchmarks (EDF scheduling, instruction cache with perfect data cache). **a** Average utilization of schedulable tasksets per nominal utilization, **b** total analysis time for 1000 tasksets

The task parameters used in our experiments were randomly generated as follows:

- The default taskset size was 10.
- Task utilizations were generated using the UUnifast (Bini and Buttazzo 2005) algorithm.
- Task periods were generated according to a log-uniform distribution with a factor of 1000 difference between the minimum and maximum possible task period and a minimum period of 5 ms. This represents a spread of task periods from 5 ms to 5 s, thus providing reasonable correspondence with real systems.
- Task execution times were set based on the utilization and period selected: $C_i=U_i \cdot T_iC_i=U_i \cdot T_i$.

- Task deadlines were implicit
- For fixed priority scheduling, priorities were assigned in Deadline Monotonic priority order.

To model the variation in the execution time, we randomly selected one of the execution time functions from our benchmarks (see Tables 1 and 3 and Figs. 1 and 2). Note that this only affects the variation of the execution time for different partition-sizes and CiCi refers to the base execution time when τiτi can use the complete cache. The tasks are indexed and processed by the partioning algorithms in decreasing priority order.

The following parameters affecting pre-emption costs were also varied, with default values given in parentheses:

- The number of cache-sets (CS=256CS=256).
- The block-reload time (BRT=8μBRT=8μs)
- The cache usage of each task, and thus, the number of ECBs, were generated using the UUnifast (Bini and Buttazzo 2005) algorithm (for a total cache utilization CU=∑i|ECB|/CS=4CU=∑i|ECB|/CS=4). UUnifast may produce values larger than 1 which means a task fills the whole cache.
- For each task, the UCBs were generated according to a uniform distribution ranging from 0 to the number of ECBs times a reuse factor: [0,RF·|ECB|][0,RF·|ECB|]. The factor *RF* was used to adapt the assumed reuse of cache-sets to account for different types of real-time applications, for example, from data processing applications with little reuse up to control-based applications with heavy reuse (default RF=0.3RF=0.3).

The parameters of the base configuration were chosen according to the actual values observed in the case studies of the PapaBench benchmarks 7.1 and the Mälardalen benchmarks 7.2. The results (Figs. 13and 14) lie between those of the case studies (Figs. 5a and 7a for fixed priority scheduling, and Figs. 6a and 8a for EDF scheduling respectively).

Overall, cache partitioning and pre-emption cost analysis with a sequential, un-optimized task layout have similar performance; however, we note that there are also a large number of tasksets that can only be scheduled with one of the two approaches, but not with the other. This shows that cache partitioning is a viable alternative in some scenarios and detrimental in others. However, we also observe that the optimal task layout with no partitioning has a clear advantage over optimal partitioning in terms of the number of schedulable tasksets (see Figs. 13b and 14b).

The choice of scheduling policy has a limited influence on the relative performance of the various approaches. Under EDF cache partitioning showed improved performance relative to no partitioning and a sequential task layout, most likely due to the higher imprecision in the cache-aware schedulability test for EDF.

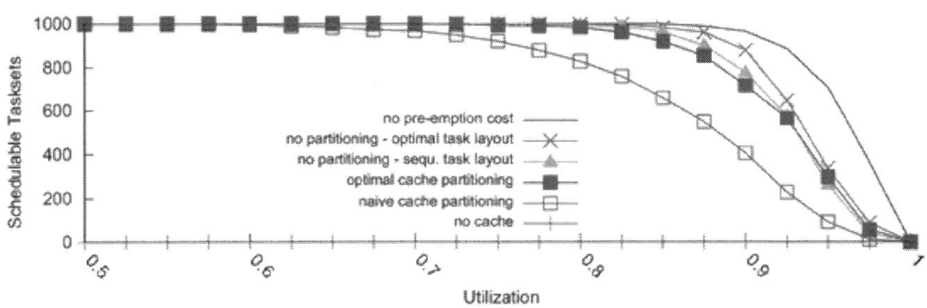


(a)

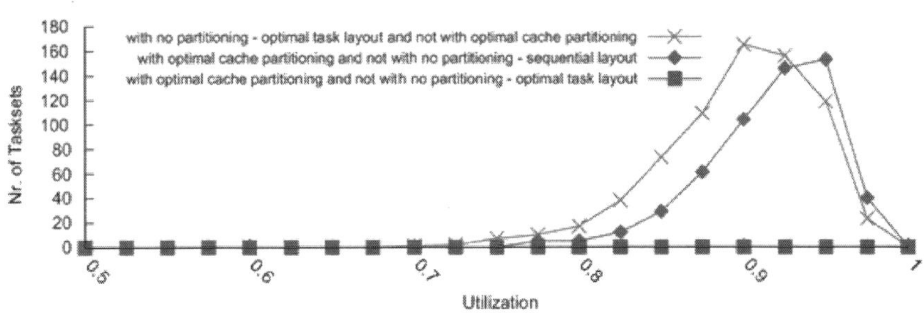


(b)

**Figure. 13** Evaluation for the base configuration, fixed priority scheduling. **a** Number of tasksets deemed schedulable at the different total utilizations, **b** number of tasksets deemed schedulable with one approach and not another

Exhaustive evaluation of all combinations of cache and taskset configuration parameters is not possible. We therefore fixed all parameters except one and varied the remaining parameter in order to see how performance depends on this value. The parameters we examined were: (i) the pre-emption cost as determined by the block reload time (BRT) and a scaling factor applied to task periods; (ii) the cache utilization, (iii) the number of tasks, and (iv) the cache size.

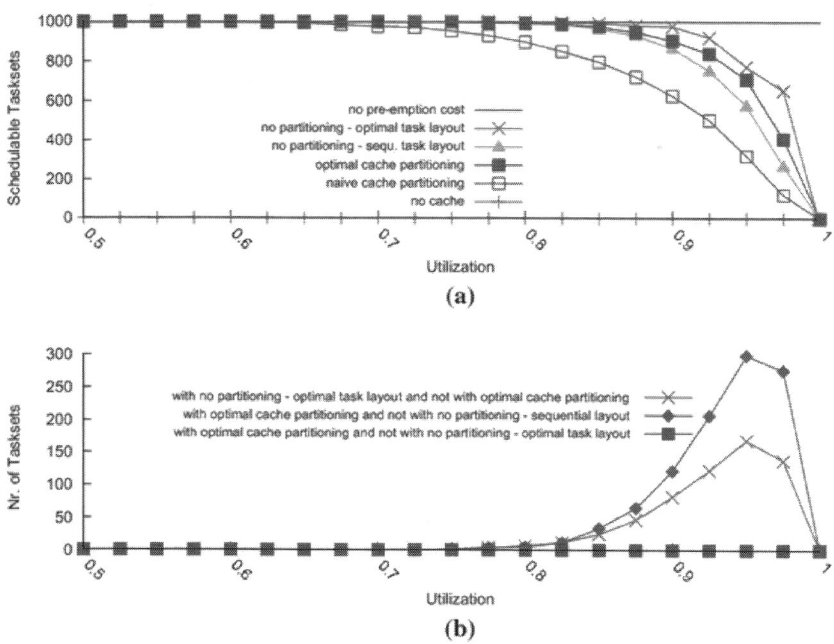


**Figure. 14** Evaluation of the base configuration, EDF scheduling. **a** Number of tasksets deemed schedulable at the different total utilizations, **b** number of tasksets deemed schedulable with one approach and not another

The graphs show the weighted schedulability measure $W_y(q)$ (Bastoni et al. 2010) for schedulability test *y*as a function of parameter *q*. For each value of *q*, this measure combines data for all of the tasksets ττgenerated for all of a set of equally spaced utilization levels. Let $S_y(\tau,q)$ be the binary result (1 or 0) of schedulability test *y* for a taskset τ and parameter value *q* then:

$$W_y(q) = \left(\sum_{\forall\tau} u(\tau) \cdot S_y(\tau, q)\right) / \sum_{\forall\tau} u(\tau) \quad (33)$$

where u(τ) is the utilization of taskset ττ. This weighted schedulability measure reduces what would otherwise be a 3-dimensional plot to 2 dimensions (Bastoni et al. 2010). Weighting the individual schedulability results by taskset utilization reflects the higher value placed on being able to schedule higher utilization tasksets.

## 9.1 Pre-emption costs

Pre-emption costs are determined by several parameters. Among those, the dominant factors are the block reload time (BRTBRT) and the range of task execution times. Figure 15 shows the weighted schedulability measure for different block reload times. In our setting, the break-even point is at a block reload time of about 10μs10μs. For larger block reload times cache partitioning becomes the more effective approach, while for smaller block reload times a non-partitioned cache is more effective.

In Fig. 16, we varied the scaling factor *w* from 0.5 to 10 and hence the range of task periods given by*w*[1, 100]ms. Given that the block reload time is constant in this experiment, the ratio of pre-emption costs to taskset utilization decreases as the task periods, deadlines and execution times are all scaled up. A lower scaling factor resembles tasks with shorter execution times (as in Tables 1 and 2), a higher scaling factor resembles tasks with higher execution times and commensurately longer periods (as in Tables 3 and 4).

The results indicate that cache partitioning is useful for control-oriented tasks with short execution times and very short periods and thus relatively high pre-emption costs compared to their WCET. When the pre-emption costs are low compared to the WCET, cache partitioning typically does not pay off.

Note that increasing the block reload time typically also leads to increased (non-pre-emptive) execution times. In these experiments, we have fixed the execution times to vary only the relation between pre-emption costs and execution time bounds.

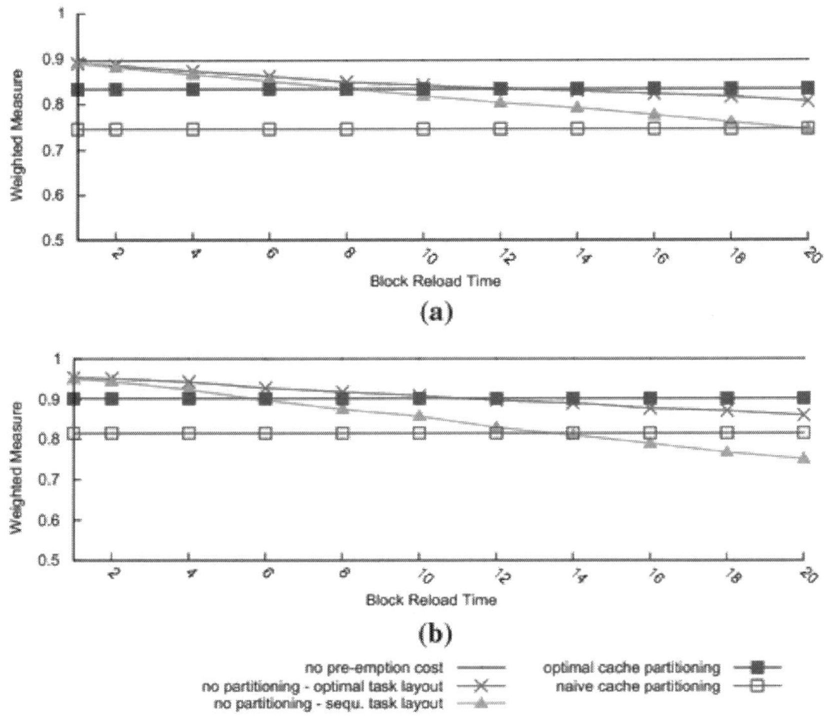


**Figure. 15** Weighted schedulability measure; varying block reload time from 1 to 20 μμs (assuming constant worst-case execution times). **a** Fixed priority scheduling, **b** EDF scheduling

The impact of the scheduling policy, i.e. fixed priority vs. EDF, on the relative performance of the various approaches remains limited.

## 9.2 Cache utilization

The cache utilization determines the ratio between the total code size of all the tasks and the overall cache size. Increasing the cache utilization leads to higher pre-emption costs, and higher execution times in the case of cache partitioning. Cache partitioning; however, suffers less from increased cache utilization as can be seen in Fig. 17a.

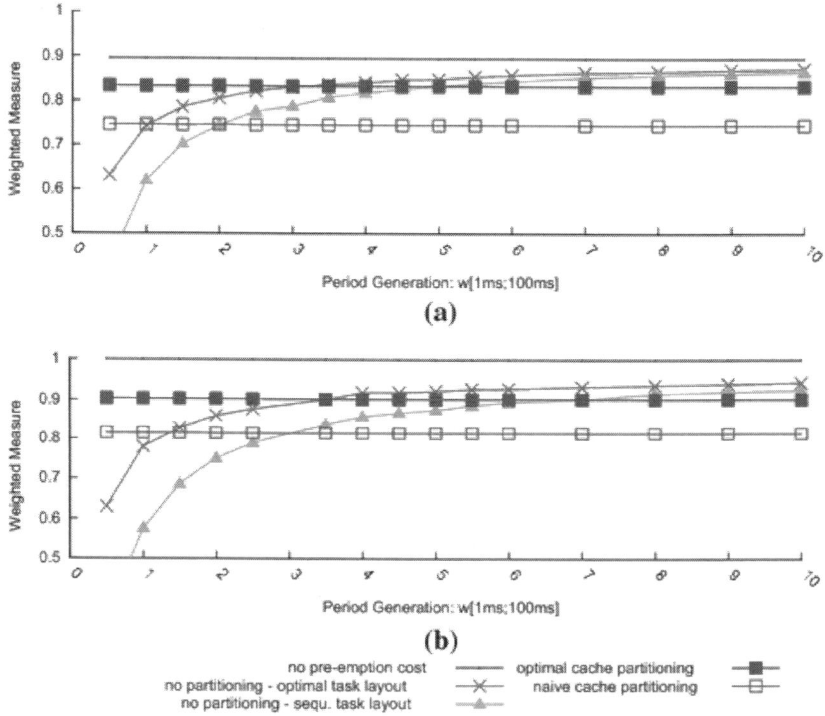


**Figure. 16** Weighted schedulability measure; varying the scale of task periods *w*[1, 100] from w=0.5w=0.5 to w=10w=10. **a**Fixed priority scheduling, **b** EDF scheduling

The results for the non-partitioned system suffer somewhat from the over-approximation of the UCB/ECB analysis and the pre-emption cost aware response time analysis: This assumes additional cache misses due to pre-emption even though the misses have already been accounted for by a prior pre-emption, providing more pessimistic results at high cache utilization levels.

## 9.3 Number of tasks

We also conducted experiments varying the number of tasks. Note that it is an unrealistic assumption to change the number of tasks without also changing the cache utilization. This would mean the cache usage of each individual task decreasing as more tasks are added to the system. Realistically, cache utilization increases with the number of tasks. Figure 18a shows the results of the evaluation if we increase the number of tasks and the cache utilization, while keeping the per task cache utilization constant.

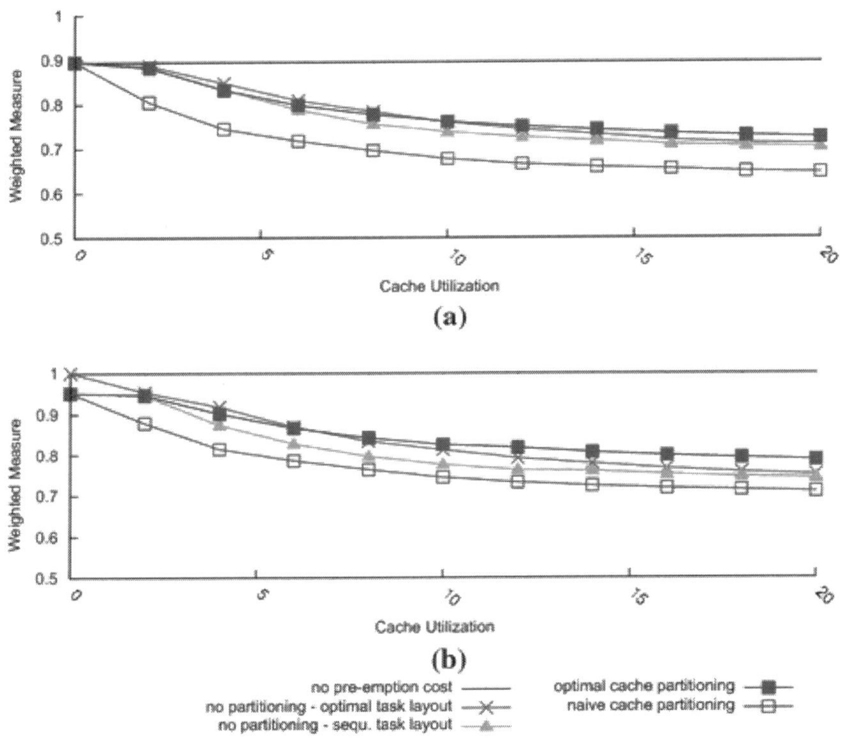


**Figure. 17** Weighted schedulability measure; varying cache utilization from 0 to 20. **a** Fixed priority scheduling, **b** EDF scheduling

Here, we see that the performance of the non-partitioned approach gradually degrades with increasing taskset size due to pessimism in the analysis of a large number of pre-emption levels. We also notice a quicker decline in the case of EDF compared to fixed priority scheduling. This validates our assumption that the relative difference is due to a larger imprecision in the cache-aware schedulability test for EDF.

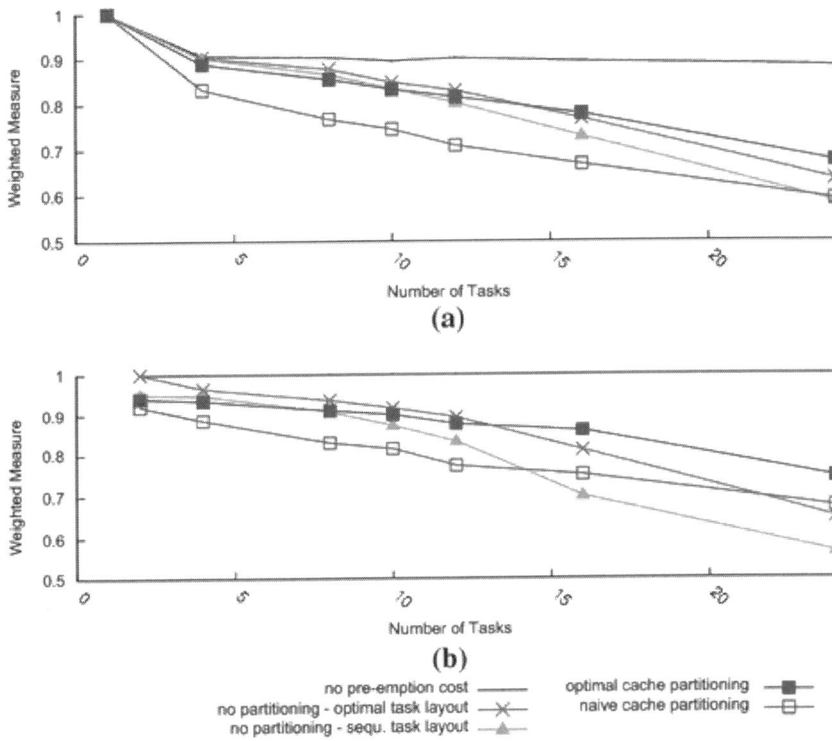


**Figure. 18** Weighted schedulability measure; varying the number of tasks from 2 to 24 with constant ratio of number of tasks to cache usage. **a** Fixed priority scheduling, **b** EDF scheduling

## 9.4 Cache size

If we only adapt the cache size without changing the relation between the execution time and the pre-emption costs (or the cache utilization), we would penalise the pre-emption cost computation: if there are more cache sets, there are also more UCBs and thus, higher pre-emption costs. The results of the cache partitioning, though, does not change. To avoid this discrimination, we have increased the number of sets, while keeping the relation of cache utilization to cache size (*CU* / *CS*) constant. The results are shown in Fig. 19a. For small cache, the partition sizes are very small which leads to high execution times and thus low schedulability for the paritioning approaches. For larger caches, the performance of partitioned and non-partitioned systems converge as the cache utilization decreases.

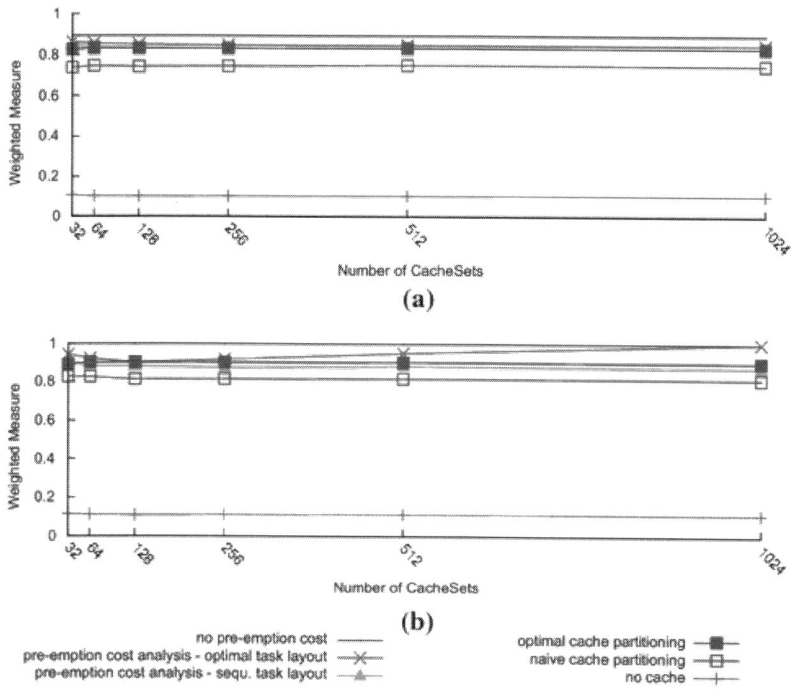


**Figure. 19** Weighted schedulability measure; varying the number of cache sets 64 to 1024 with constant ratio (*CU / CS*). **a** Fixed priority scheduling, **b** EDF scheduling

We note that small caches also lead to a reduced pre-emption overhead as the number of UCBs is upper bounded by the number of sets: The delay of additional cache reloads that would otherwise contribute to the pre-emption overhead is included in the non-pre-emptive execution time bound. The performance of the non-partitioned approaches thus declines from 32 to 128 sets (where the pre-emption overhead is maximal) as we use the task utilization (without pre-emption costs) as the baseline for each experiment.

## 9.5 Precision of the simplified execution-time model

To evaluate the precision of the simplified execution time model, and so obtain a measure of the pessimism introduced in order to obtain monotonicity of execution times, we computed for each taskset an optimal cache partitioning (using Algorithm 1) (i) assuming upper bounds (Fig. 3 blue upper line) and (ii) optimistic lower bounds on the execution times (Fig. 3 red lower line). The difference in the results—the number of tasksets that were deemed schedulable using the lower but not the upper bounds—provides a measure of the imprecision of the simplified execution time model. In the first case study (PapaBench) 0.21%0.21% of all tasksets were deemed schedulable only using lower bounds, and 1.21%1.21% (Mälardalen and SCADE) for the second case study. Note that these percentages refer to the uncertainty due to the assumed monotonicity and not due to the cache partitioning algorithm. Also note that this does not necessarily mean that 0.21%0.21%, resp. 1.21%1.21%, of the tasksets have been falsely deemed not schedulable, rather these are upper bounds on the imprecision.

# 10. CONCLUSIONS AND FUTURE WORK

In this paper, we evaluated the relative performance, in terms of taskset schedulability, of partitioning the cache on a per task basis versus allowing all tasks to share the entire cache. Our research contrasts with previous work in this area, in that we used system schedulability as the performance metric, effective techniques for analysis of cache related pre-emption delays, and code from real benchmarks as the foundation of our empirical evaluation.

The main contributions of this paper are as follow:

- Sensitivity analysis of WCET with respect to partition size, showing how the precise WCET bound as a function of the size of the partition can be effectively upper and lower bounded by monotonic functions.

- Sensitivity analysis of the schedulability of groups of tasks with respect to the size of a shared partition, showing that the precise schedulability of the task group is sustainable with respect to the size of the partition whereas the schedulability tests are not sustainable.

- The introduction of optimal algorithm for cache partitioning which finds a schedulable partioning whenever such a partitioning exists. This algorithm makes use of the monotonic WCET functions.

- The introduction of an optimal algorithm for cache partitioning which finds a schedulable partitioning with the minimum processor utilisation whenever a schedulable partitioning exists. This algorithm also makes use of the monotonic WCET functions.

- A thorough evaluation of the relative performance of optimal per task cache partitioning versus no partitioning for static and dynamic priority assignment.

- An evaluation of the trade-off of mininal processor utilization against increased analysis time.

Our results showed that for simple, short control tasks such as those from Papabench, where the pre-emption costs are relatively high compared to the WCET, the performance of partitioned and non-partitioned approaches were similar, with the use of an optimal task layout providing the non-partitioned approach with a small performance advantage. By contrast, tasks from the Mälardalen benchmark suite exhibited lower locality of memory accesses and higher amounts of computation, with larger WCETs compared to the associated cache related pre-emption delays. For tasksets based on this benchmark, the non-partitioned approach (with and without cache layout optimization) outperformed optimal partitioning. These results indicate that in most cases, the increased predictability of a partitioned cache, in terms of eliminating cache related pre-emption delays, does not compensate for the performance degradation in the WCETs.

Our extended evaluation using synthetic benchmark tasksets showed that the key parameters affecting the relative effectiveness of cache partitioning versus no partitioning are: (i) The ratio of pre-emption costs to the overall WCET (partitioning does not pay off when this ratio is small). (ii) The Block Reload Time (partitioning is most effective when the BRT is large increasing pre-emption costs). (iii) Cache utilization (the non-partitioned approach suffers from pessimism at high values of cache utilization). (iv) The number of tasks (with no partitioning the analysis suffers from increasing pessimism in the computation of pre-emption costs as the number of tasks increases). Further, we found that the relative performance of the two approaches was largely unaffected by the number of cache sets. The scheduling policy had a comparably limited impact on the overall results; however, the increased pessimism of the cache-aware schedulability analysis for EDF slightly improved the relative performance of cache partitioning in this case.

Cache partitioning often increases the utilization of the tasksets by allocating each task a partition which is less than the size of the cache, thus inflating the WCET. We found that Algorithm 2 which minimizes utilization as a secondary criterion makes small but useful gains in the average taskset utilization obtained over Algorithm 1 which only optimizes for the primary criteria of schedulability. These gains, however, come at a cost in terms of an increased runtime for the analysis. For high utilization tasksets, the differences in the utilization obtained is small, since few partitionings are schedulable and both algorithms tend towards producing very similar results.

Our evaluation shows that static cache and CRPD analyses are sufficiently precise to justify unconstrained cache usage; Cache partitioning to increase predictability is often not required but instead is detrimental to the provable system performance. Spatial isolation which reduces the certification costs and enables the integration of independently developed system components remains a strong point in favour of cache partitioning.

This paper compares two extremes, either all of the tasks share the entire cache, or every task has an individual cache partition. It is clear that between these two extremes, there is an approach which subsumes and dominates both. This intermediate approach involves allocating groups of tasks to appropriately sized cache partitions, and then controlling the layout of those tasks in memory (Lunniss et al. 2012) to enhance schedulability through a reduction in cache related pre-emption delays within each partition.

The intermediate approach in between cache partitioning and unconstrained cache usage is also fundamental for spatial isolation. Isolation is typically required between groups of tasks constituting a system component, and not in between individual tasks. The CRPD analysis has recently been extended to hierarchical scheduling to implement temporal isolation (Lunniss et al. 2014, 2015), but the integration with cache partitioning, and in particular the optimization of the cache partitioning in this context, to achieve full temporal and spatial isolation is future work.

Recent work by Wang et al. (2015) investigates an alternative intermediate approach where groups of tasks share a partition and also a preemption threshold (Wang and Saksena 1999; Saksena and Wang 2000), hence ensuring that tasks using the same partition cannot preempt each other, thus avoiding CRPD. (Analysis of CRPD has also been integrated into fixed priority scheduling with preemption thresholds assuming that the cache is shared Bril et al. 2014).

Our analysis and evaluation is restricted to a single level of cache. This restriction was necessary to single out the effect of cache partitioning and unconstrained cache usage and to reduce noise due to interferences from other parts of the cache hierarchy. Broadening the view to several cache levels, a combination of the predictability of cache partitioning on one cache level with the performance of unconstrained cache usage on another one is likely to provide optimal performance.

## FOOTNOTES

1 The concept of UCBs and ECBs cannot be applied to FIFO or PLRU replacement policies as shown by Burguière et al. (2009)

2 http://www.ti.com/product/omap-l138.

3 http://www.arm.com/products/processors/classic/arm7.

4 Esterel SCADE http://www.esterel-technologies.com/.

5 Evaluation for constrained deadlines, i.e., Di∈[2Ci;TI]Di∈[2Ci;TI] gave broadly similar results although fewer tasksets were deemed schedulable.

## REFERENCES

1. Altmeyer S, Burguière C (2009) A new notion of useful cache block to improve the bounds of cache-related preemption delay. In: ECRTS, pp 109–118

2. Altmeyer S, Maiza C, Reineke J (2010) Resilience analysis: tightening the crpd bound for set-associative caches. In: LCTES, pp 153–162

3. Altmeyer S, Davis RI, Maiza C (2011) Cache related pre-emption aware response time analysis for fixed priority pre-emptive systems. In: RTSS, pp 261–271

4. Altmeyer S, Davis RI, Maiza C (2012) Improved cache related pre-emption delay aware response time analysis for fixed priority pre-emptive systems. Real-Time Syst 48(5):499–526MATHCrossRef

5. Altmeyer S, Douma R, Lunniss W, Davis RI (2014) Evaluation of cache partitioning for hard real-time systems. In: ECRTS, pp 15–26

6. Audsley N, Burns A, Richardson M, Tindell K, Wellings AJ (1993) Applying new scheduling theory to static priority pre-emptive scheduling. Softw Eng J 8:284–292

7. Baruah S, Burns A (2006) Sustainable scheduling analysis. In: RTSS, pp 159–168

8. Baruah SK, Mok AK, Rosier LE (1990) Preemptively scheduling hard-real-time sporadic tasks on one processor. In: Proceedings of the 11th real-time systems symposium. IEEE Computer Society Press, Los Alamitos, pp 182–190

9. Bastoni A, Brandenburg B, Anderson J (2010) Cache-related preemption and migration delays: empirical approximation and impact on schedulability. In: OSPERT, pp 33–44

10. Bini E, Buttazzo G (2005) Measuring the performance of schedulability tests. Real-Time Syst 30:129–154

11. Bril RJ, Altmeyer S, van den Heuvel M, Davis R, Behnam M (2014) Integrating cache-related pre-emption delays into analysis of fixed priority scheduling with pre-emption thresholds. In: RTSS' 14

12. Bui BD, Caccamo M, Sha L, Martinez J (2008) Impact of cache partitioning on multi-tasking real time embedded systems. In: RTCSA, pp 101–110

13. Burguière C, Reineke J, Altmeyer S (2009) Cache-related preemption delay computation for set-associative caches—pitfalls and solutions. In: WCET

14. Busquets-Mataix JV, Wellings A (1997) Hybrid instruction cache partitioning for preemptive real-time systems. In: RTS

15. Busquets-Mataix JV, Serrano JJ, Ors R, Gil P, Wellings A (1996) Adding instruction cache effect to schedulability analysis of preemptive real-time systems. In: RTAS, pp 204–212

16. Davis R, Zabos A, Burns A (2008) Efficient exact schedulability tests for fixed priority real-time systems. IEEE Trans Comput 57:1261–1276

17. Dertouzos ML (1974) Control robotics: the procedural control of physical processes. In: IFIP Congress, pp 807–813

18. Ferdinand C, Heckmann R (2004) aiT: worst case execution time prediction by static program analysis. In: IFIP, pp 377–384

19. George L, Voluceau DD, BLCC (France) (1996) Preemptive and non-preemptive real-time uni-processor scheduling

20. Gustafsson J, Betts A, Ermedahl A, Lisper B (2010) The Mälardalen WCET benchmarks—past, present and future. In: WCET, pp 137–147

21. Higbee L (1990) Quick and easy cache performance analysis. SIGARCH Comput Archit News 18(2):33–44.

22. Joseph M, Pandya P (1986) Finding response times in a real-time system. Comput J 29(5):390–395

23. Kirk DB, Strosnider JK (1990) Smart (strategic memory allocation for real-time) cache design. In: RTSS, pp 322–330

24. Lee CG, Hahn J, Seo YM, Min S, Ha R, Hong S, Park CY, Lee M, Kim CS (1998) Analysis of cache-related preemption delay in fixed-priority preemptive scheduling. IEEE Trans Comput 47(6):700–713

25. Liu CL, Layland JW (1973) Scheduling algorithms for multiprogramming in a hard-real-time environment. J ACM 20:46–61

26. Lundqvist T, Stenström P (1999) Timing anomalies in dynamically scheduled microprocessors. In: RTSS, pp 12–21

27. Lunniss W, Altmeyer S, Davis RI (2012) Optimising task layout to increase schedulability via reduced cache related pre-emption delays. In: RTNS, pp 161–170

28. Lunniss W, Altmeyer S, Maiza C, Davis R (2013) Integrating cache related pre-emption delay analysis into edf scheduling. In: RTAS, pp 75–84

29. Lunniss W, Altmeyer S, Lipari G, Davis RI (2014) Accounting for cache related pre-emption delays in hierarchical scheduling. In: RTNS' 14

30. Lunniss W, Altmeyer S, Guiseppe L, Davis RI (2015) Cache related pre-emption delays in hierarchical scheduling. J Real-Time Syst

31. Meumeu Yomsi P, Sorel Y (2007) Extending rate monotonic analysis with exact cost of preemptions for hard real-time systems. In: ECRTS, pp 280–290

32. Mueller F (1995) Compiler support for software-based cache partitioning. SIGPLAN Not 30(11):125–133

33. Nemer F, Cassé H, Sainrat P, Bahsoun JP, Michiel MD (2006) Papabench: a free real-time benchmark. In: WCET. http://drops.dagstuhl.de/opus/volltexte/2006/678

34. Petters SM, Farber G (2001) Scheduling analysis with respect to hardware related preemption delay. In: Workshop on real-time embedded systems

35. Plazar S, Lokuciejewski P, Marwedel P (2009) Wcet-aware software based cache partitioning for multi-task real-time systems. In: WCET. http://drops.dagstuhl.de/opus/volltexte/2009/2286

36. Puaut I, Decotigny D (2002) Low-complexity algorithms for static cache locking in multitasking hard real-time systems. In: RTSS, pp 114–124. http://dl.acm.org/citation.cfm?id=827272.829141

37. Ripoll I, Crespo A, Mok AK (1996) Improvement in feasibility testing for real-time tasks. Real-Time Syst 11(1):19–39

38. Saksena M, Wang Y (2000) Scalable real-time system design using preemption thresholds. In: RTSS' 10

39. Staschulat J, Schliecker S, Ernst R (2005) Scheduling analysis of real-time systems with precise modeling of cache related preemption delay. In: ECRTS, pp 41–48

40. Tan Y, Mooney V (2007) Timing analysis for preemptive multitasking real-time systems with caches. Trans Embed Comput Syst 6(1):7

41. Vera X, Lisper B, Xue J (2007) Data cache locking for tight timing calculations. ACM Trans Embed Comput Syst 7(1):4:1–4:38

42. Wang C, Gu Z, Zeng H (2015) Integration of cache partitioning and preemption threshold scheduling to improve schedulability of hard real-time systems. In: ECRTS

43. Wang Y, Saksena M (1999) Scheduling fixed-priority tasks with preemption threshold. In: RTCSA, pp 328–338

44. Wolf JL, Stone HS, Thiébaut D (1992) Synthetic traces for trace-driven simulation of cache memories. IEEE Trans Comput 41(4):388–410.

45. Ye Y, West R, Cheng Z, Li Y (2014) Coloris: a dynamic cache partitioning system using page coloring. In: Proceedings of the 23rd international conference on parallel architectures and compilation, PACT '14, pp 381–392

46. Zhang F, Burns A (2009) Schedulability analysis for real-time systems with edf scheduling. IEEE Trans Comput 58(9):1250–1258

7

# FORMAL TIMING ANALYSIS OF CAN-TO-ETHERNET GATEWAY STRATEGIES IN AUTOMOTIVE NETWORKS

**Daniel Thiele , Johannes Schlatow, Philip Axer, Rolf Ernst**


## ABSTRACT

Due to increased bandwidth and scalability demands, Ethernet technology is finding its way into recent in-vehicle networks. Tomorrow's heterogeneous networks will feature legacy buses [e.g. controller area network (CAN) or FlexRay] as well as high-speed Ethernet devices, connected by switches and gateways. As Ethernet offers significantly larger frame sizes than CAN, the efficient transmission of CAN data over an Ethernet backbone depends heavily on the way this data is multiplexed into Ethernet frames. This article focuses on the timing impact introduced by various CAN/Ethernet multiplexing strategies at the gateways. We present a formal analysis method to derive upper bounds on end-to-end latencies for complex multiplexing strategies, which is key for the design of safety-critical real-time systems. We capture complex inter-domain signal paths spanning multiple buses, gateways, and switches and show the applicability in a realistic automotive setup.



## KEYWORDS

Automotive, Ethernet, Real-time, Embedded systems, Performance analysis, CAN, Gateway, Networks, Distributed systems

# 1. INTRODUCTION

The automotive network backbone, today built up on controller area network (CAN), CAN-FD (flexible data rate), or FlexRay, reaches its limits in bandwidth and scalability. New advanced driver assistance systems add an extraordinary amount of streaming data and additional control signals which cannot be handled by today's network infrastructure. Many automotive manufacturers therefore consider switched Ethernet to be used as a potential high-speed backbone, as an overlay network or, in long term perspective, even as a full replacement for most legacy buses.

In the near future, a transition phase is expected, where an Ethernet network will serve as the backbone to interconnect various vehicle domains (cf. Fig. 1). Low-speed buses (LIN, CAN) will still be used due to their competitive price and legacy compatibility. High-speed devices such as cameras, on the other hand, will be connected directly to Ethernet switches. The figure does not depict the actual Ethernet topology. A daisy-chain, a star, or a tree of arbitrary shape can be implemented, depending on bandwidth requirements and the available number of ports per switch.

One of the major challenges in automotive network design is the *timing determinism* of critical control and streaming data (Zhang et al. 2013). It is crucial that sensor and actuator data are transmitted within well-specified latency bounds to meet the constraints of time-critical driving functions and prevent controller degradation. This is especially important for safety-critical applications which put human lives at stake. Formal timing analysis, known for example from Real-Time Calculus (RTC) (Thiele et al. 2000) and Compositional Performance Analysis (CPA) (Henia et al. 2005), assists engineers to formally prove timing constraints such as network end-to-end latencies and gateway response times.

In this article we focus on the formal end-to-end timing analysis of inter-domain traffic with real-time requirements. As an example, we use traffic which is being sent over an Ethernet backbone from a CAN bus in one domain to a CAN bus in a different domain (e.g. Powertrain to Body in Fig. 1). To transport CAN frames (i.e. their ID and signal payload) over an Ethernet network, there are two extrema: (a) sending each CAN frame via a dedicated Ethernet frame and (b) multiplexing (packing) as many CAN frames as possible into an Ethernet frame. While the first approach intuitively results in low latencies (each CAN frame is sent immediately), it has a large Ethernet protocol overhead (~~90 %) and introduces a high load on the domain gateways and the Ethernet (packing and sending many small frames). The latter approach has minimal protocol overhead and might also allow the exploitation of Ethernet multicast. However, it suffers from potentially large latencies as Ethernet frames are only sent when they are full, which might take some time. An optimal solution is somewhere between these extrema and highly depends on the traffic characteristics.

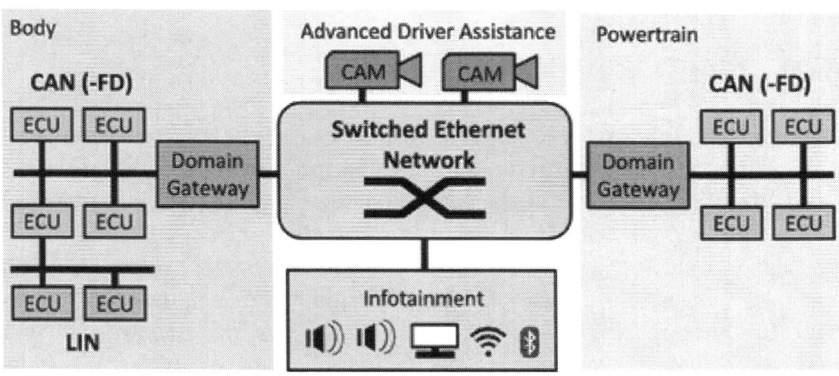


**Figure. 1** Ethernet backbone with gateways and legacy buses

While, in this article, we focus on strict-priority scheduled Ethernet (IEEE 802.1Q), our analysis methodology is scheduling agnostic and works seamlessly with Ethernet Audio/Video Bridging (AVB) or the upcoming Time Sensitive Networking (TSN) standards. As we will see in the evaluation, Ethernet has a negligible impact on the end-to-end latency. It is more important to focus on an efficient multiplexing strategy.

The main **contributions** of this article are formal methods to analyze the impact of different multiplexing strategies at the gateways on the end-to-end latency guarantees. Specifically, we focus on three different aspects of multiplexing: (a) how CAN frames are multiplexed and demultiplexed (buffering), (b) which CAN frames are multiplexed together (mapping), and (c) when an Ethernet frame is sent (triggering). Our analysis method is able to capture and quantify the (significant) differences between different multiplexing strategies.

The article is structured in the following way: First, we discuss related work in the field of system performance analysis and gateway analysis in Sect. 2. In Sect. 3, we present an overview of the CPA methodology and, in Sect. 4, we show how it can be applied to automotive networks. We extend the CPA methodology to cover the peculiarities of multiplexing CAN traffic at the gateways in Sect. 5. The applicability of our proposed approach is evaluated in Sect. 6. Finally, we conclude the article in Sect. 7.

## 2. RELATED WORK

The investigation of the timing impact of gateway strategies in heterogeneous automotive communication systems requires a multitude of analysis methods, each specialized to a specific part of the communication path. CAN buses and gateways typically utilize static-priority scheduling (non-preemptive and preemptive, respectively), which can be analyzed by the busy-period approach (e.g. Lehoczky 1990, Davis et al. 2007). Here, the worst-case response time is derived by constructing the worst-case time during which a resource is busy serving requests at a given priority.

There exists a large body of related work in timing analysis for switched networks. Most of the work uses either RTC (Thiele et al. 2000) or CPA (Henia et al. 2005). RTC has been used for Ethernet analysis in e.g. Revsbech et al. (2011). Formal timing analysis using CPA for strict-priority Ethernet was presented in Rox and Ernst (2010). In Bauer et al. (2010) the trajectory approach was applied to analyze Avionics Full Duplex Switched Ethernet (AFDX).

Different CAN to Ethernet multiplexing strategies for gateways have been studied by Kern et al. (2011), Ayed et al. (2011), Scharbarg et al. (2005), Nacer et al. (2013), and Herber et al. (2015). In Kern et al. (2011) a prototypical CAN/Ethernet multiplexing gateway has been implemented to generate experimental results for average end-to-end latencies, required network bandwidth, and resource utilization of the gateway processor for different multiplexing strategies. The authors of Ayed et al. (2011) present two simple multiplexing strategies (a 1:1 mapping and a timeout-based strategy) along with a formal analysis and propose an optimization of the timeout value regarding schedulability and gateway resources. Scharbarg et al. (2005) and Nacer et al. (2013) propose 1:1 mapping, buffer-full, and buffer-full with timeout multiplexing strategies. The evaluation of the multiplexing process, however, is only simulation based. In Herber et al. (2015) different buffering mechanisms for CAN frames at gateways are evaluated (i.e. which CAN frames are to be multiplexed first) under timeout-based triggering: FIFO, strict-priority, and earliest deadline first.

We, in contrast, model multiplexing as operations on event models (Henia et al. 2005), which can later be used seamlessly by a formal performance analysis, considering more complex triggering strategies [including the aforementioned ones and new strategies specified by AUTOSAR (2015)] and their combination. This allows us to formally derive the worst-case timing behavior on the Ethernet and the gateways, which, as we will see, has a significant impact on end-to-end timing. The importance of this work is stressed by the fact that the AUTOSAR Socket Adapter Specification (AUTOSAR 2015) already specifies multiplexed transmissions of payload data units via UDP and TCP sockets. In contrast to Herber et al. (2015), we only consider FIFO buffering and, instead, assume that time-critical CAN frames can trigger the immediate transmission of an Ethernet frame (as proposed by AUTOSAR 2015), eliminating the requirement of complex frame ordering strategies at the gateways, while also eliminating the additional delay of waiting for the next timeout to occur. Additionally, our approach supports lossy buffering, i.e. old values are overwritten by newer ones.

The multiplexing of individual control signals into (CAN) frames is discussed in e.g. Pop et al. (2005) and Saket and Navert (2006). While related to the multiplexing of CAN frames into Ethernet frames, the authors do not focus on the derivation of formal event models, but instead suggest heuristics to solve the mapping problem (which signal is packed into which frame) during multiplexing. Thus, these works are orthogonal to our approach.

Furthermore, there is work on the (hierarchical) composition and decomposition of event streams in join-fork scenarios that are applicable for the timing analysis of inter-gateway communication. In Rox and Ernst (2008), the construction and deconstruction (multiplexing and demultiplexing) of Hierarchical Event Streams (HES) was formally defined for AND-/OR-join semantics with timeout and trigger events. It also defines update functions for the modification of jitter and minimum distance of the inner event streams of an HES. Similarly, Structured Event Streams, which are characterized by so-called Event Count Curves, were introduced in Perathoner et al. (2010) and compared against HES.

# 3. COMPOSITIONAL PERFORMANCE ANALYSIS

In CPA (Henia et al. 2005), systems are modeled by sets of resources and tasks. A resource provides service (processing or transmission time) which is consumed by the tasks mapped to it. Contention for resources with multiple tasks is resolved according to the resource's scheduling policy (e.g. static-priority preemptive).

The execution behavior of a task τiτi is divided into the following steps: activation, core execution, and finally completion/propagation. After being activated, a task (or job) is ready to execute and can be scheduled. Depending on the scheduling policy and resource type, tasks may be interrupted by other tasks running on the same resource. Each invocation of a task imposes a bounded workload to the resource, i.e. its core execution time, which is bounded by the worst-case and best-case execution times denoted C+iCi+ and C−iCi−, respectively.

A distributed application consisting of multiple communicating tasks is described by a directed graph in which nodes are tasks and edges represent functional data dependencies. After a task's execution is completed, the task activates its dependent tasks (propagation). Here, forks are possible, i.e. one task can activate multiple other tasks. The opposite, i.e. a join, requires an explicit semantic. There are two common join-semantics as discussed by Henia et al. (2005): For an *OR-join* any incoming event produces one outgoing event, and for an *AND-join*, an outgoing event is produced once events are available on all incoming edges.

In CPA, the communication between tasks is abstracted by an *event model interface*. As discussed above, task activation and completion denote specific events of interest. Events can also originate from external sources, such as a timer or external devices. During the analysis, the actual data is of no further interest but rather the points in time when events occur is modeled (e.g. times when data is communicated). To keep the analysis problem tractable, an event model interface abstracts the actual event trace by only capturing worst-case and best-case behavior. An event model consists of a pair of arrival curves $\eta_i^-(\Delta t)/\eta_i^+(\Delta t)$, which return a lower/upper bound on the number of events that can arrive within any half-open time window [t,t+Δt)[t,t+Δt) Richter (2005). Thus, any trace that is between these bounds is covered by the event model representation. These functions have pseudo-inverse counterparts, the so-called maximum/minimum-distance functions $\delta_i^+(n)/\delta_i^-(n)$, which return an upper/lower bound on the time interval between the first and the last event of any sequence of *n* event arrivals. For convenience we introduce the event model interfaces $\delta_i = \{\delta_i^-, \delta_i^+\}$ and $\eta_i = \{\eta_i^+, \eta_i^-\}$ to refer to an event stream's worst-case and best-case event models. Often, it is more convenient to consider δ functions, due to their discrete domain. A conversion between δi and ηi is described by Diemer et al. (2012a).

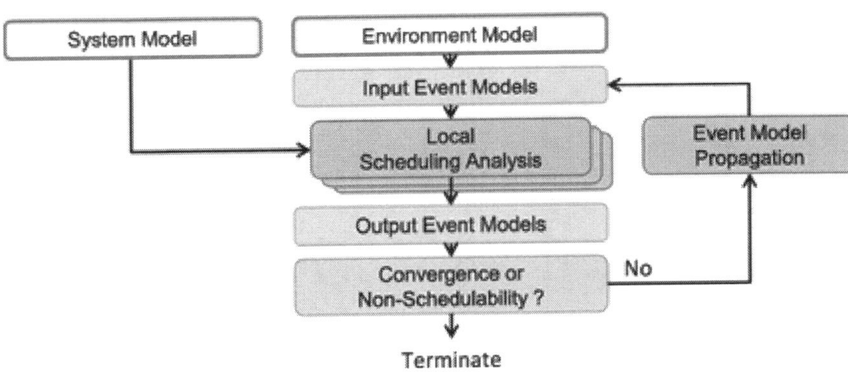


**Figure. 2** Compositional analysis flow

The CPA analysis flow, as shown in Fig. 2, consists of two interleaved steps: the *local analysis* and the*propagation* of event models. The environment model specifies the boundary conditions for each event stream under which the system is operating. This is usually given as external event models which describe the characteristics of external sources. Other, yet unknown, event models are initialized with optimistic guesses that are iteratively updated during analysis. The event models are used for the local resource analysis during which the local behavior of each resource is considered in isolation. Among other results, the local analysis yields the response-time jitter from which new output event models can be derived (Henia et al. 2005). These output event models then become the input event models of dependent task.

The iteration is stopped and a system fixed-point is found if all event models remain stable. Then, the resulting best-case/worst-case response times $(R_i^-/R_i^+)$ along a path can be added up to retrieve end-to-end path latencies $L_i^-/L_i^+$. Similarly, if we are interested in the delay of multiple activations, we can use the following equation (Diemer et al. 2011):

$$L_i^{-/+}(q) = \delta_i^-(q) + \sum_{j \in Path(i)} R_j^{-/+} \tag{1}$$

Here, Path(i) is the set of all tasks which belong to a path *i*. Equation 1 assumes a maximum injection rate at the event source, i.e. *q* events are generated within a time interval of $\delta_i^-(q)$. This will cause the system's resources to exhibit worst-case behavior such as the worst-case response times $R_i^+$. The general idea behind Eq. 1 is that the last of the *q* events will experience the worst-case on each resource. Due to causality, all q−1 previously sent events must have arrived by then.

# 4. MODELING AUTOMOTIVE NETWORKS

In this section, we discuss how a heterogeneous automotive network, consisting of multiple ECUs, buses, Ethernet switches, and gateways is modeled using CPA primitives. An exemplary architecture is shown in the upper part of Fig. 3 and the corresponding logical CPA model in the lower part. Two CAN buses are connected to an Ethernet switch via gateways. Individual communication streams are indicated by colored arrows in the upper part of the figure. One ECU is directly connected to the Ethernet switch. In this particular example, CAN frames available on CAN1 are sent to CAN2 (red arrow) and from CAN2 to CAN1 (yellow arrow). Some CAN frames from CAN1 are sent via multicast to the ECU for further processing and the result is sent back to CAN1.

The resulting CPA model is shown in the lower part of Fig. 3. Edges represent event model interfaces which are given as environment models $\delta_{1,in}$ to $\delta_{5,in}$ or are derived during analysis. Multicast traffic (CAN1 sends data to CAN2 and ECU) is modeled by forking the event stream. Most physical resources are directly modeled as CPA resources (rectangles with black name tags). An exception is the Ethernet switch, which is modeled as described by Diemer et al. (2012b). Each output port, as a point of arbitration, is modeled as a resource. We assume that all other switch delays can be modeled by constant delays Diemer et al. (2012b). Software tasks are shown as white tasks. The transmission of CAN and Ethernet frames is depicted as grey tasks.

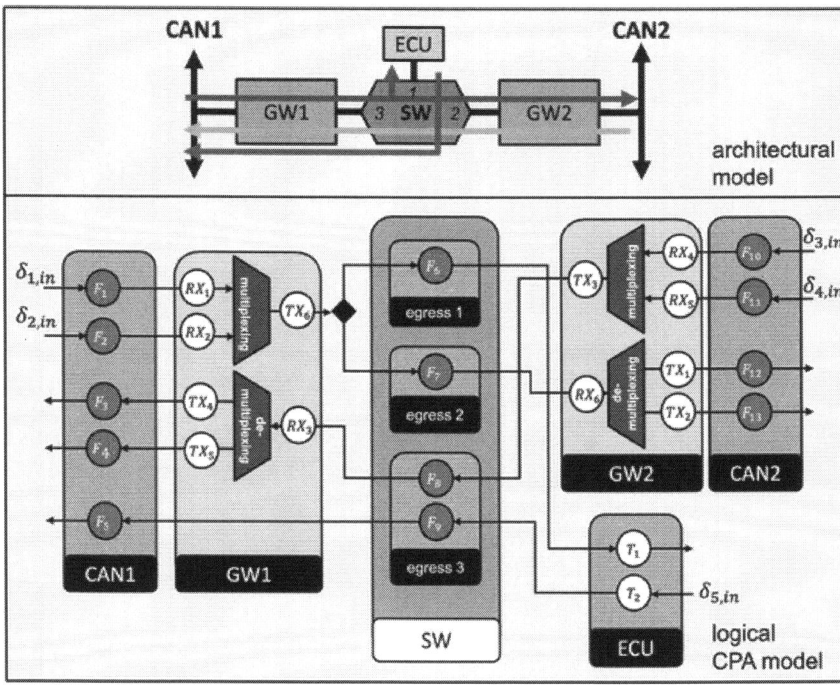


**Figure. 3** System model, consisting of two buses, two gateways, an Ethernet switch connected to the gateways, and an ECU

Due to network heterogeneity, different CPA analyses must be utilized to derive end-to-end latency guarantees, e.g. from CAN1 to CAN2. For the analysis of the CAN buses, we resort to an analysis approach based on Davis et al. (2007). We assume that frames in the Ethernet network are scheduled according to IEEE 802.1Q, i.e. in a static-priority non-preemptive way (Rox and Ernst 2010; Thiele et al. 2014). A detailed discussion of the modeling and timing analysis of the gateways is given in the following section. All analyses are interconnected by event model interfaces.

# 5. ETHERNET GATEWAYS

In this section, we present CPA techniques to model different frame multiplexing strategies, i.e. how CAN frames are buffered into an Ethernet frame, how CAN frames are mapped to Ethernet frames, when Ethernet frames are sent, as well as the demultiplexing of CAN frames from Ethernet frames.

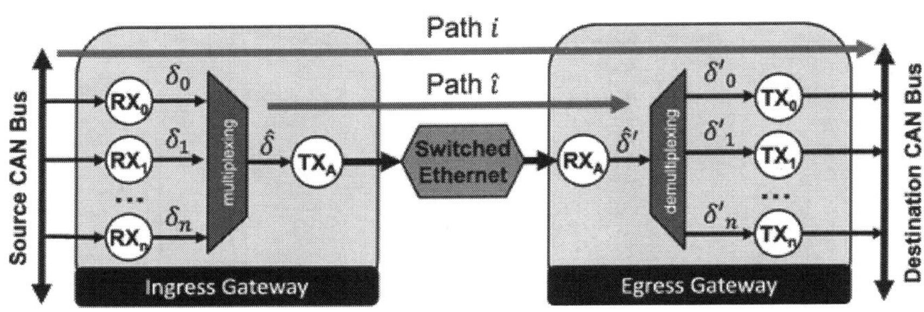


**Figure. 4** An ingress gateway sends a multiplexed CAN traffic stream via a switched Ethernet to an egress gateway. The first merges in-event models, the latter demultiplexes the stream

## 5.1 CPA gateway model

Without loss of generality, we reduce the discussion to the unidirectional scenario in Fig. 4 in which we distinguish between the ingress and the egress gateway. The ingress gateway receives CAN frames from one or multiple CAN buses and packs these frames into one or multiple Ethernet frames (multiplexing). The egress gateway receives Ethernet frames and unpacks the contained CAN frames in order to transmit them to the destination CAN bus(es) (demultiplexing). Bidirectional scenarios can be modeled by combining the task graphs of the ingress and egress gateways (cf. Fig. 3).

As we focus on CPA techniques to model different multiplexing strategies, we utilize simplified gateway models, which assume that any processing on the gateways can be split into a per-CAN-frame and a per-Ethernet-frame part. The ingress gateway comprises RX tasks for each incoming CAN frame as well as a TX task for each outgoing Ethernet frame. An RX task models the execution time that is required to process a CAN frame with a particular CAN identifier. Similarly, a TX task models the execution time of the Ethernet stack and the time that is required to transmit an Ethernet frame. The processor of the gateway is assumed to schedule tasks in static-priority preemptive (SPP) fashion (Schliecker et al. 2008). The TX task has the highest priority and RX tasks have a priority proportional to their CAN identifier below the TX task. Apart from the RX and TX tasks, a (multiplexing) join merges the event streams from multiple RX tasks to a single TX task. The semantics of this join junction depend on the multiplexing strategy and impact the *sampling delay* of the gateway (Feiertag et al. 2008). The sampling delay arises whenever multiple CAN frames are multiplexed into a single Ethernet frame during packetization, i.e. the first CAN frame in a new Ethernet frame must wait for the last CAN frame to be packed into the Ethernet frame.

The egress gateway is modeled by a task graph that basically reverses the operations of the ingress gateway. It contains an RX task for each incoming Ethernet frame and a TX task for each outgoing CAN frame. Here, the RX task has the highest priority and TX tasks have a priority proportional to their CAN identifier. In order to distribute a single activation from the RX task, which (in a multiplexing scenario) typically contains several CAN frames, to the TX tasks, a (demultiplexing) fork is required. As this fork, in contrast to the standard fork, which forwards all incoming event models to all dependent tasks, selectively distributes event models depending on the receiving task, we model the demultiplexing fork explicitly as in Perathoner et al. (2010). There is no sampling delay on the egress gateway.

## 5.2 Multiplexing strategies

We classify multiplexing strategies in terms of three fundamental parameters: *buffering, triggering* and*mapping. Buffering* takes place at the ingress gateway in order to collect incoming CAN frames. Once a certain condition is met (*triggering*), the contents of the buffer are sent as payload of an Ethernet frame. If multiple buffers are used, a *mapping* function determines to which buffer a CAN frame is forwarded.

We distinguish between lossy and lossless buffering, which fundamentally affect the timing analysis. A lossy strategy assumes that each CAN frame designated to a certain buffer has a fixed position in this buffer and will update (overwrite) the buffer content (or parts of it) with the most recent value and is suitable for transmitting sensor data. Conversely, a lossless strategy is order preserving and (non-destructively) queues data in the buffer.

Based on Kern et al. (2011), Ayed et al. (2011), Scharbarg et al. (2005), Nacer et al. (2013), and AUTOSAR (2015), Ethernet frames can be triggered by:

- *Buffer Timeout* This time-trigger is specified by a fixed timeout per buffer so that the gateway emits an Ethernet frame periodically (Kern et al. 2011; Ayed et al. 2011; Scharbarg et al. 2005; Nacer et al. 2013; AUTOSAR 2015).

- *Buffer-full Event* In case of a lossless buffering strategy, an Ethernet frame is transmitted once the queue is full (Scharbarg et al. 2005; Nacer et al. 2013; AUTOSAR 2015).

- *Trigger Frames* Incoming CAN frames with particular identifiers immediately trigger the transmission of an Ethernet frame, which corresponds to the AUTOSAR configuration TriggerMode=TRIGGER_ALWAYS (Kern et al. 2011; AUTOSAR 2015).

- *Per-frame Timeout* Incoming CAN frames set a timer, which then triggers the transmission of an Ethernet frame, i.e. to bound the sampling delay for these frames. This resembles the timed approach in Kern et al. (2011).

The last three trigger mechanisms add dependencies between all CAN frames within a buffer, i.e. the trigger condition depends on the arrival pattern of incoming CAN frames. These dependencies can be reduced by introducing multiple buffers to partition the CAN traffic (mapping), according to e.g. destination, priority, or deadline. Due to their complexity, we do not model per-frame timeouts (cf. Sect. 5.3.6 for a discussion).

CAN frames can be mapped to a buffer statically or dynamically. A static mapping assigns a CAN identifier to a buffer at design time so that each CAN frame with this identifier is always stored in the same buffer. In a dynamic mapping the assignment is not predefined and is instead determined at run-time. In such an approach the CAN frames would not be mapped statically to a fixed buffer (or set of buffers) but the gateway would rather decide at run-time which output buffer will be most suitable for an incoming CAN frame. The eligible output buffers are constrained by the CAN frame's destination(s). For this, a set of reasonable (online) strategies should be developed. However, before a formal analysis can be applied, it must be evaluated if reasonable bounds for the worst-case behavior of these online strategies can be derived. In this article, we focus on static mapping only, as dynamic mapping introduces an additional level of indeterminism and complexity to a formal analysis.

## 5.3 Multiplexing event models

We model multiplexing as an event model operator which depends on the semantics of the join (i.e. its triggering mechanism) and its input event models. More formally, we define the multiplexing function $\mathcal{M} : \mathbf{\Delta} \rightarrow \hat{\delta}$ that, given a set of input event models $\mathbf{\Delta} = \{\delta_0, \delta_1, \ldots, \delta_n\}$, calculates the combined output event model δδ^δδ^ (cf. Fig. 4). In this section, we consider buffer timeouts, trigger frames, buffer-full events, and combinations of these.

### 5.3.1 Buffer timeout

This triggering mechanism is modeled by a periodic event model δto whose period corresponds to the timeout value to. The output event model $\hat{\delta}$ is solely determined by the timeout event model.

$$\hat{\delta} = \delta_{to} \quad \text{with} \quad \begin{aligned} \delta_{to}^{-}(n) &= (n-1) \cdot t_{to} \\ \delta_{to}^{+}(n) &= (n-1) \cdot t_{to} \end{aligned} \tag{2}$$

### 5.3.2 Trigger frames

Let $\mathbf{\Delta}_{tr} \subseteq \mathbf{\Delta}$ be the subset of triggering event models. Then, the output event model is determined by event models $\delta_i \in \mathbf{\Delta}_{tr}$. As a trigger frame causes the immediate emission of an output event, an Ethernet frame can only contain, among other non-trigger frames, a single trigger frame. The output event model $\hat{\delta}$ is modeled by an OR-join (Henia et al. 2005) of all triggering event models. The OR event model is conveniently modeled in the ηη domain, which can be converted to the δδ domain to retrieve $\hat{\delta}$ (Diemer et al.2012a).

$$\hat{\eta}^{+}(\Delta t) = \sum_{\eta_i \in \Delta_{tr}} \eta_i^{+}(\Delta t)$$
$$\hat{\eta}^{-}(\Delta t) = \sum_{\eta_i \in \Delta_{tr}} \eta_i^{-}(\Delta t) \quad (3)$$

## 5.3.3 Trigger frames with buffer timeout

Here, we consider triggered frames in conjunction with a buffer timeout. If no trigger frame arrives, the data is sent after ttotto at the latest. We interpret the buffer timeout as a triggering event model, and add it to the set of triggering event models $\Delta_T = \Delta_{tr} \cup \{\delta_{to}\}$. The resulting event model can be derived analogously to Eq. 3.

This approach may introduce a certain degree of over approximation. A practical implementation would certainly omit an Ethernet frame transmission on a buffer timeout event if the buffer is empty. There are, however, also scenarios in which this behavior is desired, e.g. in lossy buffering when the latest known values should be distributed periodically (in this case the buffer is never empty but always keeps the latest values). Also, one may decide to optimize the implementation by resetting the timer once a CAN frame is placed into an empty buffer as specified by AUTOSAR (2015).

## 5.3.4 Buffer-full

At this point, we are able to analyze multiplexing scenarios with lossy buffering. For lossless buffering, however, we also need to take buffer-full events into account.

Let $\Delta_B \subseteq \Delta$ be the subset of all event models which are non-triggering and queued in the buffer. Let $\delta_B$ denote the OR-join (cf. Eq. 3) of all input event models in ΔB, and let *m* denote the size of the buffer in number of CAN frames. Now, we can construct best-case and worst-case scenarios to derive the combined output event model $\hat{\delta}$. Suppose that at time t0t0 the buffer has just been filled with $\tilde{m} \in [0, m]$ CAN frames (i.e.

frame $\tilde{m}$ just arrived), such that m−m~m−m~ additional frames are required to transmit the buffer. This implies that the last buffer transmission was $\tilde{m}+1$ frames before t0 (one frame to transmit the buffer and then m~m~ frames to fill the buffer up to time t0). So, two output frames (of $\hat{\delta}$) are $\tilde{m}+1+m-\tilde{m}=m+1$ input frames (of δB) apart. In the worst-case/best-case the minimum/maximum-distance between these two input frames is described by δ−B(m+1)δB−(m+1)/δ+B(m+1)δB+(m+1). This argumentation can be generalized to:

$$n \geq 2: \quad \hat{\delta}^-(n) = \delta_B^-((n-1)m+1)$$
$$\hat{\delta}^+(n) = \delta_B^+((n-1)m+1) \qquad (4)$$

### 5.3.5 Buffer-full, trigger frames, buffer timeout

Here, we combine the buffer-full event with trigger frames and the buffer timeout. Let δtr denote the OR-join of ΔT which contains all triggering event models, i.e. trigger frames and buffer timeout (cf. Eq. 3). Any *n*frames observed at the output of the multiplexer can be decomposed into a number of frames triggered by single trigger events ntrntr and a number of frames triggered by buffer-full events nbuf, i.e. n=ntr+nbuf. Now, the timing of the output events depends on the number of trigger frames and buffer-full events:

$$\hat{\delta}^-(n_{buf}, n_{tr}) = \max\{\delta_B^-((n_{buf}-1)\cdot m+1), \delta_{tr}^-(n_{tr})\}$$
$$\hat{\delta}^+(n_{buf}, n_{tr}) = \max\{\delta_B^+((n_{buf}-1)\cdot m+1), \delta_{tr}^+(n_{tr})\} \qquad (5)$$

As the decomposition n=ntr+nbuf is unconstrained and any combination can possibly occur, we must find the worst-case/best-case combination:

$$\hat{\delta}^-(n) = \min\{\hat{\delta}^-(n_{buf}, n_{tr}) \mid n_{buf}+n_{tr}=n\}$$
$$\hat{\delta}^+(n) = \min\{\hat{\delta}^+(n_{buf}, n_{tr}) \mid n_{buf}+n_{tr}=n\} \qquad (6)$$

Note that $\hat{\delta}^{+}(n)$, like its counterpart, is the minimum over all combinations. This is because no trigger condition that occurs within the considered time window must be missed.

### 5.3.6 Per-frame timeouts

In the per-frame timeout triggering strategy, CAN frames can be associated with an individual timeout, which then triggers the transmission of an Ethernet frame. When such a CAN frame arrives at a gateway, it is guaranteed to be sent out (as part of an Ethernet frame) after at least its timeout, i.e. the timeout allows to specify an upper bound on the CAN frame's residence time in the gateway.

Per-frame timeout triggering can be approximated by the buffer timeout strategy by using the minimum of all frame timeouts as the buffer's timeout δto. This approach assumes that, in the worst-case, a CAN frame of the stream with the shortest timeout arrives just after the buffer has been sent (cf. e1e1 Fig. 5b). Care must be taken when deriving the sampling delay for each steam (cf. Sect. 5.4 below). By definition of per-frame timeouts, the worst-case sampling delay is the frame's timeout. However, this approximation is clearly an overestimation.

Deriving tighter worst-case output event models for per-frame timeouts is hard, due to the complex interaction of the input event streams in this strategy. The triggering strategies we presented so far have in common that the trigger condition, which releases an Ethernet frame, occurs concurrently with the arrival of an input event, e.g. a timeout which acts as the exclusive trigger or the event which triggers the buffer to be sent in the buffer-full strategy. In a per-frame timeout strategy, however, this trigger condition occurs some time (i.e. the timeout) after the corresponding input event arrives. Depending on the arrival pattern of the input events and their timeouts, there can be masking effects, where one frame completely masks the actions of another frame. An example is shown in Fig. 5 where the arrival time of event e1e1 (within its jitter interval) determines whether it is masked by event e2's timeout, i.e. it is part of the Ethernet frame which is triggered by e2's timeout (at time t0t0 in Fig. 5a), or contributes to the output event model by triggering another Ethernet frame (at t1 in Fig. 5b).

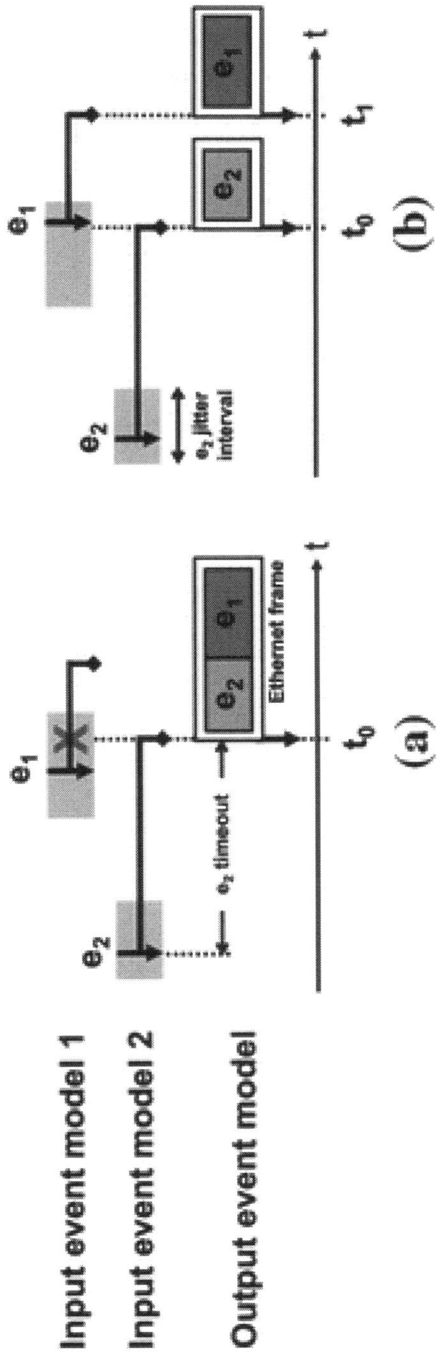


**Figure. 5** Per-frame timeout examples

Hence, to derive the worst-case output event model, we must consider the relative arrival times of the events of all input event models. Per input event, these times can be anywhere within its jitter interval. Additionally, the relative position of the jitter intervals of different input event models can be affected by an offset between these input event models. This problem is complex to solve, as we have to consider all event arrival times within their respective jitter intervals together with all offsets between the input event models to find the worst-case output event model.

If we introduce certain assumptions to simplify this problem, we can outline a constructive method to derive output event models for per-frame timeouts. First, assuming strictly periodic input event models can be used to eliminate the jitter interval problem. For each input event model, this assumption implies that the timeouts within this input event model are also periodic with the input event model's period, i.e. the (minimum) distance between any two timeouts of this input event model also is the input event model's period. Second, only trying to find the occurrence of an input event's next timeout without considering its history beyond its last timeout can be used to eliminate the offset problem between different input event models. Now, given an output event, for each per-frame timeout event model, the occurrence of its next timeout can be derived by taking into account that this timeout must occur (a) at least one period after the input event's last timeout or (b) by its timeout after the last output event (as in Fig. 5b), whichever occurs last. The next output event occurs at the minimum over all these new timeouts.

Event models from real CAN buses typically have jitter, such that this method cannot be applied directly. Moreover, if we relaxed the first assumption and allowed jitter, then the minimum distances between the timeouts of the per-frame timeout event models would decrease. If the jitter grows too large, in our argumentation above, case (b) will dominate case (a), which is equivalent to the initially presented overestimation of using the minimum of all frame timeouts as the buffer's timeout.

## 5.4 Sampling delay

As discussed in Sect. 3, the end-to-end latency along a path can be computed by summing up the response times of the contained tasks (cf. Eq. 1). The multiplexing join, however, induces an additional delay for non-trigger frames because an input event does not trigger an output event immediately. This is similar to a scenario where the inputs of a subsystem are periodically sampled, which results in a time-triggered rather than an event-triggered activation of the subsystem (Feiertag et al. 2008). In the multiplexing scenario, we therefore add a similar sampling delay (denoted Lsi) to the end-to-end latency of non-trigger frames, which results from the maximum distance between two output events of the corresponding multiplexing join:

$$L_i^s = \begin{cases} 0 & \text{if } \delta_i \in \mathbf{\Delta}_{tr} \\ \hat{\delta}^+(2) & \text{otherwise} \end{cases} \tag{7}$$

## 5.5 Demultiplexing event models

The demultiplexing problem is the inverse of the multiplexing problem: Given a combined input event model δδ^′, we have to find the set of individual output event models $\mathbf{\Delta}' = \{\delta'_0, \delta'_1, \ldots, \delta'_n\}$ (cf. Fig. 4). The individual output event models δ′i, in turn, are defined by their lower and upper bounds. In the following, we discuss how these bounds can be derived conservatively. We start with a naive approach to illustrate the general demultiplexing problem before we proceed to present a more sophisticated approach that is guaranteed to preserve the load on the egress CAN bus.

### 5.5.1 Naive bounds

The *naive* approach is based on the idea that each combined event at the demultiplexer (incoming Ethernet frame) can induce multiple demultiplexed events (CAN frames) for each stream. Hence we can establish the*naive* bounds by scaling the combined event model with the minimum/maximum number of contained events for the particular stream.

For lossy buffering, there can be at most a single CAN frame of each stream, as, during multiplexing, old CAN frames will always be updated (overwritten) by the most recent ones. Hence, the upper bounds of the demultiplexed event models $\eta'_i$ on the egress side follow the upper bound of the combined input event model from the incoming Ethernet frame: $\eta_i'^{+}(\Delta t) = \hat{\eta}'^{+}(\Delta t)$. The number of output events of a particular outgoing event model interface is lower bounded by zero at all times, i.e. $\eta_i'^{-}(\Delta t) = 0$. Again, $\eta_i'$ can be converted to δ'i (Diemer et al. 2012a).

Under lossless buffering, the number of CAN frames in a buffer (incoming Ethernet frame) depends on the multiplexing strategy (MM) and the arrival pattern of the CAN frames (δi) on the ingress gateway. We can derive an upper bound for the number of CAN frames of each stream *j* by assuming that the CAN frames of this stream arrived as fast as possible (δ−j), while the CAN frames of all other streams i≠j arrived as late as possible (δ+i). This represents the worst possible combination of event arrivals w.r.t. the number of events from stream *j*, as events from stream *j* cannot arrive faster and events from other streams cannot arrive slower. More generally, we let Δj denote this set of event models so that we can calculate a combined output event model $\hat{\delta}_j$ based on these assumptions dependent on the multiplexing strategy: $\hat{\delta}_j = \mathcal{M}(\mathbf{\Delta}_j)$. We can then bound the number of CAN frames Nj of stream *j* from above by calculating the number of events of stream *j* that can arrive between two output events: $N_j = \eta_j^+(\hat{\delta}_j^+(2))$. Thus, at the egress gateway, the maximum number of CAN frames of stream *j* in a single Ethernet frame can be upper bounded by scaling the combined input event model by $N_j$: $\eta_j'^{+}(\Delta t) = N_j \hat{\eta}_j'^{+}(\Delta t)$. As in the lossy case, the number of output events of a particular outgoing lossless event model interface is lower bounded by zero at all times, i.e. $\eta_j'^{-}(\Delta t) = 0$.

For both cases, lossy and lossless, this is an overly pessimistic approximation, as it (conservatively) underestimates/overestimates the minimum/maximum number of CAN frames for each multiplexed stream inside every incoming Ethernet frame without respecting any correlations between the scenarios. E.g. assuming the maximum number of CAN frames for each multiplexed stream (per incoming Ethernet frame) can lead to mutually exclusive worst-case scenarios for the upper event bounds: under buffer-full buffering, for example, we generally have $\sum_{0 \leq i < |\Delta|} N_i \geq m$, where *m* is the size of the buffer (number of CAN frames per Ethernet frame). Consequently, by using this naive approach, the (artificially) increased number of CAN frames on the egress side potentially induces a higher load and jitter on the egress gateway and CAN bus(es). This is a major drawback as we have observed that (especially) CAN buses can be easily overloaded, i.e. deemed unscheduable, by using this approach. Although this could be improved by deriving bounds on the number of CAN frames within multiple consecutive Ethernet frames instead of applying the same Nj on every single Ethernet frame, we present another approach that is guaranteed to preserve the load on the egress gateway and CAN bus(es) in the next section.

## 5.5.2 Load-preserving bounds

This approach is based on the assumption that the number of events entering the join must be equal to the number of events exiting the fork, i.e. we reasonably assume that no events are lost or added during multiplexing, transmission, and demultiplexing. It is similar to Perathoner et al. (2010) and Rox and Ernst (2008) as it considers a hierarchical structure of event models, i.e. inner event models that are propagated along with their outer event model. More precisely, we propagate the original (inner) input event models δδi∈ΔΔδδi∈ΔΔ of the join along with its (outer) output event model δδ^δδ^ and add the path jitter to the inner event models upon their extraction at the demultiplexing fork. Note, that under lossy buffering this approach can introduce a slight overestimation in rare cases where there might actually be desired frame loss, e.g. when the buffer timeout at the join is configured to exceed a stream's period.

Let JJFi be the path jitter, which is defined as the difference between the worst-case and best-case end-to-end latency (incl. the sampling delay Lsi) of a single event of path *i* along the subpath i^ from the join to the fork (cf. Fig. 4 and Eq. 1):

$$J_i^{JF} = l_i^+ - l_i^- \quad \text{with} \quad l_i^+ = L_i^s + L_{\hat{i}}^+(1) \qquad (8)$$
$$l_i^- = 0 + L_{\hat{i}}^-(1)$$

The path jitter is then applied as described by Rox and Ernst (2008):

$$\delta_i'^-(n) = \max(\delta_i^-(n) - J_i^{JF}, 0) \qquad (9)$$
$$\delta_i'^+(n) = \delta_i^+(n) + J_i^{JF}$$

# 6. EXPERIMENTS

Here, we evaluate the presented gateway analysis in a more complex system topology that combines video, control, and inter-gateway traffic. Our comparison metrics are the worst-case end-to-end latency guarantee and load from our analysis.

## 6.1 System topology

Figure 6 depicts the synthetic system topology on which we based our experiments. It comprises an Ethernet network of one inner switch (S center) and four outer switches (S1–S4). Moreover, there is a CAN/Ethernet gateway connected to each of the outer switches. Each of these gateways, in turn, connects a CAN bus to the system. Two cameras are assigned to S1 and S2. Further, S1, S3, and S4 each connect to a dedicated ECU. There are also two additional ECUs which are directly linked to the inner switch. All these components are interconnected by bidirectional 100 MBit/s links.

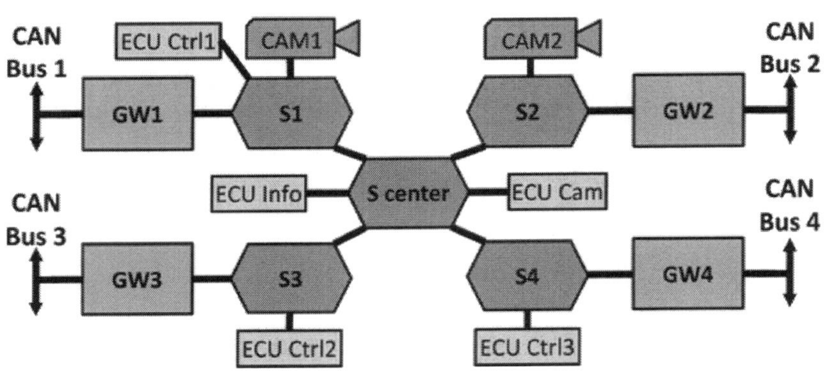


**Figure. 6** System topology for our experiments comprising a network with five switches, four gateways, two cameras and five ECUs. Ethernet links are bidirectional 100 Mbit/s links.eps

**Table 1** Ethernet traffic: three video streams and two control streams

| Name | Source | Destination | PCP | Payload (bytes) | Period | Jitter |
|---|---|---|---|---|---|---|
| Video 1 | CAM1 | ECU Cam | 2 | 786 | 250 μs | 0 |
| Video 2 | CAM2 | ECU Cam | 2 | 786 | 250 μs | 0 |
| Video 3 | ECU Cam | ECU Info | 2 | 786 | 250 μs | 0 |
| Control 1 | ECU Ctrl1 | ECU Ctrl3 | 3 | 50 | 10 ms | 10 ms |
| Control 2 | ECU Ctrl2 | ECU Ctrl3 | 3 | 100 | 50 ms | 50 ms |

PCP denotes the priority (IEEE 802.1Q)

## 6.2 Traffic streams

Table 1 specifies the *Ethernet traffic* streams in the network. There are two video streams originating from the cameras that are received and processed by ECU Cam. This ECU sends the resulting video stream to the Infotainment ECU (ECU Info). Two additional control traffic streams are sent from ECU Ctrl1 and ECU Ctrl2 to ECU Ctrl3. Control traffic is mapped to a high Ethernet priority (PCP), while video traffic is mapped to a lower one.

To model the *inter-gateway CAN traffic* streams between the gateways, we use a synthesized set of 100 periodic CAN frames with periods between 16 and 1001 ms. The periods and CAN identifiers of these frames are assigned by random according to distributions that we observed in real automotive systems. We divided this set further into two disjunct sets, which are sent from GW1 to GW3 and from GW2 to WG4, respectively. The former set contains 51 CAN traffic streams, which induce an asymptotic bus load, i.e. the (theoretical) average load over a time interval of infinite length, of about 31 % on a 500 kBit/s CAN bus, while the latter set comprises 49 streams, which induce an asymptotic bus load of about 14 %. For the later evaluation, we set the jitter of the CAN frames to half their periods to accommodate for delays within parts of the system that we do not model.

We manually assembled these inter-gateway CAN traffic streams into ten multiplexing groups as shown in Table 2. For every stream we assume an UDP/IP transport protocol (i.e. 28 bytes of additional protocol overhead) and assign it Ethernet priority 3, i.e. the same priority, we used for control traffic in Table 1. The CAN frames of these streams are statically mapped to the Ethernet frames of Table 2 according to their period, which must match the specified range. The period ranges have been chosen to match (rounded down/up to the nearest 10 μμs) the minimum/maximum periods of each group's traffic streams. For a given mapping, the Ethernet frame size can be computed as described by Diemer et al. (2012b). We also selected some of the CAN frames to be trigger frames. Table 3 shows how many frames have been assigned to which group based on this mapping scheme. Note that all frames from GW1/GW2 are transmitted to GW3/GW4 respectively, which later allows a direct comparison of the ingress and egress sides.

**Table 2** Multiplexed inter-gateway traffic by the source and destination gateway, the buffer size and the buffer timeout

| # | Source | Destination | Buffer size | Timeout (ms) | Period range (ms) |
|---|---|---|---|---|---|
| 1 | GW1 | GW3 | 10 | 20 | 0–30 |
| 2 | GW1 | GW3 | 10 | 100 | 90–110 |
| 3 | GW1 | GW3 | 10 | 120 | 110–130 |
| 4 | GW1 | GW3 | 10 | 1000 | 900–1010 |
| 5 | GW2 | GW4 | 10 | 40 | 30–50 |
| 6 | GW2 | GW4 | 10 | 60 | 50–70 |
| 7 | GW2 | GW4 | 10 | 80 | 70–90 |
| 8 | GW2 | GW4 | 10 | 140 | 130–150 |
| 9 | GW2 | GW4 | 10 | 280 | 270–290 |
| 10 | GW2 | GW4 | 10 | 480 | 470–490 |

A period range is specified, to group similar CAN frames

**Table 3** Number of trigger and total number of CAN frames assigned to the multiplexing groups

| Group # | 1 | 2 | 3 | 4 | 5 | 6 | 7 | 8 | 9 | 10 | Total |
|---|---|---|---|---|---|---|---|---|---|---|---|
| # Assigned frames | 17 | 12 | 17 | 5 | 6 | 6 | 10 | 14 | 9 | 4 | 100 |
| # Trigger frames | 0 | 0 | 1 | 1 | 0 | 0 | 1 | 0 | 1 | 0 | 4 |

For each group, we instantiate a multiplexer on the source and a demultiplexer on the destination gateway (cf. Fig. 4). Assuming a multiplexing strategy using buffer timeouts, trigger frames, and buffer-full events, the output event models can be derived from the arrival patterns of their associated CAN frames. The best-case/worst-case execution times of the ingress gateway tasks (cf. Sect. 5.1) are estimated to be 10 μμs/ 20 μμs for the RX tasks and 10 μμs/50 μμs for the TX tasks. Similarly, the execution times of the egress gateway tasks are assumed to be 10 μμs/20 μμs for the TX tasks and 10 μμs/50 μμs plus Nj·· 5 μμs for the RX tasks. For the latter, we additionally account for processing overhead depending on the maximum number Nj of packaged CAN frames within a single Ethernet frame of group *j* (cf. Sect. 5.5.1).

## 6.3 Results

We evaluate our analysis by comparing the multiplexing scenario defined by Tables 2 and 3 (i.e. buffer timeouts, trigger frames, and buffer-full events) to the two extrema discussed in the introduction: a 1:1 mapping (i.e. transmitting each CAN frame separately) as well as to an all-in-one mapping (i.e. transmitting as many CAN frames together as possible). More precisely, the latter scenario is defined by two multiplexing groups, one that transmits all CAN frames from GW1 to GW3 and one for the CAN frames from GW2 to GW4. There is no buffer timeout in the all-in-one scenario whereas the buffer size is raised to 30. In all scenarios, we use the load-preserving demultiplexing approach from Sect. 5.5.2.

**Table 4** Worst-case latency for video and control streams. 1:1 mapping, multiplexing (mux) and all-in-one mapping

| Stream: | Control 1 (μs) | Control 2 (μs) | Video 1 (μs) | Video 2 (μs) | Video 3 (μs) |
|---|---|---|---|---|---|
| 1:1 | 825 | 422 | 671 | 638 | 68 |
| mux | 349 | 201 | 333 | 313 | 68 |
| All-in-one | 246 | 131 | 299 | 280 | 68 |

**Table 5** Shared network resources (switch ports)

| Port | Traffic streams |
|---|---|
| S1→S center | Video 1, Control 1, GW1→GW3 |
| S2→S center | Video 2, GW2→GW4 |
| S center→ECU Cam | Video 1, Video 2 |
| S center→S4 | Control 1, Control 2, GW2→GW4 |
| S4→ECU Ctrl3 | Control 1, Control 2 |

Table 4 shows the resulting end-to-end latency guarantees of the Ethernet traffic streams listed in Table 1 for all three scenarios. As the inter-gateway traffic is assigned the highest Ethernet priority, it interferes with the video and control streams. The points of possible interference (i.e. shared resources) are listed in Table 5. As multiplexing reduces the number of traffic streams injected by the gateways considerably, the interference with other traffic streams decreases as well. Hence their end-to-end latency improves by at least 50 % except for stream Video 3, which does not experience any interference from other streams. As expected, the all-in-one scenario minimizes the interference on other streams.

Table 6 shows the asymptotic load for the gateways and selected ports on the central switch as a result of the worst-case analysis. Due to the low bandwidth requirements of the inter-gateway traffic, there is only a small improvement on the network load in the multiplexing scenario. The gateway load, in contrast, is significantly lower under multiplexing, as less Ethernet packets must be processed. Note that the load increase on the egress gateways (GW3 and GW4) results from the higher execution times of the RX tasks (which depend on the number of CAN frames in an Ethernet frame) in comparison to the corresponding TX tasks on the ingress gateways (GW1 and GW2). This additional load, however, is only required during the demultiplexing process on the egress gateway. The asymptotic load induced by the demultiplexed CAN streams on the egress CAN buses (CAN buses 2 and 4), in contrast, is preserved and equals the asymptotic load on the corresponding ingress CAN buses.

**Table 6** Load comparison between 1:1 mapping, multiplexing (mux) and all-in-one mapping on the gateways and the ports of the central switch

| Res.: | GW1 (%) | GW2 (%) | GW3 (%) | GW4 (%) | S center→ ECU Cam (%) | S center→ ECU Info (%) | S center →S3 (%) | S center →S4 (%) |
|---|---|---|---|---|---|---|---|---|
| 1:1 | 8.2 | 3.7 | 8.2 | 3.7 | 54.9 | 27.4 | 0.78 | 0.48 |
| mux | 3.3 | 1.7 | 4.2 | 2.3 | 54.9 | 27.4 | 0.23 | 0.28 |
| All-in-one | 2.6 | 1.2 | 3.3 | 1.7 | 54.9 | 27.4 | 0.12 | 0.21 |

Each multiplexing strategy introduces a certain amount of jitter, which is caused by the sampling delay (if present) and the Ethernet latency difference during frame transmissions. This jitter can (potentially) lead to transient overload peaks on the egress side. Figure 7 illustrates how the different approaches affect the (transient) worst-case load induced by the inter-gateway CAN frames on the pretended ingress and egress CAN buses. Specifically, the figure shows the transient worst-case load (on the y-axis) versus the time interval in which this load can be observed (on the x-axis). Note that, as the traffic on ingress CAN buses 1 and 2 is not multiplexed, all approaches perform the same on these two buses. As expected, the latency a CAN frame experiences on the path between the ingress and egress gateway results in additional output jitter and therefore (potentially) a bursty arrival at the egress CAN bus. Asymptotically, there is no difference between the load on the ingress and egress buses as our analysis is load preserving, i.e., although not shown, the asymptotic load on egress buses 3 and 4 approaches loads of 31 and 14 % (respectively) as the time interval approaches infinity. The lowest (transient) overload can be seen for the 1:1 mapping whereas the all-in-one mapping results in the highest overload. This is also reflected in the latency results for the inter-gateway traffic.

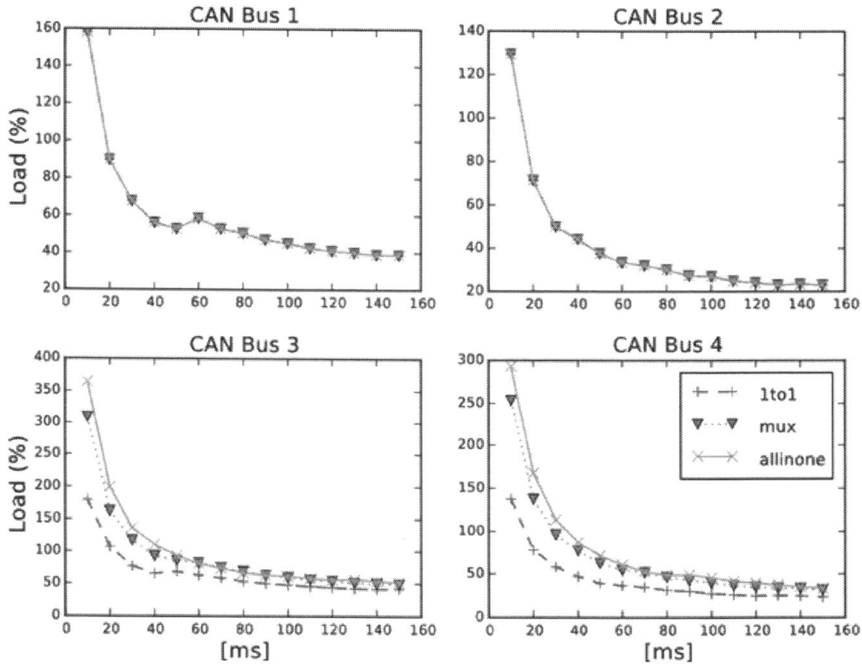


**Figure. 7** Worst-case transient load on the (pretended) ingress (Bus 1, Bus 2) and egress (Bus 3, Bus 4) CAN buses

Figure 8 shows the worst-case end-to-end (i.e. gateway-to-gateway) latency guarantees of the inter-gateway traffic in all scenarios *relative to the periods* of the frames. The frames are sorted by their period. In 1:1 mapping, the worst-case response times of the corresponding gateway tasks dominate, which, in turn, are affected by their priority assignment (CAN frames with lower IDs have higher priority). This becomes clear by looking at the frames of the first group (first 17 bars in Fig. 8) that all have similar periods of 16–23 ms but quite different latencies (cf. Fig. 9, which shows the absolute latencies for the 8-th (#671) and 9-th (#1854) frames of the group). Looking at the longer-periodic frames, we can identify some room for improvement to exploit in the multiplexing scenario as their latency is much lower than their period. In the multiplexing scenario, for non-trigger frames, the buffer timeouts, i.e. the sampling delays, dominate. The latency of trigger frames (#1420, #822, #1966, #1462) is improved over the latency from 1:1 multiplexing (e.g. compare the absolute latencies of frame #1420 in Fig. 9a, b). Contrastingly, the all-in-one scenario is dominated by the buffer-full events and trigger frames, resulting in large latencies for the lower-periodic frames. Figure 8 clearly shows that we can influence the frame latencies (in both directions) by multiplexing. We will continue this train of thought when we discuss the impact of different multiplexing parameters in Fig. 10.

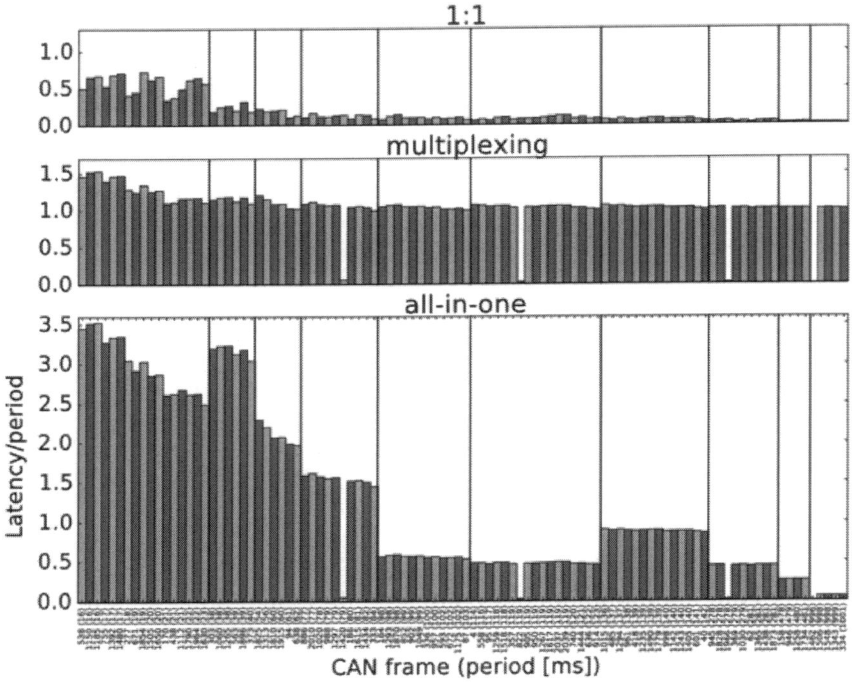


**Figure. 8** Period-relative worst-case end-to-end latency of CAN frames in the 1:1, multiplexing, and all-in-one scenarios. The *vertical lines* represent the group boundaries from Table 2

Figure 9 depicts the latency contributions of the Ethernet, the ingress and egress gateways, as well as the sampling delay for four selected frames and thereby further illustrates the dominating factors. The frames are selected from two different groups in the multiplexing and all-in-one scenario. We notice that the sampling delay in Fig. 9 equals the corresponding buffer timeouts and that the trigger frame #1420 is not affected by the sampling delay. In the all-in-one scenario (Fig. 9), we observe that frames #671 and #1854 experience a sampling delay of ~~53 ms that results from the buffer-full event whereas frame #1297 has a sampling delay of ~~119 ms resulting from the period (79 ms) and jitter (39.5 ms) of trigger frame #1420.

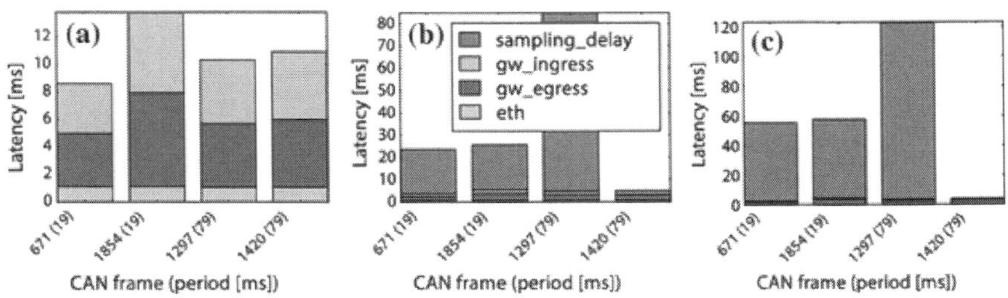


**Figure. 9** Worst-case end-to-end latency contributions of selected CAN frames for 1:1 mapping (**a**), multiplexing (**b**), and all-in-one mapping (**c**)

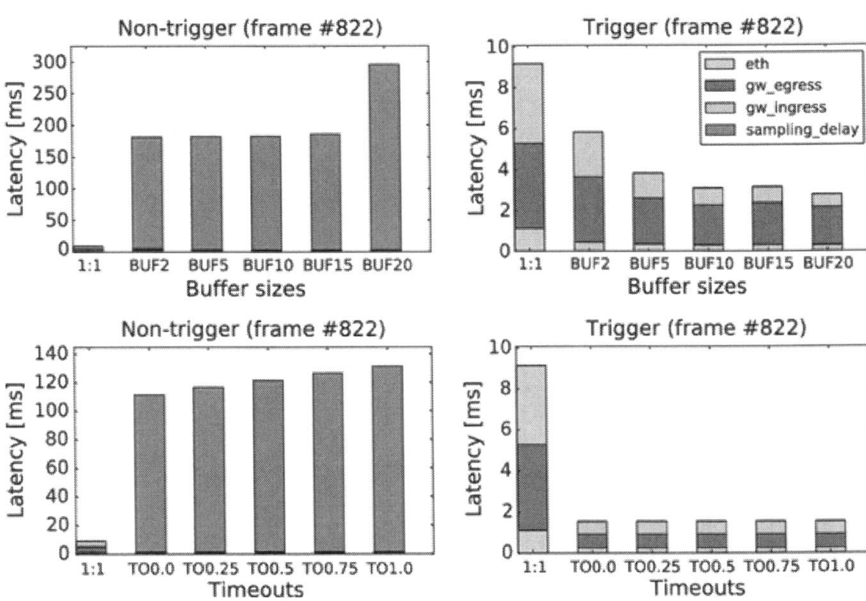


**Figure. 10** Worst-case end-to-end latency guarantees of frame #822 for different buffer sizes and timeouts

Next, we evaluate the effect of different multiplexing parameters on the end-to-end latencies guarantees. In the following, we focus on frame

#822, which is the only trigger frame of group 3. The buffers for all groups in Table 3 are evaluated for sizes 2, 5, 10, 15, and 20 (named BUF2 to BUF20). We vary the timeouts for each group within 0, 25, 50, 75, and 100 % of their period range (named TO0.0 to TO1.0). For group 3, 0 % corresponds to 110 ms and 100 % to 130 ms. At the same time, these parameters lead to 90 and 110 ms for group 2. For group 1 the 0 % bound is set to 5 ms to prevent overload at the gateways.

Figure 10 shows the effect of these parameters on the end-to-end latency guarantees of frame #822. The subgraphs on the right show the latencies when frame #822 is considered as a trigger frame (as originally specified), whereas for the subgraphs on the left, we consider frame #822 as a non-trigger frame, i.e. in this scenario group 3 does not contain any trigger frames.

The latencies of the non-trigger setup are dominated by the sampling delay $\delta+(2)$, which is the longest distance between any two output events (Eq. 7). Thus, during timeout evaluation, the sampling delay corresponds to the timeouts. In the buffer size evaluation, the sampling delay increases with buffer size, but there is a plateau between BUF2 and BUF15. This is because many frames in group 3 have roughly the same $\delta+(n)$ leading to a burst in $\delta+B(n)$ ) (Eq. 4), which is large enough to generate the output events for BUF2 to BUF15 at nearly the same time.

In the trigger setup, smaller buffers induce more gateway and Ethernet load, leading to higher interference, and thus, longer latencies. At the same time, as long as the buffer-full events are dominating, a larger buffer size also increases the execution time of the RX tasks on the egress gateway in our model, as this time depends on the number of CAN frames in an incoming Ethernet frame. At BUF15, we can observe that the increased execution time overbalances the reduced interference. From BUF15, the group's trigger event begins to dominate buffer-full events. There is effectively no influence of different timeouts on the latency for frame #822. This is expected, as, in this scenario, frame #822 is a trigger frame whose period is in the order of the smallest timeout (TO0.0).

In all scenarios, the gateway load is lower than in the 1:1 scenario (~~ 8 %). Short timeouts and small buffers induce a high load, while large timeouts and big buffers result in lower loads.

## 6.4 Discussion

The focus of our evaluation was to demonstrate how multiplexing affects the design metrics worst-case end-to-end latency and load. In general (and unsurprisingly), latency can be reduced at the cost of increased load and vice versa. However, our formal analysis allows to quantify this trade-off, which enables future optimizations to find the best multiplexing parameters for a given problem.

Multiplexing (compared to a 1:1 mapping of CAN frames to Ethernet frames) can reduce the number of transmitted Ethernet frames, which leads to less load on the gateways (less frames require processing) and less interfering frames in the Ethernet network (cf. Table 6). Consequently, less interfering Ethernet frames lead to smaller end-to-end latencies of other (non-inter-gateway) Ethernet traffic (cf. Table 4). For inter-gateway traffic, however, multiplexing can introduce sampling delay, which negatively affects its end-to-end latencies (compared to a 1:1 mapping). This sampling delay can be controlled via different multiplexing parameters, e.g. timeouts or buffer sizes (cf. Figs. 8, 10). In general, smaller timeouts or smaller buffer sizes decrease the sampling delay at the cost of increased load and an increased number of interfering Ethernet frames. By making frames triggering, the sampling delay can be avoided entirely (cf. Figs. 8, 9). In fact, the 1:1 mapping is a scenario where all frames are trigger frames.

We have also shown that there can be complex interdependencies between different multiplexing parameters (cf. Fig. 10). Larger buffer sizes, for example, can reduce the number of Ethernet frames, which need to be processed. This can reduce the load, but at the same time more time is required at the egress gateway to extract individual CAN frames from larger Ethernet frames. Some triggering strategies also introduce dependencies of the output event models on the input event models, e.g. buffer-full triggering (cf. sampling delay plateau in the upper left subfigure of Fig. 10), while for others the output event models are independent of the input event models, e.g. buffer timeouts, or are dominated by a single trigger frame (cf. Fig. 10, lower right subfigure).

# 7. CONCLUSION

In this article, we presented a formal system-level analysis approach of heterogeneous, in-vehicle Ethernet-based systems, focusing on CAN-to-Ethernet gateway strategies. We considered complex frame packing effects with various triggering strategies such as buffer timeout, buffer-full as well as trigger frames. We modeled and analyzed an Ethernet-based backbone under different gateway multiplexing strategies. However, the additional latency introduced by gateway effects such as sampling latency is significantly larger than Ethernet effects. We showed that end-to-end latency can be adjusted by trading it for Ethernet and gateway load via different multiplexing parameters and vice versa. Formal analysis is able to reflect such design decisions enabling Ethernet network optimization guided by formal timing guarantees. This will help to establish Ethernet-based backbone networks for safety critical systems.

# REFERENCES

1. AUTOSAR (2015) Release 4.2.2, Specification of socket adapter

2. Ayed H, Mifdaoui A, Fraboul C (2011) Gateway optimization for an heterogeneous avionics network afdx-can. In: IEEE real-time systems symposium (RTSS)

3. Bauer H, Scharbarg JL, Fraboul C (2010) Improving the worst-case delay analysis of an afdx network using an optimized trajectory approach. IEEE Trans Ind Inf 6:521–533

4. Davis R, Burns A, Bril R, Lukkien J (2007) Controller area network (can) schedulability analysis: refuted, revisited and revised. Real-Time Syst 35(3):239–272

5. Diemer J, Rox J, Negrean M, Stein S, Ernst R (2011) Real-time communication analysis for networks with two-stage arbitration. In: Proceedings of EMSOFT, pp 243–252

6. Diemer J, Axer P, Ernst R (2012a) Compositional performance analysis in python with pycpa. In: Proceedings of WATERS. http://retis.sssup.it/waters2012/WATERS-2012-Proceedings.pdf

7. Diemer J, Rox J, Ernst R (2012b) Modeling of ethernet avb networks for worst-case timing analysis. In: Proceedings of MATHMOD

8. Feiertag N, Richter K, Nordlander J, Jonsson J (2008) A compositional framework for end-to-end path delay calculation of automotive systems under different path semantics. In: Work on compositional theory and technology for real-time embedded systems CRTS

9. Henia R, Hamann A, Jersak M, Racu R, Richter K, Ernst R (2005) System level performance analysis—-the SymTA/S approach. IEE Proc Comput Digit Tech 152(2):148–166

10. Herber C, Richter A, Wild T, Herkersdorf A (2015) Real-time capable can to avb ethernet gateway using frame aggregation and scheduling. In: Proceedings of design, automation and test in Europe (DATE)

11. Kern A, Reinhard D, Streichert T, Teich J (2011) Gateway strategies for embedding of automotive CAN-frames into ethernet-packets and vice versa. In: Architecture of computing systems, pp 259–270

12. Lehoczky J (1990) Fixed priority scheduling of periodic task sets with arbitrary deadlines. In: Proceedings of 11th RTSS, pp 201–209.

13. Nacer A, Jaffres-Runser K, Scharbarg JL, Fraboul C (2013) Strategies for the interconnection of can buses through an ethernet switch. In: IEEE international symposium on industrial embedded systems (SIES), pp 77–80

14. Perathoner S, Rein T, Thiele L, Lampka K, Rox J (2010) Modeling structured event streams in system level performance analysis. In: ACM SIGPLAN/SIGBED conference on languages, compilers and tools for embedded systems (LCTES). ACM, Sweden, pp 37–46

15. Pop P, Eles P, Peng Z (2005) Schedulability-driven frame packing for multicluster distributed embedded systems. ACM Trans Embed Comput Syst 4(1):112–140

16. Revsbech K, Schiøler H, Madsen TK, Nielsen JJ (2011) Worst-case traversal time modelling of ethernet based in-car networks using real time calculus. In: Proceedings of NEW2AN, pp 219–230

17. Richter K (2005) Compositional scheduling analysis using standard event models. Ph.D. Thesis, TU Braunschweig

18. Rox J, Ernst R (2008) Modeling event stream hierarchies with hierarchical event models. In: Proceedings of design, automation and test in Europe DATE'08, pp 492–497.

19. Rox J, Ernst R (2010) Formal timing analysis of full duplex switched based ethernet network architectures. In: SAE World Congress, vol System level architecture design tools and methods

20. Saket R, Navet N (2006) Frame packing algorithms for automotive applications. J Embed Comput 2:93–102

21. Scharbarg J, Boyer M, Fraboul C (2005) Can-ethernet architectures for real-time applications. In: IEEE conference on emerging technologies and factory automation (ETFA), vol 2, pp 8–252

22. Schliecker S, Rox J, Ivers M, Ernst R (2008) Providing accurate event models for the analysis of heterogeneous multiprocessor systems. In: Proceedings of CODES-ISSS, pp 185–190

23. Thiele D, Axer P, Ernst R, Seyler JR (2014) Improving formal timing analysis of switched ethernet by exploiting traffic stream correlations. In: Proceedings of CODE+ISSS, New Delhi

24. Thiele L, Chakraborty S, Naedele M (2000) Real-time calculus for scheduling hard real-time systems. In: Proceedings of IEEE international symposium on circuits and systems (ISCAS), vol 4, pp 101–104.

25. Zhang L, Gao H, Kaynak O (2013) Network-induced constraints in networked control systems—a survey. IEEE Trans Ind Inf 9(1):403–416

# INDEX